Daily 6-Trait Writing

GRADE 5

Manufacturer	Evan-Moor Corporation 10 Harris Court, Suite C-3 Monterey, CA 93940, USA www.evan-moor.com
EU Rep.	Authorised Rep Compliance Ltd., Ground Floor, 71 Lower Baggot Street, Dublin, D02 P593, Ireland www.arccompliance.com

Editorial Development: Roseann Erwin, Gail Blasser Riley, Leslie Sorg, Andrea Weiss
Copy Editing: Cathy Harber
Art Direction: Cheryl Puckett
Cover Design: Liliana Potigian
Illustrator: Lauren Scheuer
Design/Production: Susan Bigger, Carolina Caird

Evan-Moor Educational Publishers

EMC 6025

Visit *teaching-standards.com* to view a correlation of this book.

Correlated to Current Standards

Congratulations on your purchase of some of the finest teaching materials in the world.

For information about other Evan-Moor products, call 1-800-777-4362, fax 1-800-777-4332, or visit our website, www.evan-moor.com.

10 Harris Court, Suite C-3, Monterey, CA 93940-5773. Printed in China.

009

CPSIA: Cre8 Direct (Ningbo) Co., Ltd., Beilun, Ningbo, China [3/2026]

Contents

How to Use This Book

Daily 6-Trait Writing contains 25 weeks of mini-lessons divided into five units. Each unit provides five weeks of scaffolded instruction focused on one of the following traits: **Ideas, Organization, Word Choice, Sentence Fluency,** and **Voice**. (See pages 6–9 for more information about each of these, as well as the sixth trait, **Conventions**.) You may wish to teach each entire unit in consecutive order, or pick and choose the lessons within the unit.

Each week of *Daily 6-Trait Writing* focuses on a specific skill within the primary trait, as well as one Convention skill. The weeks follow a consistent five-day format, making *Daily 6-Trait Writing* easy to use.

Teacher Overview Pages

Trait Skill

A specific writing skill for each trait is targeted.

Reduced Pages

Reduced student pages provide sample answers.

Convention Skill

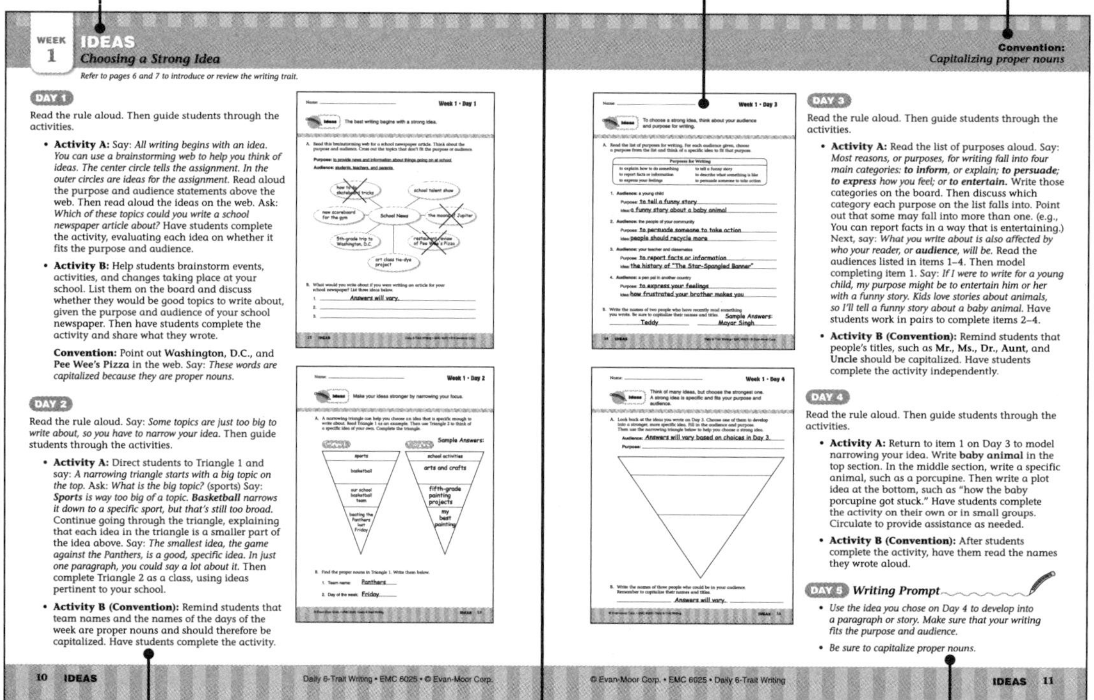
WEEK 1 IDEAS
Choosing a Strong Idea
Refer to pages 6 and 7 to introduce or review the writing trait.

Convention:
Capitalizing proper nouns

DAY 1
Read the rule aloud. Then guide students through the activities.

- **Activity A:** Say: *All writing begins with an idea. You can use a brainstorming web to help you think of ideas. The center circle tells the assignment. In the outer circles are ideas for the assignment.* Read aloud the purpose and audience statements above the web. Then read aloud the ideas on the web. Ask: *Which of these topics could you write a school newspaper article about?* Have students complete the activity, evaluating each idea on whether it fits the purpose and audience.
- **Activity B:** Help students brainstorm events, activities, and changes taking place at your school. List them on the board and discuss whether they would be good topics to write about, given the purpose and audience of your school newspaper. Then have students complete the activity and share what they wrote.

Convention: Point out **Washington, D.C.,** and **Pee Wee's Pizza** in the web. Say: *These words are capitalized because they are proper nouns.*

DAY 2
Read the rule aloud. Say: *Some topics are just too big to write about, so you have to narrow your idea.* Then guide students through the activities.

- **Activity A:** Direct students to Triangle 1 and say: *A narrowing triangle starts with a big topic on the top.* Ask: *What is the big topic?* (sports) Say: ***Sports** is way too big of a topic. **Basketball** narrows it down to a specific sport, but that's still too broad.* Continue going through the triangle, explaining that each idea in the triangle is a smaller part of the idea above. Say: *The smallest idea, the game against the Panthers, is a good, specific idea. In just one paragraph, you could say a lot about it.* Then complete Triangle 2 as a class, using ideas pertinent to your school.
- **Activity B (Convention):** Remind students that team names and the names of the days of the week are proper nouns and should therefore be capitalized. Have students complete the activity.

DAY 3
Read the rule aloud. Then guide students through the activities.

- **Activity A:** Read the list of purposes aloud. Say: *Most reasons, or purposes, for writing fall into four main categories: **to inform**, or explain; **to persuade**; **to express** how you feel; or **to entertain**.* Write those categories on the board. Then discuss which category each purpose on the list falls into. Point out that some may fall into more than one. (e.g., You can report facts in a way that is entertaining.) Next, say: *What you write about is also affected by who your reader, or **audience**, will be.* Read the audiences listed in items 1–4. Then model completing item 1. Say: *If I were to write for a young child, my purpose might be to entertain him or her with a funny story. Kids love stories about animals, so I'll tell a funny story about a baby animal.* Have students work in pairs to complete items 2–4.
- **Activity B (Convention):** Remind students that people's titles, such as **Mr., Ms., Dr., Aunt,** and **Uncle** should be capitalized. Have students complete the activity independently.

DAY 4
Read the rule aloud. Then guide students through the activities.

- **Activity A:** Return to item 1 on Day 3 to model narrowing your idea. Write **baby animal** in the top section. In the middle section, write a specific animal, such as a porcupine. Then write a plot idea at the bottom, such as "how the baby porcupine got stuck." Have students complete the activity on their own or in small groups. Circulate to provide assistance as needed.
- **Activity B (Convention):** After students complete the activity, have them read the names they wrote aloud.

DAY 5 *Writing Prompt*

- *Use the idea you chose on Day 4 to develop into a paragraph or story. Make sure that your writing fits the purpose and audience.*
- *Be sure to capitalize proper nouns.*

10 IDEAS Daily 6-Trait Writing • EMC 6025 • © Evan-Moor Corp.

© Evan-Moor Corp. • EMC 6025 • Daily 6-Trait Writing IDEAS 11

Lesson Plans

Use the lesson plans to teach the trait and Convention skills and guide students through the activities on Days 1–4. The plans are structured to enable you to differentiate and tailor lessons for your own class, but still provide the explanation and support you need. You may choose to have students complete the activities as a class, in small groups, or independently.

Day 5 Writing Prompt

Give your students the writing prompt to apply the trait and Convention skills in their own writing. Provide students with paper, or use the page provided for Day 5 in the student practice book. You may also wish to expand the writing prompt into a more fully developed assignment that takes students through the writing process.

Student Activity Pages

Trait and Rule (Skill Summary)

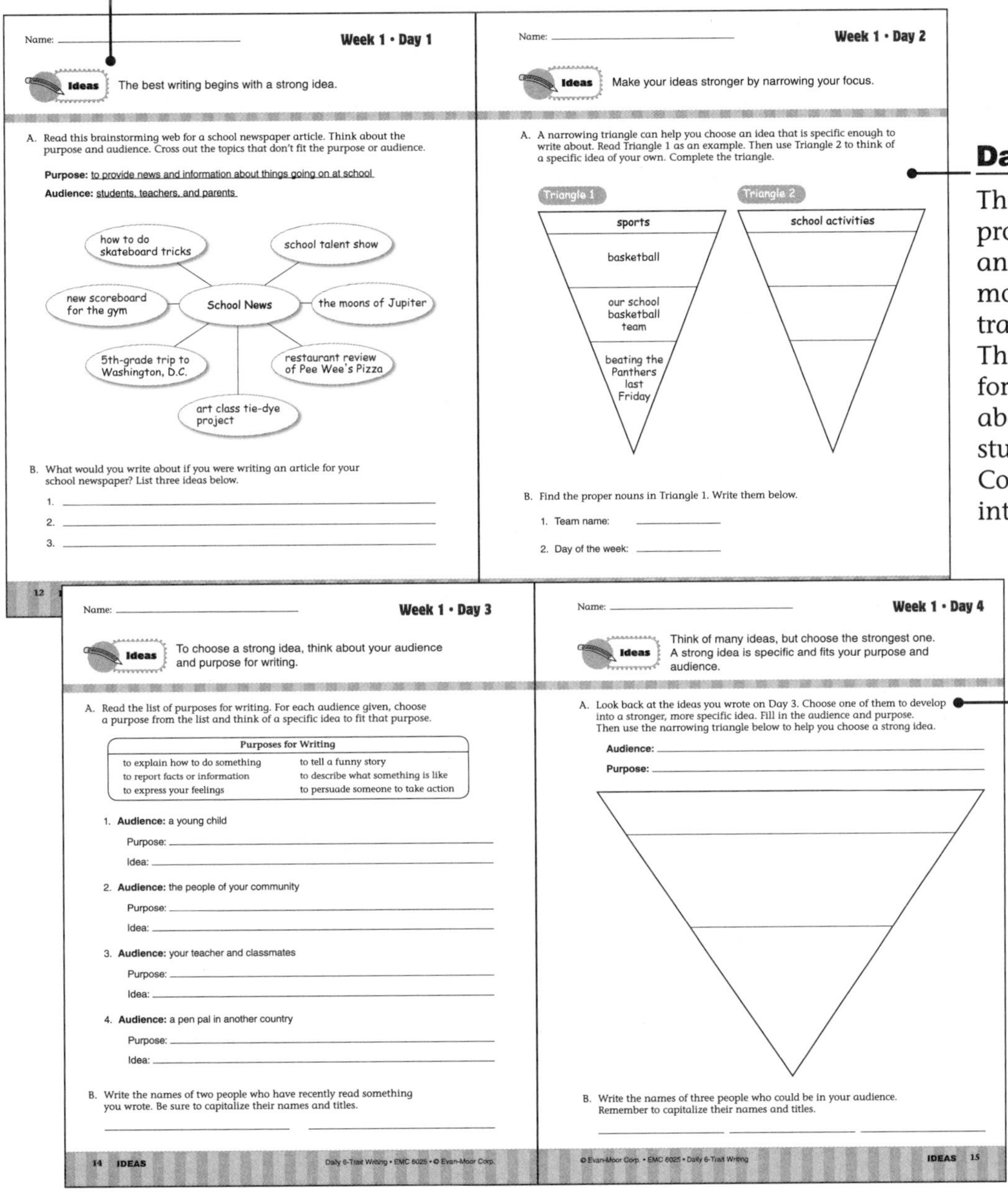

Name: ______ **Week 1 • Day 1**

Ideas The best writing begins with a strong idea.

A. Read this brainstorming web for a school newspaper article. Think about the purpose and audience. Cross out the topics that don't fit the purpose or audience.

Purpose: to provide news and information about things going on at school

Audience: students, teachers, and parents

School News: how to do skateboard tricks; school talent show; new scoreboard for the gym; the moons of Jupiter; 5th-grade trip to Washington, D.C.; restaurant review of Pee Wee's Pizza; art class tie-dye project

B. What would you write about if you were writing an article for your school newspaper? List three ideas below.

1. ______
2. ______
3. ______

Name: ______ **Week 1 • Day 2**

Ideas Make your ideas stronger by narrowing your focus.

A. A narrowing triangle can help you choose an idea that is specific enough to write about. Read Triangle 1 as an example. Then use Triangle 2 to think of a specific idea of your own. Complete the triangle.

Triangle 1: sports; basketball; our school basketball team; beating the Panthers last Friday

Triangle 2: school activities

B. Find the proper nouns in Triangle 1. Write them below.

1. Team name: ______
2. Day of the week: ______

Name: ______ **Week 1 • Day 3**

Ideas To choose a strong idea, think about your audience and purpose for writing.

A. Read the list of purposes for writing. For each audience given, choose a purpose from the list and think of a specific idea to fit that purpose.

Purposes for Writing	
to explain how to do something	to tell a funny story
to report facts or information	to describe what something is like
to express your feelings	to persuade someone to take action

1. **Audience:** a young child
   Purpose: ______
   Idea: ______
2. **Audience:** the people of your community
   Purpose: ______
   Idea: ______
3. **Audience:** your teacher and classmates
   Purpose: ______
   Idea: ______
4. **Audience:** a pen pal in another country
   Purpose: ______
   Idea: ______

B. Write the names of two people who have recently read something you wrote. Be sure to capitalize their names and titles.

14 IDEAS Daily 6-Trait Writing • EMC 6025 • © Evan-Moor Corp.

Name: ______ **Week 1 • Day 4**

Ideas Think of many ideas, but choose the strongest one. A strong idea is specific and fits your purpose and audience.

A. Look back at the ideas you wrote on Day 3. Choose one of them to develop into a stronger, more specific idea. Fill in the audience and purpose. Then use the narrowing triangle below to help you choose a strong idea.

Audience: ______

Purpose: ______

B. Write the names of three people who could be in your audience. Remember to capitalize their names and titles.

© Evan-Moor Corp. • EMC 6025 • Daily 6-Trait Writing IDEAS 15

Days 1–3 Activities

The activities on Days 1–3 provide models for students to analyze, revise, or add to. These models expose students to the traits in many forms of writing. They also provide opportunities for students to think critically about writing, enhancing students' own proficiency. The Convention skill is integrated into the activities.

Day 4 Activity

The Day 4 activity provides a prewriting form for the Day 5 writing prompt.

Ways to Use

There are many ways to integrate *Daily 6-Trait Writing* into your classroom:

- Teach the lessons trait by trait.
- Target and practice specific skills students need help with.
- Use the lessons to enhance writing workshops.
- Incorporate the lessons into your other writing programs.

Introducing the Six Traits

Use these ideas to introduce or review the trait at the beginning of each unit.

Ideas

Explain to students that good writing starts with good ideas.

Say: *A good idea is clear, interesting, and original. It makes the reader say, "Wow!" or "I never would have thought of that!" Without good ideas, your writing would not have much of a point. Your reader would be bored!*

Organization

Explain to students that good writing is organized in a way that helps the reader understand the information and follow what the writer is saying.

Say: *The organization of your writing is what holds everything together. It puts your ideas in an order that makes sense, and it gives your writing a strong introduction, body, and conclusion. When your writing is not organized, your reader can grow confused and lose interest.*

Word Choice

Explain to students that good writers choose their words carefully in order to get their ideas across.

Say: *When you write, choose just the right words and use them correctly. Make them fun and interesting so they help your readers "see" what you are talking about. Try not to use the same words over and over again. If you don't choose your words carefully, your reader may not understand what you're trying to say.*

Sentence Fluency

Explain to students that good writers make their writing flow by using different kinds of sentences.

Say: *You want your writing to be easy to read and follow. It should flow so smoothly and sound so interesting that people want to read it aloud! When your sentences don't flow, your writing sounds choppy and flat. Your reader would not want to read it aloud.*

Voice

Explain to students that when they write, their personality, or who they are, should shine through.

Say: *You want your writing to sound like you, and no one else! When you write, you show who you are through words. No matter what type of writing you do, always make sure it sounds like you. Otherwise, your reader may not care about what you have to say. In fact, your reader may not even know who wrote it!*

Conventions

Explain to students that good writers follow all the rules, or conventions, of writing, so their readers can easily read and understand the writing.

Say: *Using correct grammar, spelling, and punctuation when you write is important. When you don't follow the rules, your reader can become lost or confused. He or she may not know where one idea starts and another begins.*

Using the Rubric

Use the rubric on pages 8 and 9 to evaluate and assess your students' skill acquisition.

- Each week, evaluate the student responses to the Day 5 writing prompt using the criteria that correspond to the skills taught that week.
- For Week 5, use all the trait criteria to assess students' understanding of that trait as a whole.
- Use the entire set of criteria to occasionally assess students' writing across the traits.
- In student- and parent-teacher conferences, use the rubric to accurately and clearly explain what a student does well in writing, as well as what he or she needs to improve.

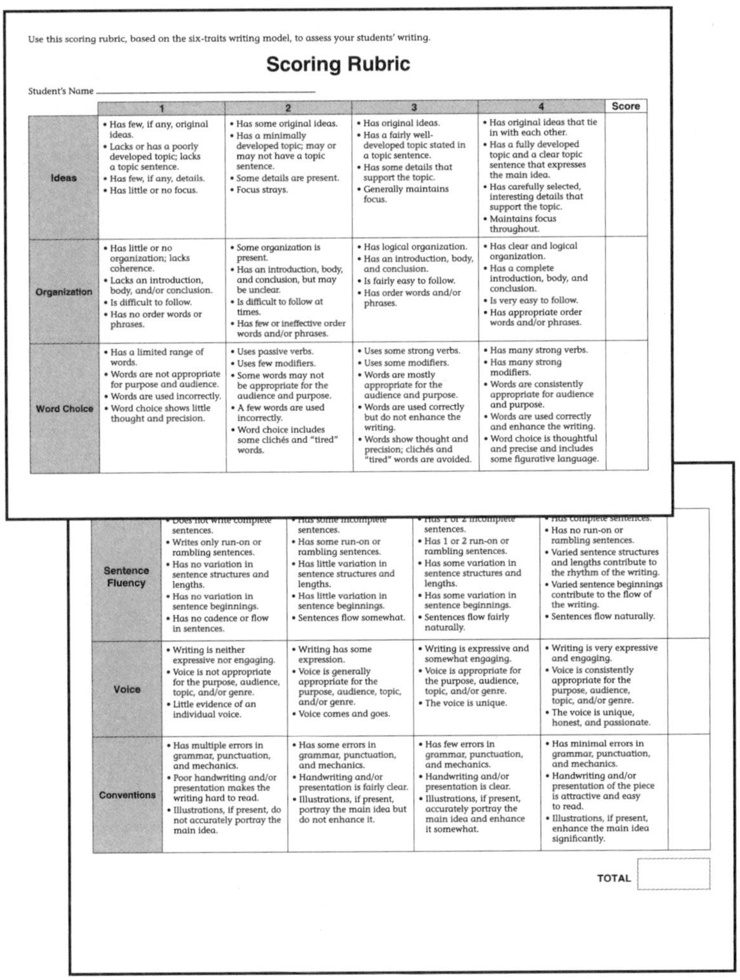

Use this scoring rubric, based on the six-traits writing model, to assess your students' writing.

Scoring Rubric

Student's Name ____________________

	1	2	3	4	Score
Ideas	• Has few, if any, original ideas. • Lacks or has a poorly developed topic; lacks a topic sentence. • Has few, if any, details. • Has little or no focus.	• Has some original ideas. • Has a minimally developed topic; may or may not have a topic sentence. • Some details are present. • Focus strays.	• Has original ideas. • Has a fairly well-developed topic stated in a topic sentence. • Has some details that support the topic. • Generally maintains focus.	• Has original ideas that tie in with each other. • Has a fully developed topic and a clear topic sentence that expresses the main idea. • Has carefully selected, interesting details that support the topic. • Maintains focus throughout.	
Organization	• Has little or no organization; lacks coherence. • Lacks an introduction, body, and/or conclusion. • Is difficult to follow. • Has no order words or phrases.	• Some organization is present. • Has an introduction, body, and conclusion, but may be unclear. • Is difficult to follow at times. • Has few or ineffective order words and/or phrases.	• Has logical organization. • Has an introduction, body, and conclusion. • Is fairly easy to follow. • Has order words and/or phrases.	• Has clear and logical organization. • Has a complete introduction, body, and conclusion. • Is very easy to follow. • Has appropriate order words and/or phrases.	
Word Choice	• Has a limited range of words. • Words are not appropriate for purpose and audience. • Words are used incorrectly. • Word choice shows little thought and precision.	• Uses passive verbs. • Uses few modifiers. • Some words may not be appropriate for the audience and purpose. • A few words are used incorrectly. • Word choice includes some clichés and "tired" words.	• Uses some strong verbs. • Uses some modifiers. • Words are mostly appropriate for the audience and purpose. • Words are used correctly but do not enhance the writing. • Words show thought and precision; clichés and "tired" words are avoided.	• Has many strong verbs. • Has many strong modifiers. • Words are consistently appropriate for audience and purpose. • Words are used correctly and enhance the writing. • Word choice is thoughtful and precise and includes some figurative language.	
Sentence Fluency	• Does not write complete sentences. • Writes only run-on or rambling sentences. • Has no variation in sentence structures and lengths. • Has no variation in sentence beginnings. • Has no cadence or flow in sentences.	• Has some incomplete sentences. • Has some run-on or rambling sentences. • Has little variation in sentence structures and lengths. • Has little variation in sentence beginnings. • Sentences flow somewhat.	• Has 1 or 2 incomplete sentences. • Has 1 or 2 run-on or rambling sentences. • Has some variation in sentence structures and lengths. • Has some variation in sentence beginnings. • Sentences flow fairly naturally.	• Has complete sentences. • Has no run-on or rambling sentences. • Varied sentence structures and lengths contribute to the rhythm of the writing. • Varied sentence beginnings contribute to the flow of the writing. • Sentences flow naturally.	
Voice	• Writing is neither expressive nor engaging. • Voice is not appropriate for the purpose, audience, topic, and/or genre. • Little evidence of an individual voice.	• Writing has some expression. • Voice is generally appropriate for the purpose, audience, topic, and/or genre. • Voice comes and goes.	• Writing is expressive and somewhat engaging. • Voice is appropriate for the purpose, audience, topic, and/or genre. • The voice is unique.	• Writing is very expressive and engaging. • Voice is consistently appropriate for the purpose, audience, topic, and/or genre. • The voice is unique, honest, and passionate.	
Conventions	• Has multiple errors in grammar, punctuation, and mechanics. • Poor handwriting and/or presentation makes the writing hard to read. • Illustrations, if present, do not accurately portray the main idea.	• Has some errors in grammar, punctuation, and mechanics. • Handwriting and/or presentation is fairly clear. • Illustrations, if present, portray the main idea but do not enhance it.	• Has few errors in grammar, punctuation, and mechanics. • Handwriting and/or presentation is clear. • Illustrations, if present, accurately portray the main idea and enhance it somewhat.	• Has minimal errors in grammar, punctuation, and mechanics. • Handwriting and/or presentation of the piece is attractive and easy to read. • Illustrations, if present, enhance the main idea significantly.	

TOTAL ______

Use this scoring rubric, based on the six-traits writing model, to assess your students' writing.

Scoring Rubric

Student's Name ______________________________

	1	2	3	4	Score
Ideas	• Has few, if any, original ideas. • Lacks or has a poorly developed topic; lacks a topic sentence. • Has few, if any, details. • Has little or no focus.	• Has some original ideas. • Has a minimally developed topic; may or may not have a topic sentence. • Some details are present. • Focus strays.	• Has original ideas. • Has a fairly well-developed topic stated in a topic sentence. • Has some details that support the topic. • Generally maintains focus.	• Has original ideas that tie in with each other. • Has a fully developed topic and a clear topic sentence that expresses the main idea. • Has carefully selected, interesting details that support the topic. • Maintains focus throughout.	
Organization	• Has little or no organization; lacks coherence. • Lacks an introduction, body, and/or conclusion. • Is difficult to follow. • Has no order words or phrases.	• Some organization is present. • Has an introduction, body, and conclusion, but may be unclear. • Is difficult to follow at times. • Has few or ineffective order words and/or phrases.	• Has logical organization. • Has an introduction, body, and conclusion. • Is fairly easy to follow. • Has order words and/or phrases.	• Has clear and logical organization. • Has a complete introduction, body, and conclusion. • Is very easy to follow. • Has appropriate order words and/or phrases.	
Word Choice	• Has a limited range of words. • Words are not appropriate for purpose and audience. • Words are used incorrectly. • Word choice shows little thought and precision.	• Uses passive verbs. • Uses few modifiers. • Some words may not be appropriate for the audience and purpose. • A few words are used incorrectly. • Word choice includes some clichés and "tired" words.	• Uses some strong verbs. • Uses some modifiers. • Words are mostly appropriate for the audience and purpose. • Words are used correctly but do not enhance the writing. • Words show thought and precision; clichés and "tired" words are avoided.	• Has many strong verbs. • Has many strong modifiers. • Words are consistently appropriate for audience and purpose. • Words are used correctly and enhance the writing. • Word choice is thoughtful and precise and includes some figurative language.	

Sentence Fluency	• Does not write complete sentences. • Writes only run-on or rambling sentences. • Has no variation in sentence structures and lengths. • Has no variation in sentence beginnings. • Has no cadence or flow in sentences.	• Has some incomplete sentences. • Has some run-on or rambling sentences. • Has little variation in sentence structures and lengths. • Has little variation in sentence beginnings. • Sentences flow somewhat.	• Has 1 or 2 incomplete sentences. • Has 1 or 2 run-on or rambling sentences. • Has some variation in sentence structures and lengths. • Has some variation in sentence beginnings. • Sentences flow fairly naturally.	• Has complete sentences. • Has no run-on or rambling sentences. • Varied sentence structures and lengths contribute to the rhythm of the writing. • Varied sentence beginnings contribute to the flow of the writing. • Sentences flow naturally.	
Voice	• Writing is neither expressive nor engaging. • Voice is not appropriate for the purpose, audience, topic, and/or genre. • Little evidence of an individual voice.	• Writing has some expression. • Voice is generally appropriate for the purpose, audience, topic, and/or genre. • Voice comes and goes.	• Writing is expressive and somewhat engaging. • Voice is appropriate for the purpose, audience, topic, and/or genre. • The voice is unique.	• Writing is very expressive and engaging. • Voice is consistently appropriate for the purpose, audience, topic, and/or genre. • The voice is unique, honest, and passionate.	
Conventions	• Has multiple errors in grammar, punctuation, and mechanics. • Poor handwriting and/or presentation makes the writing hard to read. • Illustrations, if present, do not accurately portray the main idea.	• Has some errors in grammar, punctuation, and mechanics. • Handwriting and/or presentation is fairly clear. • Illustrations, if present, portray the main idea but do not enhance it.	• Has few errors in grammar, punctuation, and mechanics. • Handwriting and/or presentation is clear. • Illustrations, if present, accurately portray the main idea and enhance it somewhat.	• Has minimal errors in grammar, punctuation, and mechanics. • Handwriting and/or presentation of the piece is attractive and easy to read. • Illustrations, if present, enhance the main idea significantly.	

TOTAL ______

WEEK 1 IDEAS

Choosing a Strong Idea

Refer to pages 6 and 7 to introduce or review the writing trait.

DAY 1

Read the rule aloud. Then guide students through the activities.

- **Activity A:** Say: *All writing begins with an idea. You can use a brainstorming web to help you think of ideas. The center circle tells the assignment. In the outer circles are ideas for the assignment.* Read aloud the purpose and audience statements above the web. Then read aloud the ideas on the web. Ask: *Which of these topics could you write a school newspaper article about?* Have students complete the activity, evaluating each idea on whether it fits the purpose and audience.
- **Activity B:** Help students brainstorm events, activities, and changes taking place at your school. List them on the board and discuss whether they would be good topics to write about, given the purpose and audience of your school newspaper. Then have students complete the activity and share what they wrote.

  Convention: Point out **Washington, D.C.,** and **Pee Wee's Pizza** in the web. Say: *These words are capitalized because they are proper nouns.*

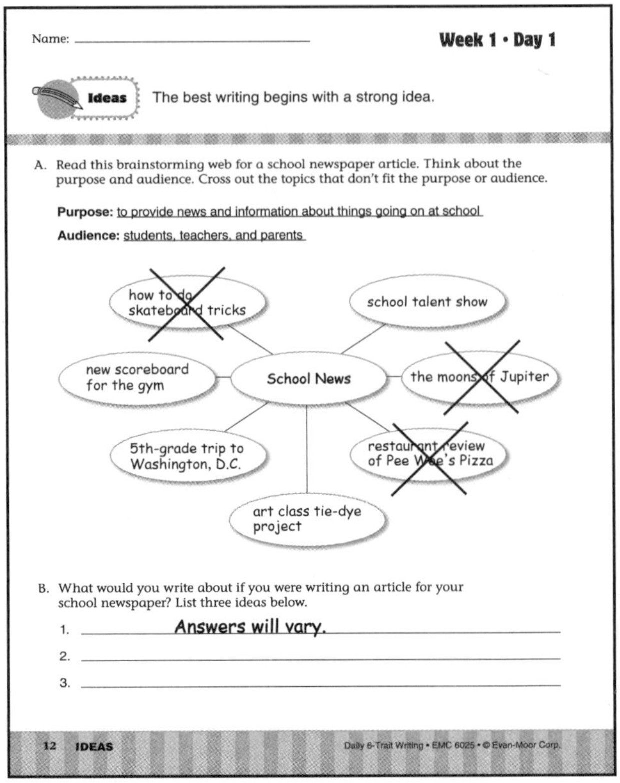

Name: ____________ **Week 1 • Day 1**

Ideas The best writing begins with a strong idea.

A. Read this brainstorming web for a school newspaper article. Think about the purpose and audience. Cross out the topics that don't fit the purpose or audience.

Purpose: to provide news and information about things going on at school

Audience: students, teachers, and parents

B. What would you write about if you were writing an article for your school newspaper? List three ideas below.

1. Answers will vary.
2. ____________
3. ____________

12 IDEAS Daily 6-Trait Writing • EMC 6025 • © Evan-Moor Corp.

DAY 2

Read the rule aloud. Say: *Some topics are just too big to write about, so you have to narrow your idea.* Then guide students through the activities.

- **Activity A:** Direct students to Triangle 1 and say: *A narrowing triangle starts with a big topic on the top.* Ask: *What is the big topic?* (sports) Say: ***Sports** is way too big of a topic. **Basketball** narrows it down to a specific sport, but that's still too broad.* Continue going through the triangle, explaining that each idea in the triangle is a smaller part of the idea above. Say: *The smallest idea, the game against the Panthers, is a good, specific idea. In just one paragraph, you could say a lot about it.* Then complete Triangle 2 as a class, using ideas pertinent to your school.
- **Activity B (Convention):** Remind students that team names and the names of the days of the week are proper nouns and should therefore be capitalized. Have students complete the activity.

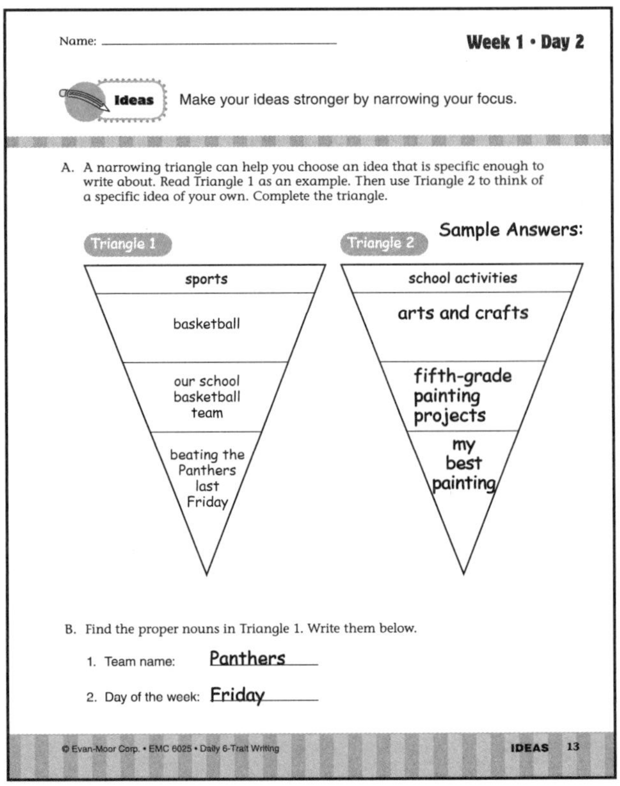

Name: ____________ **Week 1 • Day 2**

Ideas Make your ideas stronger by narrowing your focus.

A. A narrowing triangle can help you choose an idea that is specific enough to write about. Read Triangle 1 as an example. Then use Triangle 2 to think of a specific idea of your own. Complete the triangle.

B. Find the proper nouns in Triangle 1. Write them below.

1. Team name: Panthers
2. Day of the week: Friday

© Evan-Moor Corp. • EMC 6025 • Daily 6-Trait Writing IDEAS 13

Name: ______________________ **Week 1 • Day 3**

Ideas To choose a strong idea, think about your audience and purpose for writing.

A. Read the list of purposes for writing. For each audience given, choose a purpose from the list and think of a specific idea to fit that purpose.

Purposes for Writing	
to explain how to do something	to tell a funny story
to report facts or information	to describe what something is like
to express your feelings	to persuade someone to take action

1. **Audience:** a young child
   Purpose: to tell a funny story
   Idea: a funny story about a baby animal
2. **Audience:** the people of your community
   Purpose: to persuade someone to take action
   Idea: people should recycle more
3. **Audience:** your teacher and classmates
   Purpose: to report facts or information
   Idea: the history of "The Star-Spangled Banner"
4. **Audience:** a pen pal in another country
   Purpose: to express your feelings
   Idea: how frustrated your brother makes you

B. Write the names of two people who have recently read something you wrote. Be sure to capitalize their names and titles. Sample Answers:
Teddy Mayor Singh

14 IDEAS Daily 6-Trait Writing • EMC 6025 • © Evan-Moor Corp.

Name: ______________________ **Week 1 • Day 4**

Ideas Think of many ideas, but choose the strongest one. A strong idea is specific and fits your purpose and audience.

A. Look back at the ideas you wrote on Day 3. Choose one of them to develop into a stronger, more specific idea. Fill in the audience and purpose. Then use the narrowing triangle below to help you choose a strong idea.
Audience: Answers will vary based on choices in Day 3.
Purpose: ______________________

B. Write the names of three people who could be in your audience. Remember to capitalize their names and titles.
Answers will vary.

© Evan-Moor Corp. • EMC 6025 • Daily 6-Trait Writing IDEAS 15

DAY 3

Read the rule aloud. Then guide students through the activities.

- **Activity A:** Read the list of purposes aloud. Say: *Most reasons, or purposes, for writing fall into four main categories:* ***to inform****, or explain;* ***to persuade****;* ***to express*** *how you feel; or* ***to entertain.*** Write those categories on the board. Then discuss which category each purpose on the list falls into. Point out that some may fall into more than one. (e.g., You can report facts in a way that is entertaining.) Next, say: *What you write about is also affected by who your reader, or* ***audience****, will be.* Read the audiences listed in items 1–4. Then model completing item 1. Say: *If I were to write for a young child, my purpose might be to entertain him or her with a funny story. Kids love stories about animals, so I'll tell a funny story about a baby animal.* Have students work in pairs to complete items 2–4.
- **Activity B (Convention):** Remind students that people's titles, such as **Mr., Ms., Dr., Aunt,** and **Uncle** should be capitalized. Have students complete the activity independently.

DAY 4

Read the rule aloud. Then guide students through the activities.

- **Activity A:** Return to item 1 on Day 3 to model narrowing your idea. Write **baby animal** in the top section. In the middle section, write a specific animal, such as a porcupine. Then write a plot idea at the bottom, such as "how the baby porcupine got stuck." Have students complete the activity on their own or in small groups. Circulate to provide assistance as needed.
- **Activity B (Convention):** After students complete the activity, have them read the names they wrote aloud.

DAY 5 *Writing Prompt*

- *Use the idea you chose on Day 4 to develop into a paragraph or story. Make sure that your writing fits the purpose and audience.*
- *Be sure to capitalize proper nouns.*

Name: ______________________________

Week 1 • Day 1

Ideas The best writing begins with a strong idea.

A. Read this brainstorming web for a school newspaper article. Think about the purpose and audience. Cross out the topics that don't fit the purpose or audience.

Purpose: to provide news and information about things going on at school

Audience: students, teachers, and parents

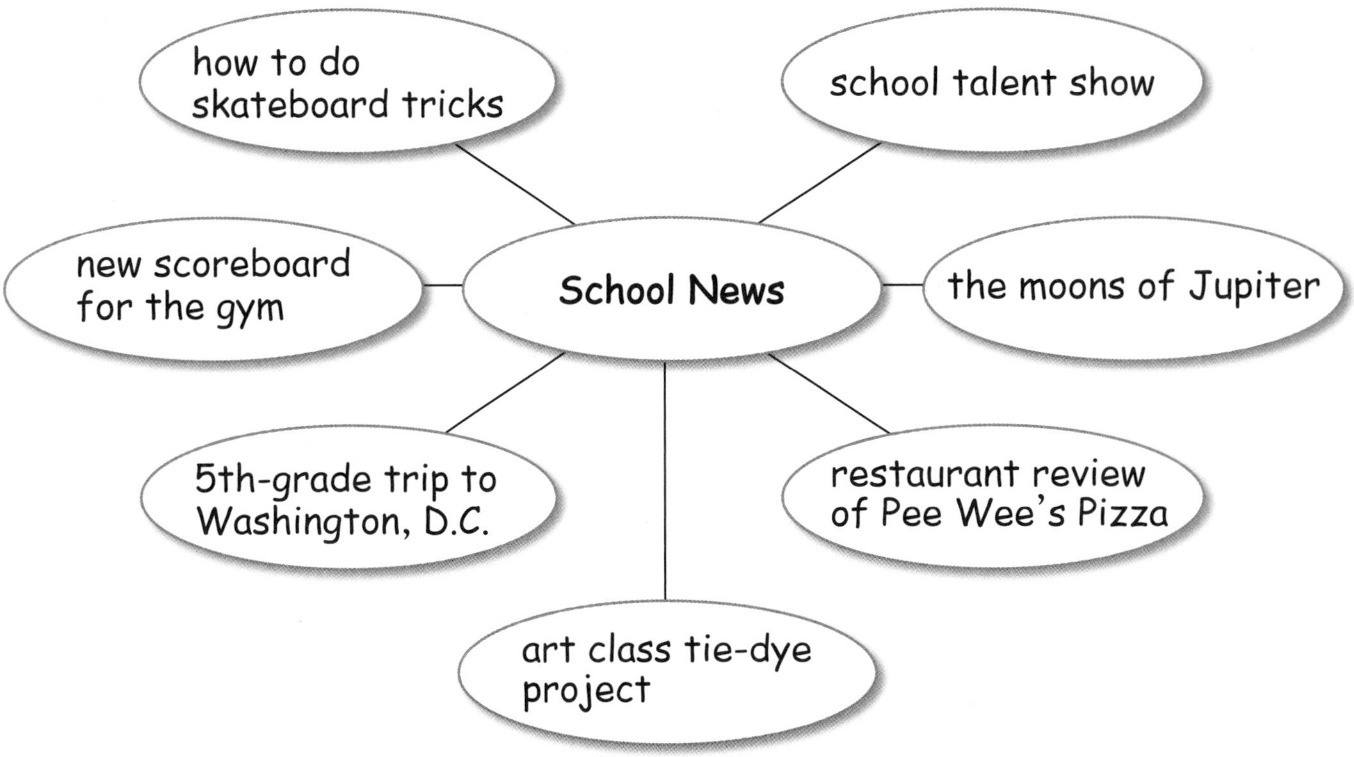

B. What would you write about if you were writing an article for your school newspaper? List three ideas below.

1. ______________________________

2. ______________________________

3. ______________________________

Name: ____________________

Ideas Make your ideas stronger by narrowing your focus.

A. A narrowing triangle can help you choose an idea that is specific enough to write about. Read Triangle 1 as an example. Then use Triangle 2 to think of a specific idea of your own. Complete the triangle.

Triangle 1

- sports
- basketball
- our school basketball team
- beating the Panthers last Friday

Triangle 2

- school activities
-
-
-

B. Find the proper nouns in Triangle 1. Write them below.

1. Team name: ____________________
2. Day of the week: ____________________

Name: ______________________________

Ideas

To choose a strong idea, think about your audience and purpose for writing.

A. Read the list of purposes for writing. For each audience given, choose a purpose from the list and think of a specific idea to fit that purpose.

Purposes for Writing	
to explain how to do something	to tell a funny story
to report facts or information	to describe what something is like
to express your feelings	to persuade someone to take action

1. **Audience:** a young child

   Purpose: ______________________________

   Idea: ______________________________

2. **Audience:** the people of your community

   Purpose: ______________________________

   Idea: ______________________________

3. **Audience:** your teacher and classmates

   Purpose: ______________________________

   Idea: ______________________________

4. **Audience:** a pen pal in another country

   Purpose: ______________________________

   Idea: ______________________________

B. Write the names of two people who have recently read something you wrote. Be sure to capitalize their names and titles.

______________________________ ______________________________

Name: ______________________

Week 1 • Day 4

Ideas

Think of many ideas, but choose the strongest one. A strong idea is specific and fits your purpose and audience.

A. Look back at the ideas you wrote on Day 3. Choose one of them to develop into a stronger, more specific idea. Fill in the audience and purpose. Then use the narrowing triangle below to help you choose a strong idea.

Audience: ______________________

Purpose: ______________________

B. Write the names of three people who could be in your audience. Remember to capitalize their names and titles.

______________ ______________ ______________

IDEAS
Writing a Topic Sentence and Supporting Details

DAY 1

Read the rule aloud. Review the definition of main idea. Then say: *A topic sentence expresses the main idea, but it doesn't have to come at the beginning of a paragraph. Sometimes the paragraph leads up to the topic sentence.* Then guide students through the activities.

- **Activity A:** Read aloud Paragraph 1. Then ask: *Which topic sentence tells what the paragraph is mainly about?* (the first) Say: *Hurricanes do cause flooding, but the whole paragraph is not about flooding. It also tells about roofs blowing away. So the main idea is that hurricanes are dangerous.* Ask: *Where is the best place to put the topic sentence in this case?* (the beginning) Have students read and complete Paragraph 2 on their own.
- **Activity B (Convention):** Read aloud the first pair of sentences. Ask: *What is the difference between the sentences?* (verbs) Say: ***Lakes** is the subject of both sentences. It is a plural noun. We use **are** with plural nouns.* Have students read the correct sentence aloud. Repeat for item 2.

Name: ______________________ **Week 2 • Day 1**

Ideas A topic sentence clearly states the main idea of a paragraph.

A. Read each paragraph and pair of topic sentences beneath it. Choose the best topic sentence for the paragraph and write it where you think it should go in the paragraph.

Paragraph 1

Hurricanes are dangerous storms.
^Hurricanes blow through with very high winds. The winds often lift roofs from buildings and send cars sailing through the air. Flooding is very common during hurricanes. The large amounts of rain they bring can make the water level of lakes, oceans, and other bodies of water rise quickly and flood streets, homes, and businesses.

Topic Sentences: Hurricanes are dangerous storms.
Hurricanes cause flooding.

Paragraph 2

Thousands of years ago, during the Ice Age, glaciers crawled across North America. These sheets of ice were so heavy that they carved out giant valleys. Then the glaciers melted, leaving behind rocks and gravel. These changes in the land created the Great Lakes: Huron, Ontario, Michigan, Erie, and Superior. These are some of the largest lakes in the world! Without them, the land would look a lot different. ^**The Great Lakes are proof of the power of glaciers.**

Topic Sentences: Glaciers are slow-moving masses of ice.
The Great Lakes are proof of the power of glaciers.

B. Read each sentence. Which one uses verbs correctly? Write an *X* next to it.

1. ___ The lakes is full of fresh water.
   X The lakes are full of fresh water.
2. **X** A hurricane sometimes has 100-mile-per-hour winds.
   ___ A hurricane sometimes have 100-mile-per-hour winds.

18 IDEAS Daily 6-Trait Writing • EMC 6025 • © Evan-Moor Corp.

DAY 2

Read the rule aloud. Explain: *Good details in a paragraph support the topic sentence by telling more about the main idea.* Guide students through the activities.

- **Activity A:** Have students read the paragraph and look for the topic sentence. Remind them that it may be anywhere in the paragraph. After they have identified it as the third sentence, ask: *What details support that main idea?* (e.g., He has illustrated many books; children write to him.) Say: *These details are good. They give examples of why Carle is successful and well-known.* Have students complete the activities.
- **Activity B:** Read aloud the paragraph. Ask: *What is the main idea of this paragraph? What do all the details tell about?* (making a bowl out of clay) Have students turn the main idea into a topic sentence.

  Convention: Ask: *Which sentence has an incorrect verb?* (the last one) Ask: *What should the verb change to?* (**dries**) Model using proofreading marks to change **dry** to **dries**.

Name: ______________________ **Week 2 • Day 2**

Ideas Clearly state the main idea in the topic sentence. Give strong details to support the main idea.

A. Read this paragraph. Circle its topic sentence. Underline three details that support its main idea.

When you were younger, did you ever read the books **The Very Hungry Caterpillar** or **Brown Bear, Brown Bear, What Do You See?** If so, then you have seen the art of Eric Carle. (Eric Carle is a successful artist whose style is known all over the world.) To make his illustrations, he paints papers. Then he cuts the papers and makes them into a collage. Since the 1950s, he has illustrated more than 70 books. Now, 75 million copies of his books exist all over the world. That's a lot of books! Carle has inspired children everywhere to make collages of their own. Sometimes they send him pictures of their art. **Underlining will vary. Any sentences after the circled topic sentence can be considered a detail.**

B. This paragraph is missing a topic sentence. Figure out the main idea of the paragraph, and write a topic sentence for it. Then fix any verbs that do not agree with their subjects.

First, form a ball of clay. Then press your thumb halfway into the ball. Use your other hand to pinch the clay around your thumb. Keep pinching as you turn the ball of clay. Soon, you will have a clay bowl! After your bowl ~~dry~~ **dries**, you can paint it any color you wish.

Topic Sentence:
Sample Answer: Making a clay bowl is easy.

© Evan-Moor Corp. • EMC 6025 • Daily 6-Trait Writing IDEAS 19

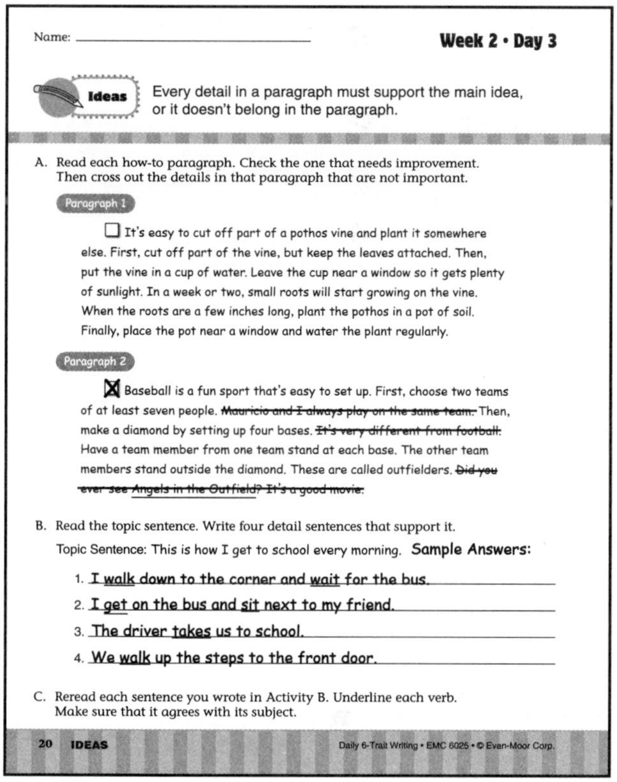

Name: ______________________ **Week 2 • Day 3**

Ideas Every detail in a paragraph must support the main idea, or it doesn't belong in the paragraph.

A. Read each how-to paragraph. Check the one that needs improvement. Then cross out the details in that paragraph that are not important.

Paragraph 1

☐ It's easy to cut off part of a pothos vine and plant it somewhere else. First, cut off part of the vine, but keep the leaves attached. Then, put the vine in a cup of water. Leave the cup near a window so it gets plenty of sunlight. In a week or two, small roots will start growing on the vine. When the roots are a few inches long, plant the pothos in a pot of soil. Finally, place the pot near a window and water the plant regularly.

Paragraph 2

☒ Baseball is a fun sport that's easy to set up. First, choose two teams of at least seven people. ~~Mauricio and I always play on the same team.~~ Then, make a diamond by setting up four bases. ~~It's very different from football.~~ Have a team member from one team stand at each base. The other team members stand outside the diamond. These are called outfielders. ~~Did you ever see Angels in the Outfield? It's a good movie.~~

B. Read the topic sentence. Write four detail sentences that support it.

Topic Sentence: This is how I get to school every morning. **Sample Answers:**

1. I walk down to the corner and wait for the bus.
2. I get on the bus and sit next to my friend.
3. The driver takes us to school.
4. We walk up the steps to the front door.

C. Reread each sentence you wrote in Activity B. Underline each verb. Make sure that it agrees with its subject.

20 IDEAS Daily 6-Trait Writing • EMC 6025 • © Evan-Moor Corp.

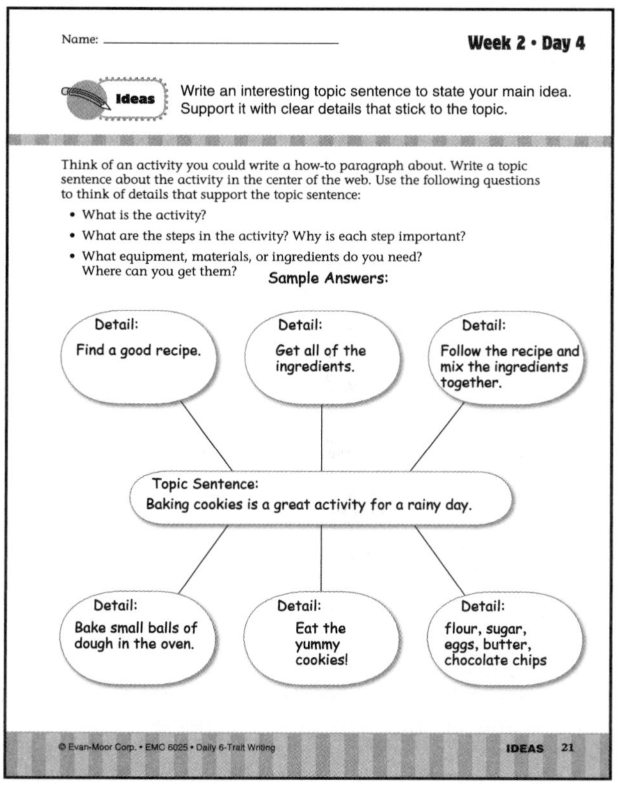

Name: ______________________ **Week 2 • Day 4**

Ideas Write an interesting topic sentence to state your main idea. Support it with clear details that stick to the topic.

Think of an activity you could write a how-to paragraph about. Write a topic sentence about the activity in the center of the web. Use the following questions to think of details that support the topic sentence:

- What is the activity?
- What are the steps in the activity? Why is each step important?
- What equipment, materials, or ingredients do you need? Where can you get them?

Sample Answers:

© Evan-Moor Corp. • EMC 6025 • Daily 6-Trait Writing IDEAS 21

DAY 3

Read the rule aloud. Then guide students through the activities.

- **Activity A:** Say: *In a good paragraph, all details tell more about the topic sentence.* Have students read the paragraphs. Ask: *What is Paragraph 1 about?* (growing a new pothos plant) *Are all sentences about that main idea?* (yes) *What is the main idea of Paragraph 2?* (how to play baseball) Say: *The writer mentions his friend Mauricio. Does that help you understand how to play the sport?* (no) Have students complete the activity.
- **Activity B:** Read aloud the topic sentence. Invite students to give details that could support it. Then ask: *What if I said, "I like cereal for breakfast"? Does that support the topic sentence?* (no) Say: *It may also be about the morning, but this paragraph should only have details about coming to school.* Have students complete the activity.
- **Activity C (Convention):** After students underline their verbs, invite volunteers to read their sentences aloud. Have other students confirm that the correct verbs were used.

DAY 4

Read the rule aloud. Then guide students through the activity.

- Help students brainstorm topics. Ask: *Is there a sport or musical instrument you play? Is there anything you like to make or cook?*
- Model filling out the web. Say: *If I were going to write about making vegetable soup, my topic sentence might be "You can make vegetable soup with the leftovers in your fridge."* Then model answering the bulleted questions to generate details. Have students confirm that each detail supports your topic. Then have students fill out their own webs.

DAY 5 *Writing Prompt*

- *Use the web you completed on Day 4 to write a how-to paragraph with a clear topic sentence and supporting details.*
- *Be sure that your subjects and verbs agree.*

Name: ____________________

Week 2 • Day 1

Ideas A topic sentence clearly states the main idea of a paragraph.

A. Read each paragraph and pair of topic sentences beneath it. Choose the best topic sentence for the paragraph and write it where you think it should go in the paragraph.

Paragraph 1

Hurricanes blow through with very high winds. The winds often lift roofs from buildings and send cars sailing through the air. Flooding is very common during hurricanes. The large amounts of rain they bring can make the water level of lakes, oceans, and other bodies of water rise quickly and flood streets, homes, and businesses.

Topic Sentences: Hurricanes are dangerous storms.
Hurricanes cause flooding.

Paragraph 2

Thousands of years ago, during the Ice Age, glaciers crawled across North America. These sheets of ice were so heavy that they carved out giant valleys. Then the glaciers melted, leaving behind rocks and gravel. These changes in the land created the Great Lakes: Huron, Ontario, Michigan, Erie, and Superior. These are some of the largest lakes in the world! Without them, the land would look a lot different.

Topic Sentences: Glaciers are slow-moving masses of ice.
The Great Lakes are proof of the power of glaciers.

B. Read each sentence. Which one uses verbs correctly? Write an *X* next to it.

1. ____ The lakes is full of fresh water.

   ____ The lakes are full of fresh water.

2. ____ A hurricane sometimes has 100-mile-per-hour winds.

   ____ A hurricane sometimes have 100-mile-per-hour winds.

Name: ______________________________

Week 2 • Day 2

Ideas Clearly state the main idea in the topic sentence.
Give strong details to support the main idea.

A. Read this paragraph. Circle its topic sentence. Underline three details that support its main idea.

When you were younger, did you ever read the books **The Very Hungry Caterpillar** or **Brown Bear, Brown Bear, What Do You See?** If so, then you have seen the art of Eric Carle. Eric Carle is a successful artist whose style is known all over the world. To make his illustrations, he paints papers. Then he cuts the papers and makes them into a collage. Since the 1950s, he has illustrated more than 70 books. Now, 75 million copies of his books exist all over the world. That's a lot of books! Carle has inspired children everywhere to make collages of their own. Sometimes they send him pictures of their art.

B. This paragraph is missing a topic sentence. Figure out the main idea of the paragraph, and write a topic sentence for it. Then fix any verbs that do not agree with their subjects.

First, form a ball of clay. Then press your thumb halfway into the ball. Use your other hand to pinch the clay around your thumb. Keep pinching as you turn the ball of clay. Soon, you will have a clay bowl! After your bowl dry, you can paint it any color you wish.

Topic Sentence:

____

____

Name: ______________________________

Ideas Every detail in a paragraph must support the main idea, or it doesn't belong in the paragraph.

A. Read each how-to paragraph. Check the one that needs improvement. Then cross out the details in that paragraph that are not important.

Paragraph 1

☐ It's easy to cut off part of a pothos vine and plant it somewhere else. First, cut off part of the vine, but keep the leaves attached. Then, put the vine in a cup of water. Leave the cup near a window so it gets plenty of sunlight. In a week or two, small roots will start growing on the vine. When the roots are a few inches long, plant the pothos in a pot of soil. Finally, place the pot near a window and water the plant regularly.

Paragraph 2

☐ Baseball is a fun sport that's easy to set up. First, choose two teams of at least seven people. Mauricio and I always play on the same team. Then, make a diamond by setting up four bases. It's very different from football. Have a team member from one team stand at each base. The other team members stand outside the diamond. These are called outfielders. Did you ever see Angels in the Outfield? It's a good movie.

B. Read the topic sentence. Write four detail sentences that support it.

Topic Sentence: This is how I get to school every morning.

1. ______________________________

2. ______________________________

3. ______________________________

4. ______________________________

C. Reread each sentence you wrote in Activity B. Underline each verb. Make sure that it agrees with its subject.

Name: ______________________________

Ideas

Write an interesting topic sentence to state your main idea. Support it with clear details that stick to the topic.

Think of an activity you could write a how-to paragraph about. Write a topic sentence about the activity in the center of the web. Use the following questions to think of details that support the topic sentence:

- What is the activity?
- What are the steps in the activity? Why is each step important?
- What equipment, materials, or ingredients do you need? Where can you get them?

Detail:

Detail:

Detail:

Topic Sentence:

Detail:

Detail:

Detail:

IDEAS
Developing Character, Setting, and Plot Ideas

DAY 1

Review the basic elements of a story (character, setting, plot). Then read the rule aloud and guide students through the activities.

- **Activity A:** Ask: *Who is your favorite book character? Why do you like him or her?* Help students understand that good authors give their characters interesting qualities and traits.

  Say: *Let's make a boring character more interesting.* Read the story aloud, and explain the questions as needed. For example, say: *His goals are what he wants to do. His strengths are what he is good at. His weaknesses are what he's not good at, or the personality traits that cause him to make mistakes.* Students may brainstorm and complete the activity in small groups.

- **Activity B (Convention):** Write the word **could've** on the board and say: ***Could've** is a contraction for **could have.** Don't write **could of** when you mean **could have.** The same is true for **would've** and **might've.*** Then write the contractions **he'd** and **she'd** on the board. Say: *The **'d** can stand for the helping verb **had** or **would.** You have to use context clues to decide which one is meant.* Have students complete the activity.

Name: ______________________ **Week 3 • Day 1**

Ideas Use interesting details to make your characters come to life.

A. Read the story. Then use your imagination to answer the questions about the character. Try to think of details that would make George more interesting.

George sat on the steps of his apartment building. The steaming sun beat down on his shoulders, and the street was almost deserted. George heard the old grandfather clock inside the apartment chime noon. He thought about his sister's request. She wanted him to enter a local talent contest. Before the accident, he would've done it in a heartbeat. But now he'd do just about anything to get out of it.

Sample Answers:

1. What is George's full name? How old is he?
   George Vincent Liu
2. What does George look like?
   He is tall, with brown hair and a scar on his arm from when he broke his arm dancing.
3. What are George's goals?
   He wants to be a professional dancer, but he broke his arm while dancing. He also wants to earn prize money to help his family.
4. What are George's strengths?
   He is a good dancer. He also loves his family very much and would do anything for them.
5. What are George's weaknesses?
   His arm has not healed all the way, so he is scared to dance again. Sometimes he does dangerous things, such as flips and headspins. He could really get hurt.

B. Reread the story. Find the two contractions and write them below. Then write the two words that form each contraction.

1. would've = would + have
2. he'd = he + would

24 IDEAS — Daily 6-Trait Writing • EMC 6025 • © Evan-Moor Corp.

DAY 2

Read the rule aloud. Review the definition of setting (where and when a story takes place). Have students discuss what makes the settings of their favorite books interesting. Then guide students through the activities.

- **Activity A:** Read the story aloud. Say: *This story sounds interesting, but the setting isn't very clear. Let's use our imaginations to think of possible details.* Read aloud the questions and model answering them, using the sample answers on the reduced page to the right. For example, say: *The story doesn't say exactly what Greta's experiment was, but I bet something exploded. So I imagine there is glass on the floor.* Students may brainstorm and complete the activity in small groups.

- **Activity B (Convention):** Review the helping verbs **have, had,** and **would.** Then have students complete the activity.

Name: ______________________ **Week 3 • Day 2**

Ideas Use vivid details to make your setting interesting.

A. Read the story. Then use your imagination to answer the questions about the setting.

Greta looked around with dread. She couldn't believe her eyes! She let out a long sigh. This wouldn't be the first time her science experiments had gotten her into trouble. She could've gone to summer camp, but instead she'd spent her entire vacation trying to earn enough money to pay for the damage her last experiment caused. And now, she had made an even bigger mess! When her parents got home, they'd ground her for life!

Sample Answers:

1. At what time of day does the story take place?
   The story happens in the late afternoon, before Greta's parents come home from work.
2. Where does the story take place? Be specific.
   The story takes place in Greta's kitchen, in a small town in Arizona.
3. What does the place look like? Describe it.
   There is broken glass all over the floor. Green slime drips from the walls and ceiling. The stove is covered with soot, and a couple of cabinet doors are hanging off their hinges.
4. What can you hear in the setting? Smell? Feel? Touch?
   You can hear the microwave beeping. The kitchen smells like burnt rubber and rotten eggs. The floor feels sticky.

B. Reread the story. Find the contractions formed from *have, had,* or *would* and write them below. Then write the two words that form each contraction.

1. could've = could + have
2. she'd = she + had
3. they'd = they + would

© Evan-Moor Corp. • EMC 6025 • Daily 6-Trait Writing — IDEAS 25

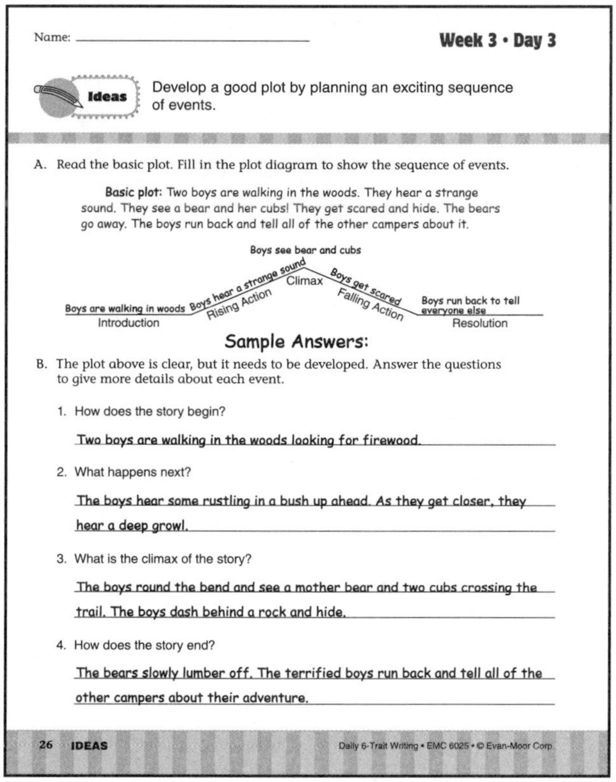

Name: ______________________ **Week 3 • Day 3**

Ideas Develop a good plot by planning an exciting sequence of events.

A. Read the basic plot. Fill in the plot diagram to show the sequence of events.

Basic plot: Two boys are walking in the woods. They hear a strange sound. They see a bear and her cubs! They get scared and hide. The bears go away. The boys run back and tell all of the other campers about it.

Sample Answers:

B. The plot above is clear, but it needs to be developed. Answer the questions to give more details about each event.

1. How does the story begin?

   Two boys are walking in the woods looking for firewood.

2. What happens next?

   The boys hear some rustling in a bush up ahead. As they get closer, they hear a deep growl.

3. What is the climax of the story?

   The boys round the bend and see a mother bear and two cubs crossing the trail. The boys dash behind a rock and hide.

4. How does the story end?

   The bears slowly lumber off. The terrified boys run back and tell all of the other campers about their adventure.

26 IDEAS Daily 6-Trait Writing • EMC 6025 • © Evan-Moor Corp.

DAY 3

Read the rule aloud. Say: *A plot is a sequence of events. In the* ***introduction****, or beginning, the reader learns about the characters and setting. The* ***rising action*** *is what happens that leads up to the* ***climax****, which is the turning point of the story. This is usually where the most important, or biggest, action happens. The* ***falling action*** *is what happens as a result of the climax, and the* ***resolution*** *is how the story ends.* Then guide students through the activities.

- **Activity A:** Read the basic plot aloud. Say: *A plot diagram is used to plan a plot before you write.* Draw a plot diagram on the board and model filling in the introduction. Have students complete the activity on their own. Go over the completed diagram as a class.
- **Activity B:** Read the questions aloud. Help students brainstorm ways to develop each plot point. For example, ask: *Why are the boys walking in the woods? What sounds do they hear? Where do they hide? Why do the bears go away?*

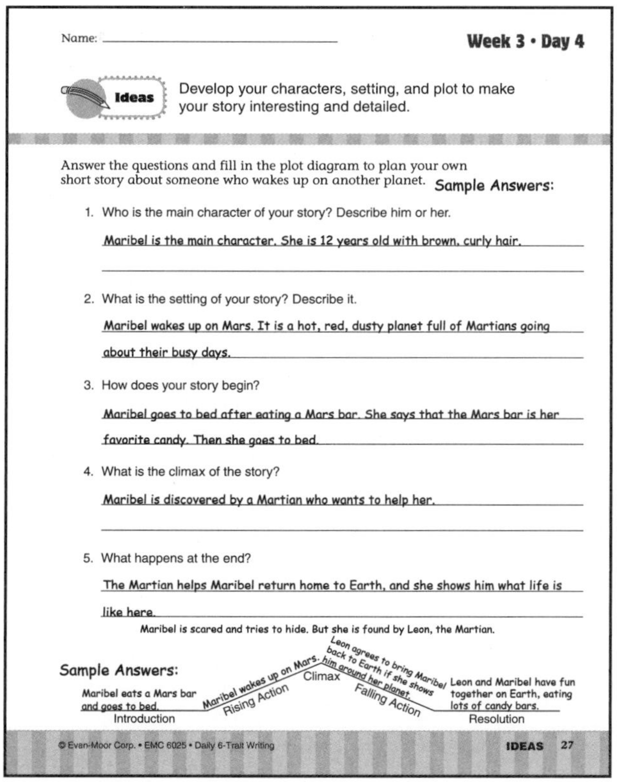

Name: ______________________ **Week 3 • Day 4**

Ideas Develop your characters, setting, and plot to make your story interesting and detailed.

Answer the questions and fill in the plot diagram to plan your own short story about someone who wakes up on another planet. **Sample Answers:**

1. Who is the main character of your story? Describe him or her.

   Maribel is the main character. She is 12 years old with brown, curly hair.

2. What is the setting of your story? Describe it.

   Maribel wakes up on Mars. It is a hot, red, dusty planet full of Martians going about their busy days.

3. How does your story begin?

   Maribel goes to bed after eating a Mars bar. She says that the Mars bar is her favorite candy. Then she goes to bed.

4. What is the climax of the story?

   Maribel is discovered by a Martian who wants to help her.

5. What happens at the end?

   The Martian helps Maribel return home to Earth, and she shows him what life is like here.

Sample Answers:

© Evan-Moor Corp. • EMC 6025 • Daily 6-Trait Writing IDEAS 27

DAY 4

Read the rule aloud. Then guide students through the activity.

- Say: *Plan the main character, setting, and plot for your own story about someone who wakes up on another planet. Remember to use what you've learned this week about developing story parts.*
- While students answer the questions and complete the diagram, circulate to ensure that they are using well-developed ideas. You may want to have students work with a partner to generate ideas and details.

DAY 5 *Writing Prompt*

- *Write a short story about someone who wakes up on another planet. Include the plot, character, and setting ideas you developed on Day 4.*
- *Use at least one contraction with* ***have****,* ***had****, or* ***would*** *in your story.*

Name: ________________________________

Ideas Use interesting details to make your characters come to life.

A. Read the story. Then use your imagination to answer the questions about the character. Try to think of details that would make George more interesting.

George sat on the steps of his apartment building. The steaming sun beat down on his shoulders, and the street was almost deserted. George heard the old grandfather clock inside the apartment chime noon. He thought about his sister's request. She wanted him to enter a local talent contest. Before the accident, he would've done it in a heartbeat. But now he'd do just about anything to get out of it.

1. What is George's full name? How old is he?

 ____

2. What does George look like?

 ____

3. What are George's goals?

 ____

4. What are George's strengths?

 ____

5. What are George's weaknesses?

 ____

B. Reread the story. Find the two contractions and write them below. Then write the two words that form each contraction.

1. ____________ = ____________ + ____________

2. ____________ = ____________ + ____________

Name: ______________________________

Ideas Use vivid details to make your setting interesting.

A. Read the story. Then use your imagination to answer the questions about the setting.

Greta looked around with dread. She couldn't believe her eyes! She let out a long sigh. This wouldn't be the first time her science experiments had gotten her into trouble. She could've gone to summer camp, but instead she'd spent her entire vacation trying to earn enough money to pay for the damage her last experiment caused. And now, she had made an even bigger mess! When her parents got home, they'd ground her for life!

1. At what time of day does the story take place?

____

2. Where does the story take place? Be specific.

____

3. What does the place look like? Describe it.

____

____

4. What can you hear in the setting? Smell? Feel? Touch?

____

B. Reread the story. Find the contractions formed from *have, had,* or *would* and write them below. Then write the two words that form each contraction.

1. __________ = __________ + __________

2. __________ = __________ + __________

3. __________ = __________ + __________

Name: ____________________ **Week 3 • Day 3**

Ideas Develop a good plot by planning an exciting sequence of events.

A. Read the basic plot. Fill in the plot diagram to show the sequence of events.

Basic plot: Two boys are walking in the woods. They hear a strange sound. They see a bear and her cubs! They get scared and hide. The bears go away. The boys run back and tell all of the other campers about it.

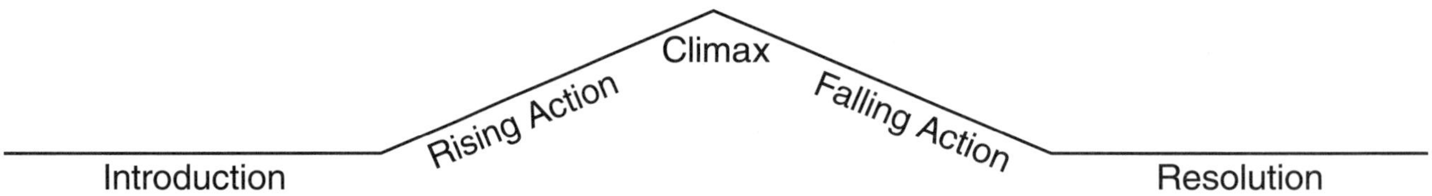

B. The plot above is clear, but it needs to be developed. Answer the questions to give more details about each event.

1. How does the story begin?

____

2. What happens next?

____

____

3. What is the climax of the story?

____

____

4. How does the story end?

____

____

Name: ______________________

Ideas

Develop your characters, setting, and plot to make your story interesting and detailed.

Answer the questions and fill in the plot diagram to plan your own short story about someone who wakes up on another planet.

1. Who is the main character of your story? Describe him or her.

____

____

2. What is the setting of your story? Describe it.

____

____

3. How does your story begin?

____

____

4. What is the climax of the story?

____

____

5. What happens at the end?

____

____

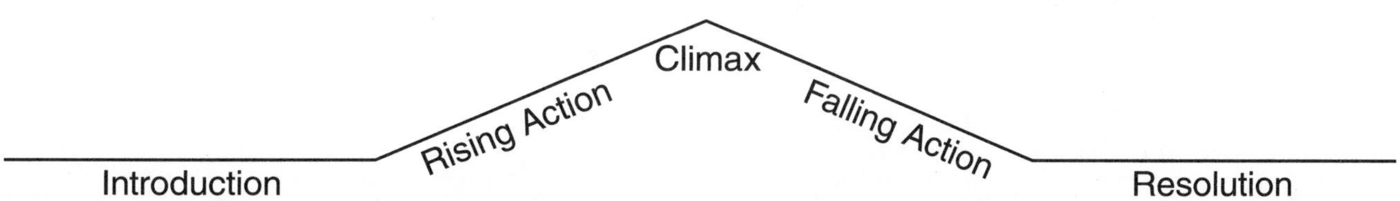

WEEK 4

IDEAS

Elaborating on Ideas and Details

DAY 1

Read the rule aloud. Explain that **to elaborate** means "to develop further or tell more about something." Then guide students through the activities.

- **Activity A:** Have students read both letters. Then say: *Pat's letter says the students used to have fun in the writer's club. Rula's letter says the club members used to have fun staying after school and thinking up stories to write. Which writer elaborated on the details more?* (Rula) Continue to go through the letters, comparing details. Then have students write their answers to the question.
- **Activity B (Convention):** Say: *Negative words are words such as* ***no, not, never, nothing, nobody,*** *and* ***nowhere****. Using two negatives in a sentence is called using a double negative. When you see double negatives, you should remove one, because you only need one.* Read sentence 1 aloud and ask: *What is the double negative?* ("don't live nowhere") *How could we change that sentence to make it correct?* ("The students don't live anywhere near..." or "The students live nowhere near...") Model using proofreading marks to correct the sentence. Repeat the process for the second sentence.

DAY 2

Read the rule aloud. Then guide students through the activities.

- **Activity A:** Read the essay aloud. Say: *This essay's ideas are too general. The lack of specific examples makes the paragraph boring.* Point out the word **things** and ask: *What are some specific things that a photograph can help you remember?* Use the students' answers to model filling in the first box. Have students complete the rest of the chart independently. Then review the answers.
- **Activity B (Convention):** Review the definition of double negatives. Then read aloud sentence 1 and say: ***Never*** *is a negative because it means "not ever."* ***Couldn't*** *is a negative because it is a contraction for* ***could not.*** *So, what is the double negative?* (**couldn't never**) Say: *There are two ways to fix this: "I could never give up my camera" or "I couldn't ever give up my camera."* Have students complete the activity independently.

Name: ______________________ **Week 4 • Day 1**

Ideas Good writers elaborate on ideas and details to paint a meaningful picture for the reader.

A. Two students wrote letters to their principal. Read the letters and answer the question.

Dear Ms. Wong,

We want the Writer's Club to come back. We used to have fun. Now we don't have anyplace to meet, and it's hard to find times to get together. Some teachers said they could help. We need to meet sometime at school.

Sincerely,
Pat Johnston

Dear Ms. Wong,

We don't want the Writer's Club to end. The other club members and I used to have fun after school, thinking of plots and characters. Now there's nowhere for us to meet. We want to talk about our stories and read each other's work, but we live miles from each other. There's no way to get together after school except for the Writer's Club. Mr. Gonzales and Ms. Zane have both said we can use their rooms.

Sincerely,
Rula Paz

Which writer did a better job of elaborating? Give at least two examples of specific details to support your answer. **Sample Answer:**

Rula's letter has better details. She tells what the Writer's Club used to do. She also tells exactly which teachers will help.

B. Use proofreading marks to correct the double negatives in these sentences.

Delete mark over "don't" OR delete mark over "nowhere"
1. The students don't live nowhere near each other.

Delete mark over "not" OR delete mark over "never" and insertion of "ever"
2. We're not never going to have a place to meet.

30 IDEAS Daily 6-Trait Writing • EMC 6025 • © Evan-Moor Corp.

Name: ______________________ **Week 4 • Day 2**

Ideas Look for ways to elaborate on your ideas by making your details and examples more specific.

A. Read this short essay. The words in bold are not very specific. How could the writer have elaborated more on her ideas? Use the chart below to write more specific examples the writer might have included instead.

Photographs are a good way to help remember **things**. **Important events** in my life are shown through photos. Photos help me remember the **fun times** with my friends.

Sample Answers:

Too General	More Specific
things	people, places, and events that are special to you
important events	the day I was born, the first time I rode a bike, starring in the school play
fun times	parties, trips, holiday celebrations

B. Rewrite each sentence to fix the double negative.

1. I couldn't never give up my camera.
   I could never (OR couldn't ever) give up my camera.
2. Stacey doesn't want nobody to take her picture.
   Stacey doesn't want anybody to take her picture.
3. There's not nothing better than taking pictures.
   There isn't anything (OR There is nothing) better than taking pictures.

© Evan-Moor Corp. • EMC 6025 • Daily 6-Trait Writing IDEAS 31

Name: ____________________ **Week 4 • Day 3**

Ideas Elaborate on your ideas to be persuasive. Use specific details and examples that support your argument.

A. Read Joey's first draft of a letter to a newspaper. Use proofreading marks to fix any sentences that have double negatives. Then underline vague words and phrases that Joey could improve to provide details that support his argument.

> **Sample Answers:**
>
> Dear Editor:
>
> I heard that the city wants to close the Bevington Library because it doesn't have ~~no more~~ anymore money to pay the staff or buy ~~no more~~ anymore books. We need to keep the library open. My family uses the library a lot. We check out lots of things. We go there a lot in the summer. Whenever I write a report, people help me find information there. If the library closes, where will kids go?

B. Read Joey's revision. Underline the specific details and examples he added to support his argument.

> I heard that the city wants to close the Bevington Library because it doesn't have anymore money to pay the staff or buy anymore books. We need to keep the library open so students like me can use it. My family goes to the library every Saturday. My dad checks out books to read, and my brothers rent CDs and DVDs that they can't afford to buy. In the summer, my sister and I always join the reading program and earn prizes for reading books. And, whenever I need to write a report, Mr. Jue helps me find tons of information about my topic. If the library closes, where will kids go to get help like that?

C. Imagine that a library in your area has to close. Write two reasons why you think it shouldn't.

Answers will vary.

32 IDEAS Daily 6-Trait Writing • EMC 6025 • © Evan-Moor Corp.

Name: ____________________ **Week 4 • Day 4**

Ideas When you want to be persuasive, choose meaningful details that support your reasons.

Think of a change you would like to see in your community or school and prepare to write a letter to the editor of your local newspaper about it. Use the questions below to plan your ideas. **Sample Answers:**

1. What change or action would you like to see taken?
   I want the city to build a skateboard park.
2. Why is this change or action necessary?
   Kids need a place to skateboard safely.
3. How could the change or action take place? Who would be involved?
   The skateboard park could be built where the old playground was. It would be built by the City Recreation Department. Then the city could charge admission to help pay for the park.
4. Who might be against the idea? What would you say to them?
   People who live near the park might worry that it will be too noisy. But we could limit the park hours to certain times or build a wall to keep noise down. People might think it costs too much, but if we charge admission, the city will actually make money.

© Evan-Moor Corp. • EMC 6025 • Daily 6-Trait Writing IDEAS 33

DAY 3

Read the rule aloud. Then guide students through the activities.

- **Activity A (Convention):** Read the letter aloud and have students correct the double negatives. Then say: *Joey wrote this letter because he wants to persuade other people that the library shouldn't be closed. He has given several reasons but hasn't elaborated on them very well.* Direct students to the sentence "My family uses the library a lot." Ask: *Is this sentence specific? Does it tell us exactly how often or when they use the library?* (no) Guide students through the rest of the paragraph, underlining similarly vague statements.
- **Activity B:** Read the paragraph aloud. Then call students' attention to the third sentence ("My family goes to...") and ask: *What did Joey change?* (the word **a lot** to **every Saturday**) Ask: *Why is this better?* (It's more specific and meaningful.) Have students complete the activity in pairs.
- **Activity C:** After students write their reasons, invite volunteers to share what they wrote.

DAY 4

Read the rule aloud. Then guide students through the activity.

- Say: *A letter to a newspaper editor is often written to persuade readers to do something.* Point out that letters to the editor are typically about issues related to neighborhood improvement, recreation, public transportation, the environment, or crime. Help students brainstorm specific topics.
- Use the sample answers on the reduced page to the left to model answering the questions. For question 4, point out that it's important to think of possible arguments against your position so you can address them.

DAY 5 *Writing Prompt*

- *Use your answers to the questions on Day 4 to write a letter to the editor about an important issue. Include specific details, examples, and reasons that elaborate on your opinion.*
- *Be sure to fix any double negatives in your letter.*

Name: ______________________________

Ideas Good writers elaborate on ideas and details to paint a meaningful picture for the reader.

A. Two students wrote letters to their principal. Read the letters and answer the question.

> Dear Ms. Wong,
>
> We want the Writer's Club to come back. We used to have fun. Now we don't have anyplace to meet, and it's hard to find times to get together. Some teachers said they could help. We need to meet sometime at school.
>
> Sincerely,
> Pat Johnston

> Dear Ms. Wong,
>
> We don't want the Writer's Club to end. The other club members and I used to have fun after school, thinking of plots and characters. Now there's nowhere for us to meet. We want to talk about our stories and read each other's work, but we live miles from each other. There's no way to get together after school except for the Writer's Club. Mr. Gonzales and Ms. Zane have both said we can use their rooms.
>
> Sincerely,
> Rula Paz

Which writer did a better job of elaborating? Give at least two examples of specific details to support your answer.

____

____

B. Use proofreading marks to correct the double negatives in these sentences.

1. The students don't live nowhere near each other.

2. We're not never going to have a place to meet.

Name: ______________________________

Ideas

Look for ways to elaborate on your ideas by making your details and examples more specific.

A. Read this short essay. The words in bold are not very specific. How could the writer have elaborated more on her ideas? Use the chart below to write more specific examples the writer might have included instead.

Photographs are a good way to help remember **things**. **Important events** in my life are shown through photos. Photos help me remember the **fun times** with my friends.

Too General	More Specific
things	
important events	
fun times	

B. Rewrite each sentence to fix the double negative.

1. I couldn't never give up my camera.

____

2. Stacey doesn't want nobody to take her picture.

____

3. There's not nothing better than taking pictures.

____

Name: ______________________

Ideas

Elaborate on your ideas to be persuasive. Use specific details and examples that support your argument.

A. Read Joey's first draft of a letter to a newspaper. Use proofreading marks to fix any sentences that have double negatives. Then underline vague words and phrases that Joey could improve to provide details that support his argument.

> Dear Editor:
>
> I heard that the city wants to close the Bevington Library because it doesn't have no more money to pay the staff or buy no more books. We need to keep the library open. My family uses the library a lot. We check out lots of things. We go there a lot in the summer. Whenever I write a report, people help me find information there. If the library closes, where will kids go?

B. Read Joey's revision. Underline the specific details and examples he added to support his argument.

> I heard that the city wants to close the Bevington Library because it doesn't have anymore money to pay the staff or buy anymore books. We need to keep the library open so students like me can use it. My family goes to the library every Saturday. My dad checks out books to read, and my brothers rent CDs and DVDs that they can't afford to buy. In the summer, my sister and I always join the reading program and earn prizes for reading books. And, whenever I need to write a report, Mr. Jue helps me find tons of information about my topic. If the library closes, where will kids go to get help like that?

C. Imagine that a library in your area has to close. Write two reasons why you think it shouldn't.

____

____

Name: ______________________

Ideas

When you want to be persuasive, choose meaningful details that support your reasons.

Think of a change you would like to see in your community or school and prepare to write a letter to the editor of your local newspaper about it. Use the questions below to plan your ideas.

1. What change or action would you like to see taken?

____

____

2. Why is this change or action necessary?

____

____

____

3. How could the change or action take place? Who would be involved?

____

____

____

____

4. Who might be against the idea? What would you say to them?

____

____

____

____

IDEAS
Maintaining Your Focus

DAY 1

Read the rule aloud. Say: *When you stay focused on a topic, you stick to the subject. Staying on topic makes your writing clear.* Guide students through the activities.

- **Activity A:** Have students read each paragraph and check the one they think does not keep its focus. (Paragraph 1) Confirm students' understanding by asking: *What is the subject of both paragraphs?* (trip to a flower shop) *Are all of the sentences in Paragraph 1 about being at the flower shop?* (no) Have students identify the sentences that should be deleted. Read the paragraph again, without the irrelevant details.
- **Activity B (Convention):** Review the rules for spelling plural forms of nouns that end in **y, lf,** or **x**. (change **y** to **ies**; **lf** to **lves**; **x** to **xes**) Point out that Paragraph 1 also contains "regular" plural nouns in which only an **s** was added. Have students complete the activity, and go over the answers together.

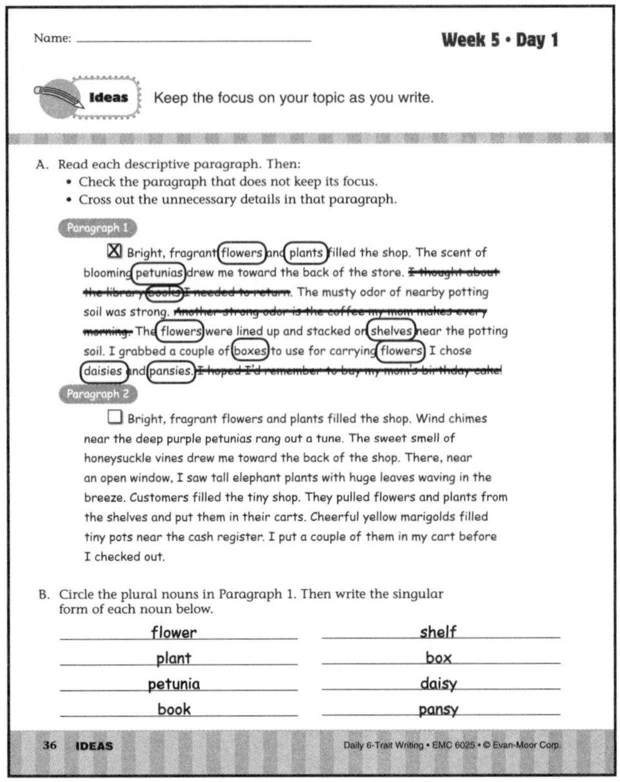

Name: ____________________ **Week 5 • Day 1**

Ideas Keep the focus on your topic as you write.

A. Read each descriptive paragraph. Then:
- Check the paragraph that does not keep its focus.
- Cross out the unnecessary details in that paragraph.

Paragraph 1

☒ Bright, fragrant flowers and plants filled the shop. The scent of blooming petunias drew me toward the back of the store. ~~I thought about the library books I needed to return~~. The musty odor of nearby potting soil was strong. ~~Another strong odor is the coffee my mom makes every morning.~~ The flowers were lined up and stacked on shelves near the potting soil. I grabbed a couple of boxes to use for carrying flowers. I chose daisies and pansies. ~~I hoped I'd remember to buy my mom's birthday cake!~~

Paragraph 2

☐ Bright, fragrant flowers and plants filled the shop. Wind chimes near the deep purple petunias rang out a tune. The sweet smell of honeysuckle vines drew me toward the back of the shop. There, near an open window, I saw tall elephant plants with huge leaves waving in the breeze. Customers filled the tiny shop. They pulled flowers and plants from the shelves and put them in their carts. Cheerful yellow marigolds filled tiny pots near the cash register. I put a couple of them in my cart before I checked out.

B. Circle the plural nouns in Paragraph 1. Then write the singular form of each noun below.

flower	shelf
plant	box
petunia	daisy
book	pansy

36 IDEAS — Daily 6-Trait Writing • EMC 6025 • © Evan-Moor Corp.

DAY 2

Review the rule. Say: *When you finish writing, always check to make sure that all of your sentences focus on the topic.* Then guide students through the activities.

- **Activity A:** Have students read the paragraph. Then ask: *What is the topic of the paragraph?* (the trip to New York City) Have students identify the topic sentence. (the first) Then have them compare the remaining sentences against the topic. For example, say: *The second sentence mentions that some students wanted to go to Washington, D.C. Does that sentence support the topic?* (no) Have students cross it out, as well as the other irrelevant sentences.

  Read the sentences in the box aloud, and discuss how each one sticks to the topic. Guide students in deciding where each sentence best fits in the paragraph. For example, ask: *Where should we add the sentence about the food that the students bought?* (after "They offered many kinds of food.")
- **Activity B (Convention):** Explain: *To form the plural of a word that ends in* **ss** *or* **ch**, *add* **es**. *To form the plural of a word that ends in* **ey**, *add* **s**. Then have students complete the activity.

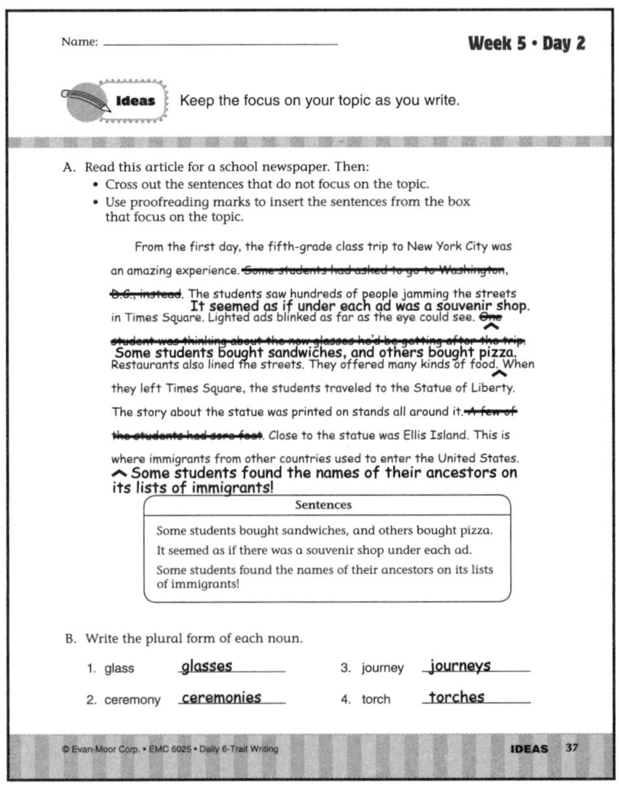

Name: ____________________ **Week 5 • Day 2**

Ideas Keep the focus on your topic as you write.

A. Read this article for a school newspaper. Then:
- Cross out the sentences that do not focus on the topic.
- Use proofreading marks to insert the sentences from the box that focus on the topic.

From the first day, the fifth-grade class trip to New York City was an amazing experience. ~~Some students had asked to go to Washington, D.C., instead~~. The students saw hundreds of people jamming the streets in Times Square. Lighted ads blinked as far as the eye could see. ^It seemed as if under each ad was a souvenir shop. ~~One student was thinking about the new glasses he'd be getting after the trip.~~ Restaurants also lined the streets. They offered many kinds of food. ^Some students bought sandwiches, and others bought pizza. When they left Times Square, the students traveled to the Statue of Liberty. The story about the statue was printed on stands all around it. ~~A few of the students had sore feet~~. Close to the statue was Ellis Island. This is where immigrants from other countries used to enter the United States. ^Some students found the names of their ancestors on its lists of immigrants!

Sentences

Some students bought sandwiches, and others bought pizza.
It seemed as if there was a souvenir shop under each ad.
Some students found the names of their ancestors on its lists of immigrants!

B. Write the plural form of each noun.

1. glass glasses
2. ceremony ceremonies
3. journey journeys
4. torch torches

© Evan-Moor Corp. • EMC 6025 • Daily 6-Trait Writing — IDEAS 37

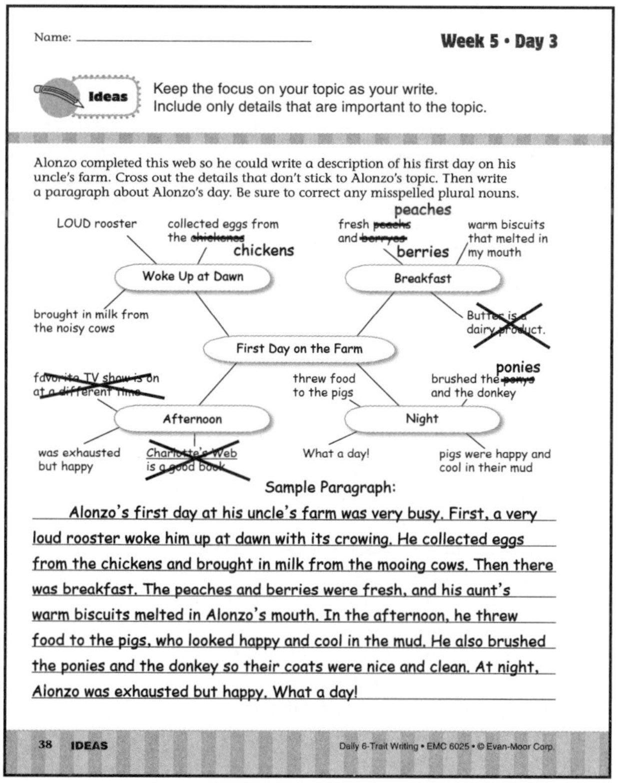

Name: ____________ **Week 5 • Day 3**

Ideas Keep the focus on your topic as your write. Include only details that are important to the topic.

Alonzo completed this web so he could write a description of his first day on his uncle's farm. Cross out the details that don't stick to Alonzo's topic. Then write a paragraph about Alonzo's day. Be sure to correct any misspelled plural nouns.

Sample Paragraph:

Alonzo's first day at his uncle's farm was very busy. First, a very loud rooster woke him up at dawn with its crowing. He collected eggs from the chickens and brought in milk from the mooing cows. Then there was breakfast. The peaches and berries were fresh, and his aunt's warm biscuits melted in Alonzo's mouth. In the afternoon, he threw food to the pigs, who looked happy and cool in the mud. He also brushed the ponies and the donkey so their coats were nice and clean. At night, Alonzo was exhausted but happy. What a day!

38 IDEAS Daily 6-Trait Writing • EMC 6025 • © Evan-Moor Corp.

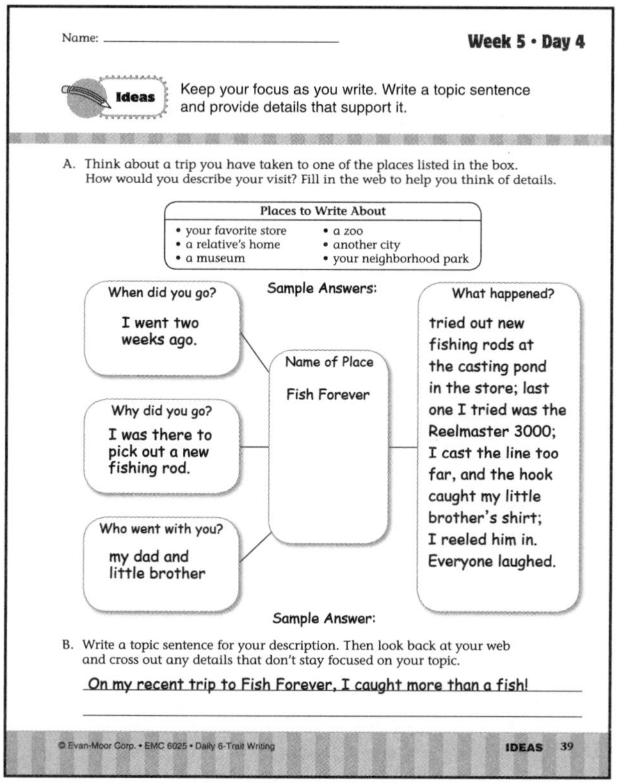

Name: ____________ **Week 5 • Day 4**

Ideas Keep your focus as you write. Write a topic sentence and provide details that support it.

A. Think about a trip you have taken to one of the places listed in the box. How would you describe your visit? Fill in the web to help you think of details.

Places to Write About	
• your favorite store	• a zoo
• a relative's home	• another city
• a museum	• your neighborhood park

Sample Answer:

B. Write a topic sentence for your description. Then look back at your web and cross out any details that don't stay focused on your topic.

On my recent trip to Fish Forever, I caught more than a fish!

© Evan-Moor Corp. • EMC 6025 • Daily 6-Trait Writing IDEAS 39

DAY 3

Read the rule aloud. Then guide students through the activity.

- Say: *When you are prewriting, or planning what to write, you may think of details that do not relate to your topic. That's OK to do when you're just getting your thoughts down on paper. After that, read your ideas again. If they don't stick to your topic, cross them out.* Then read aloud the web and ask: *What is the topic of Alonzo's description?* (his first day on the farm) *Which details are probably not important to the topic?* (e.g., butter; his favorite show; etc.) Have students cross out the irrelevant details.
- Before students use the remaining details to write their paragraphs, remind them that the paragraph needs a topic sentence. You may wish to brainstorm possible topic sentences as a class.
- **Convention:** Have students read aloud their completed paragraphs, identifying the plural nouns they corrected. List the plural nouns on the board and review the rules for forming them.

DAY 4

Read the rule aloud. Then guide students through the activities.

- **Activity A:** Read the list aloud and help students brainstorm specific topics. Once students have decided on a topic, have them complete their webs. When finished, have students review their webs to make sure that each detail is focused on their topic.
- **Activity B:** Remind students: *A topic sentence will help you keep your focus. Look at all of the details you have written. What is the main idea of your description? Which details don't focus on that main idea?* Model turning the main idea into a topic sentence and crossing out irrelevant details.

DAY 5 *Writing Prompt*

- *Use the details you wrote on Day 4 to write a descriptive paragraph about a place you have been. Remember to stay focused on your topic.*
- *Be sure to spell plural nouns correctly.*

Name: ______________________________

Ideas Keep the focus on your topic as you write.

A. Read each descriptive paragraph. Then:
- Check the paragraph that does not keep its focus.
- Cross out the unnecessary details in that paragraph.

Paragraph 1

☐ Bright, fragrant flowers and plants filled the shop. The scent of blooming petunias drew me toward the back of the store. I thought about the library books I needed to return. The musty odor of nearby potting soil was strong. Another strong odor is the coffee my mom makes every morning. The flowers were lined up and stacked on shelves near the potting soil. I grabbed a couple of boxes to use for carrying flowers. I chose daisies and pansies. I hoped I'd remember to buy my mom's birthday cake!

Paragraph 2

☐ Bright, fragrant flowers and plants filled the shop. Wind chimes near the deep purple petunias rang out a tune. The sweet smell of honeysuckle vines drew me toward the back of the shop. There, near an open window, I saw tall elephant plants with huge leaves waving in the breeze. Customers filled the tiny shop. They pulled flowers and plants from the shelves and put them in their carts. Cheerful yellow marigolds filled tiny pots near the cash register. I put a couple of them in my cart before I checked out.

B. Circle the plural nouns in Paragraph 1. Then write the singular form of each noun below.

______________________ ______________________

______________________ ______________________

______________________ ______________________

______________________ ______________________

Name: ______________________________

Ideas Keep the focus on your topic as you write.

A. Read this article for a school newspaper. Then:
- Cross out the sentences that do not focus on the topic.
- Use proofreading marks to insert the sentences from the box that focus on the topic.

From the first day, the fifth-grade class trip to New York City was an amazing experience. Some students had asked to go to Washington, D.C., instead. The students saw hundreds of people jamming the streets in Times Square. Lighted ads blinked as far as the eye could see. One student was thinking about the new glasses he'd be getting after the trip. Restaurants also lined the streets. They offered many kinds of food. When they left Times Square, the students traveled to the Statue of Liberty. The story about the statue was printed on stands all around it. A few of the students had sore feet. Close to the statue was Ellis Island. This is where immigrants from other countries used to enter the United States.

Sentences
Some students bought sandwiches, and others bought pizza.
It seemed as if there was a souvenir shop under each ad.
Some students found the names of their ancestors on its lists of immigrants!

B. Write the plural form of each noun.

1. glass ______________
2. ceremony ______________
3. journey ______________
4. torch ______________

Name: ____________________

Ideas

Keep the focus on your topic as your write.
Include only details that are important to the topic.

Alonzo completed this web so he could write a description of his first day on his uncle's farm. Cross out the details that don't stick to Alonzo's topic. Then write a paragraph about Alonzo's day. Be sure to correct any misspelled plural nouns.

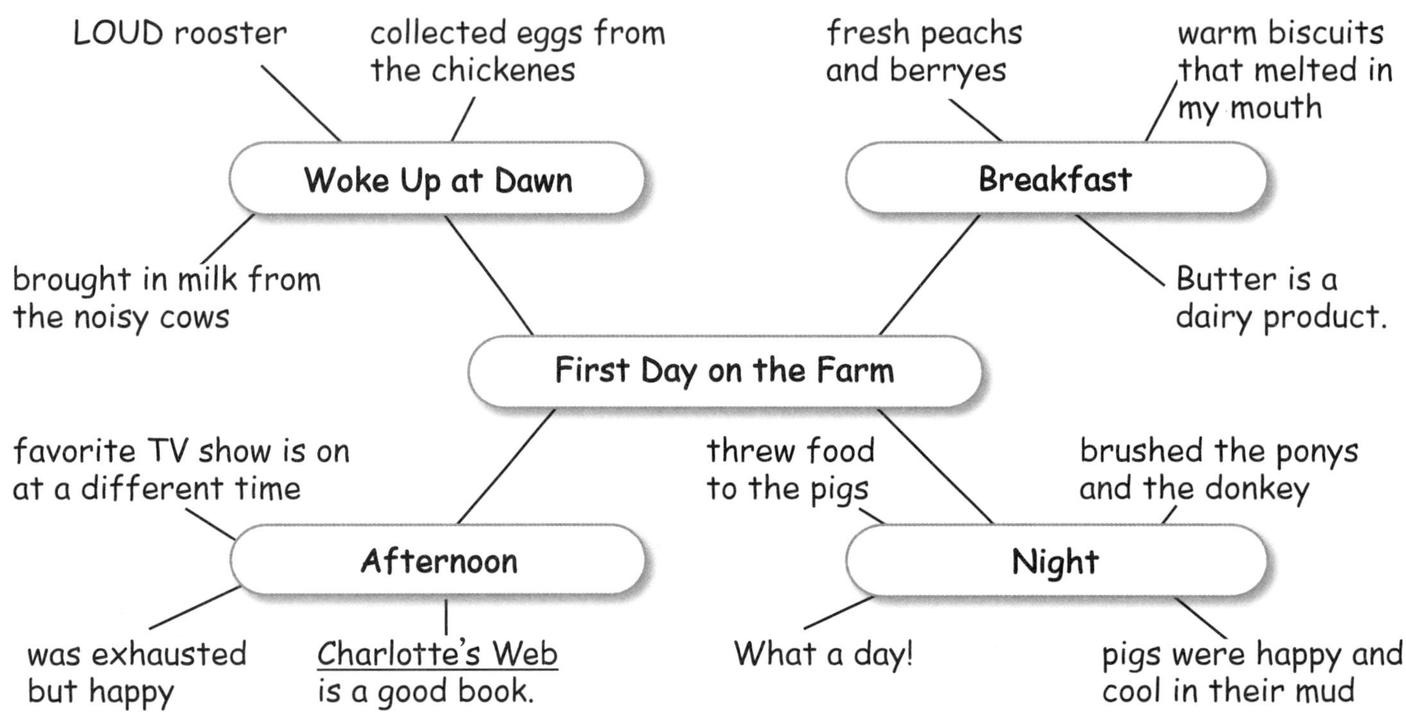

____

____

____

____

____

____

____

____

Name: ______________________________

Week 5 • Day 4

Ideas Keep your focus as you write. Write a topic sentence and provide details that support it.

A. Think about a trip you have taken to one of the places listed in the box. How would you describe your visit? Fill in the web to help you think of details.

Places to Write About	
• your favorite store	• a zoo
• a relative's home	• another city
• a museum	• your neighborhood park

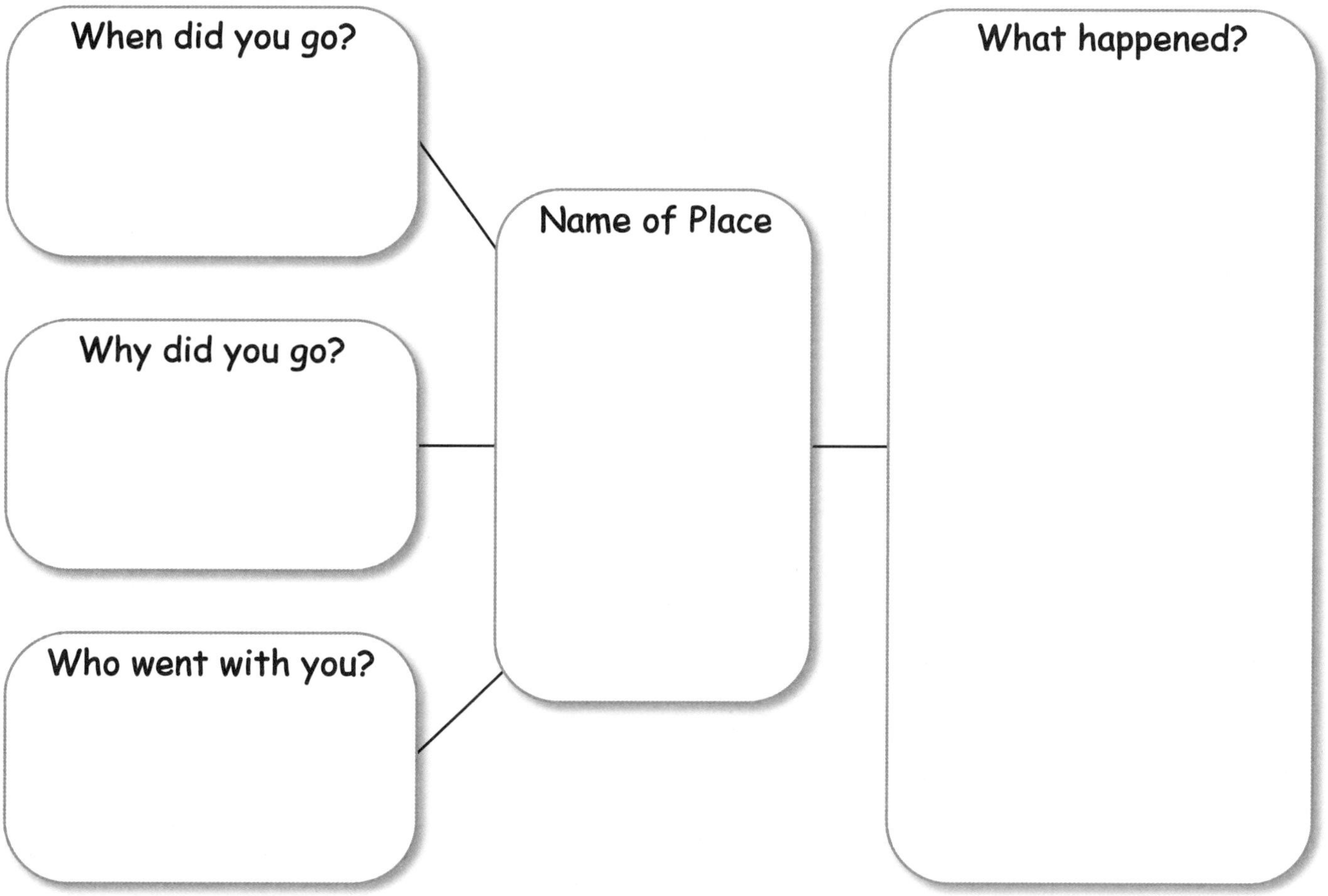

B. Write a topic sentence for your description. Then look back at your web and cross out any details that don't stay focused on your topic.

____

____

WEEK 1 ORGANIZATION

Sequencing

Refer to pages 6 and 7 to introduce or review the writing trait.

DAY 1

Say: *When you write, you have to organize your information. For instance, if you're writing about how to make or do something, or how to get somewhere, you have to describe the steps in the right order, or sequence. This is called* ***sequential order.*** Then read the rule aloud and guide students through the activities.

- **Activity A:** Say: *When you write in sequential order, you tell what happens first, next, and so on.* Read aloud the steps for making a burrito. Then ask: *Which step should be the first?* (the third listed) *How do you know?* (the other steps involve doing something to the tortilla) Have students write a **1** next to that step. Then have students complete the activity independently.

  Convention: Write **to, too,** and **two** on the board. Say: *These words are homophones.* (words that sound alike but have different spellings and meanings) *People often use them incorrectly in writing.* Point out **two** in the title of the recipe and say: *This word means the number two. Does that word make sense with the title?* (no) *How should the word be spelled?* (**to**) Have students correct the other errors.

- **Activity B:** Read aloud the words in the box. Say: *These words are also called* ***transition words.*** *They provide transitions between steps and signal what happens next.* Have students complete the activity. Invite volunteers to share their paragraphs.

Name: ______________________ **Week 1 • Day 1**

Organization When you write about steps in a process, be sure to put the steps in sequential order.

A. In the recipe below, the steps for making a burrito are out of order. Reorder the steps by writing the number that each step should be. Then correct the misspellings of *to, too,* and *two.*

to
How ~~two~~ Make a Burrito

4 Sprinkle cheese on top of the beans.
6 Eat and enjoy your burrito.
1 Place a soft tortilla flat on a plate. too
2 Spoon salsa onto the flat tortilla. Don't use ~~to~~ much!
5 Roll up the tortilla with all of the fillings inside.
two
3 Place ~~too~~ spoonfuls of beans on top of the salsa.

B. Using the numbered steps in Activity A and the transition words and phrases in the box below, write a paragraph explaining how to make a burrito. Be sure to spell *to, too,* and *two* correctly.

Transition Words				
next	then	after that	finally	first

Sample Answer: How to Make a Burrito

Making a burrito is easy! First, place a soft tortilla flat on a plate. Then, spoon salsa onto the tortilla. Don't use too much! Next, place two spoonfuls of beans on top of the salsa and sprinkle some cheese on top of the beans. After that, roll up the tortilla with all of the fillings inside. Finally, eat and enjoy your burrito!

42 ORGANIZATION Daily 6-Trait Writing • EMC 6025 • © Evan-Moor Corp.

DAY 2

Read the rule aloud. Say: ***Chronological order*** *means "the order in which things happen in time."* Then guide students through the activity.

- **Convention:** Read aloud the timeline and the paragraph. Say: *Some of the words in this paragraph are misspelled.* Review the homophones **to, too,** and **two**. Then write **threw** and **through** on the board. Say: *These are also homophones.* ***T-h-r-e-w*** *is the past tense of* ***throw. T-h-r-o-u-g-h*** *is a preposition, as in "We fly* ***through*** *the air."*
- Have students complete the activity independently. Invite volunteers to read aloud their revised paragraphs, checking for the correct organization.

Name: ______________________ **Week 1 • Day 2**

Organization In an autobiography, the events of someone's life should be in the order in which they happened.

The timeline below shows events in Adrienne's life. Read her autobiography. Then use proofreading marks to insert the missing events, based on her timeline. Find and correct the misspelled words in the paragraph.

1997 Born in Philadelphia
1998 Said my first word: "cat"
2001 Started ballet class; my brother, Saul, was born
2002 Moved to Oshkosh, Wisconsin; missed Grandma
2004 Grandma came to visit from Philadelphia; we made rocky road ice cream together
2006 Auditioned for lead role in ballet, but didn't get it
2007 Won the lead role in ballet!

Sample Answers:

I came into this world on August 5, 1997, in Philadelphia. My parents
I said my first word, "cat," in 1998. two
said I loved animals from the time I was born. When I was four, ~~to~~
important things happened: I started ballet class, and my little brother,
Saul, was born. I had always wanted a little brother. Now I had someone to
A year later, we moved to Oshkosh, Wisconsin. I missed my grandma!
call me "Big Sis" for the rest of my life. We had fun when Grandma Merrill
While she was here, we made homemade rocky road ice cream together.
came ~~too~~ visit from Philadelphia in 2004. In 2006, I auditioned for the lead
to
role in a ballet, but I didn't get it. However, I auditioned for the role again
in 2007, and finally I got it! I had achieved my dreams ~~threw~~ hard work.
through

© Evan-Moor Corp. • EMC 6025 • Daily 6-Trait Writing ORGANIZATION 43

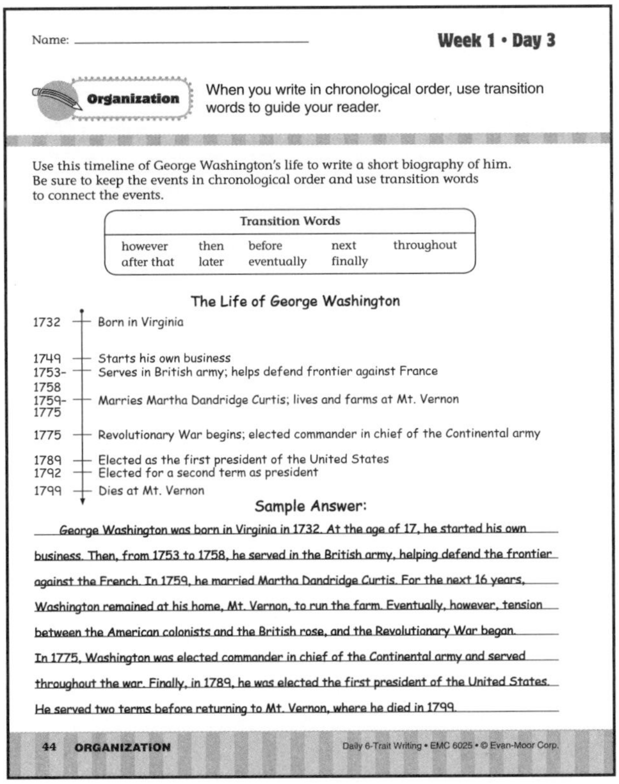

Name: ______________________ **Week 1 • Day 3**

Organization When you write in chronological order, use transition words to guide your reader.

Use this timeline of George Washington's life to write a short biography of him. Be sure to keep the events in chronological order and use transition words to connect the events.

Transition Words				
however	then	before	next	throughout
after that	later	eventually	finally	

The Life of George Washington

1732	Born in Virginia
1749	Starts his own business
1753-1758	Serves in British army; helps defend frontier against France
1759-1775	Marries Martha Dandridge Curtis; lives and farms at Mt. Vernon
1775	Revolutionary War begins; elected commander in chief of the Continental army
1789	Elected as the first president of the United States
1792	Elected for a second term as president
1799	Dies at Mt. Vernon

Sample Answer:

George Washington was born in Virginia in 1732. At the age of 17, he started his own business. Then, from 1753 to 1758, he served in the British army, helping defend the frontier against the French. In 1759, he married Martha Dandridge Curtis. For the next 16 years, Washington remained at his home, Mt. Vernon, to run the farm. Eventually, however, tension between the American colonists and the British rose, and the Revolutionary War began. In 1775, Washington was elected commander in chief of the Continental army and served throughout the war. Finally, in 1789, he was elected the first president of the United States. He served two terms before returning to Mt. Vernon, where he died in 1799.

44 ORGANIZATION Daily 6-Trait Writing • EMC 6025 • © Evan-Moor Corp.

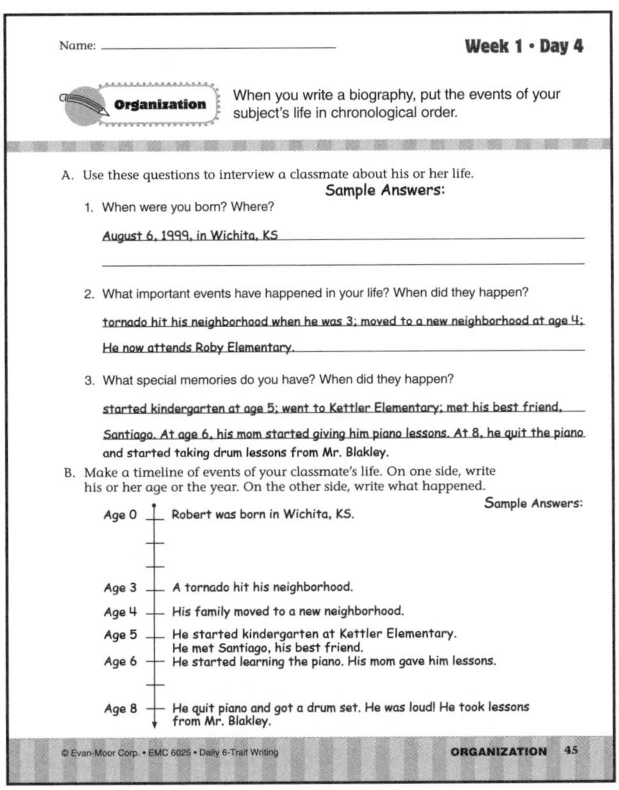

Name: ______________________ **Week 1 • Day 4**

Organization When you write a biography, put the events of your subject's life in chronological order.

A. Use these questions to interview a classmate about his or her life.

Sample Answers:

1. When were you born? Where?

   August 6, 1999, in Wichita, KS

2. What important events have happened in your life? When did they happen?

   tornado hit his neighborhood when he was 3; moved to a new neighborhood at age 4; He now attends Roby Elementary.

3. What special memories do you have? When did they happen?

   started kindergarten at age 5; went to Kettler Elementary; met his best friend, Santiago. At age 6, his mom started giving him piano lessons. At 8, he quit the piano and started taking drum lessons from Mr. Blakley.

B. Make a timeline of events of your classmate's life. On one side, write his or her age or the year. On the other side, write what happened.

Sample Answers:

Age 0	Robert was born in Wichita, KS.
Age 3	A tornado hit his neighborhood.
Age 4	His family moved to a new neighborhood.
Age 5	He started kindergarten at Kettler Elementary. He met Santiago, his best friend.
Age 6	He started learning the piano. His mom gave him lessons.
Age 8	He quit piano and got a drum set. He was loud! He took lessons from Mr. Blakley.

© Evan-Moor Corp. • EMC 6025 • Daily 6-Trait Writing ORGANIZATION 45

DAY 3

Read the rule aloud. Then guide students through the activity.

- Have a volunteer read aloud the entries on the timeline. Say: *Use this timeline to write a short biography of George Washington. Be sure to write about events in the correct order.* Then read the transition words in the box. Say: *Remember that transition words guide your readers and make your writing flow. But be careful not to use the same transition words* (e.g., **Then,**) *or phrases* (e.g., **In [year],**) *over and over again.*
- Have students write their biographies. Circulate to provide assistance as necessary. When students have finished, invite volunteers to share their biographies. Comment on the proper organization of each one.

DAY 4

Read the rule aloud. Then guide students through the activities.

- **Activity A:** Have students work in pairs to interview each other using the questions provided. Encourage students to list as many answers as possible for the second and third questions.
- **Activity B:** Model completing the timeline using events from your own life or the sample answers to the left. Then have students complete their timelines independently. After they have finished, have students give their timelines to their partners to make sure the events and dates are correct.

DAY 5 *Writing Prompt*

- *Use the timeline you created on Day 4 to write a short biography of your classmate. Remember to keep the events in chronological order.*
- *Check your writing for the words* ***to, too, two, threw,*** *and* ***through.*** *Make sure that you have spelled them correctly.*

Name: ______________________________

Organization When you write about steps in a process, be sure to put the steps in sequential order.

A. In the recipe below, the steps for making a burrito are out of order. Reorder the steps by writing the number that each step should be. Then correct the misspellings of *to, too,* and *two.*

How two Make a Burrito

___ Sprinkle cheese on top of the beans.

___ Eat and enjoy your burrito.

___ Place a soft tortilla flat on a plate.

___ Spoon salsa onto the flat tortilla. Don't use to much!

___ Roll up the tortilla with all of the fillings inside.

___ Place too spoonfuls of beans on top of the salsa.

B. Using the numbered steps in Activity A and the transition words and phrases in the box below, write a paragraph explaining how to make a burrito. Be sure to spell *to, too,* and *two* correctly.

Transition Words				
next	then	after that	finally	first

How to Make a Burrito

____

____

____

____

____

____

____

Name: ______________________

Organization

In an autobiography, the events of someone's life should be in the order in which they happened.

The timeline below shows events in Adrienne's life. Read her autobiography. Then use proofreading marks to insert the missing events, based on her timeline. Find and correct the misspelled words in the paragraph.

1997	Born in Philadelphia
1998	Said my first word: "cat"
2001	Started ballet class; my brother, Saul, was born
2002	Moved to Oshkosh, Wisconsin; missed Grandma
2004	Grandma came to visit from Philadelphia; we made rocky road ice cream together
2006	Auditioned for lead role in ballet, but didn't get it
2007	Won the lead role in ballet!

I came into this world on August 5, 1997, in Philadelphia. My parents said I loved animals from the time I was born. When I was four, to important things happened: I started ballet class, and my little brother, Saul, was born. I had always wanted a little brother. Now I had someone to call me "Big Sis" for the rest of my life. We had fun when Grandma Merrill came too visit from Philadelphia in 2004. In 2006, I auditioned for the lead role in a ballet, but I didn't get it. However, I auditioned for the role again in 2007, and finally I got it! I had achieved my dreams threw hard work.

Organization When you write in chronological order, use transition words to guide your reader.

Use this timeline of George Washington's life to write a short biography of him. Be sure to keep the events in chronological order and use transition words to connect the events.

Transition Words				
however	then	before	next	throughout
after that	later	eventually	finally	

The Life of George Washington

1732	Born in Virginia
1749	Starts his own business
1753-1758	Serves in British army; helps defend frontier against France
1759-1775	Marries Martha Dandridge Curtis; lives and farms at Mt. Vernon
1775	Revolutionary War begins; elected commander in chief of the Continental army
1789	Elected as the first president of the United States
1792	Elected for a second term as president
1799	Dies at Mt. Vernon

____

____

____

____

____

____

____

____

Name: ______________________________

Organization

When you write a biography, put the events of your subject's life in chronological order.

A. Use these questions to interview a classmate about his or her life.

1. When were you born? Where?

____

____

2. What important events have happened in your life? When did they happen?

____

____

3. What special memories do you have? When did they happen?

____

____

B. Make a timeline of events of your classmate's life. On one side, write his or her age or the year. On the other side, write what happened.

WEEK 2 ORGANIZATION
Organizing Information Logically

DAY 1

Read the rule aloud. Then guide students through the activities.

- **Activity A (Convention):** Read the letter aloud. Say: *A complete sentence needs a subject and a predicate. Which sentence is incomplete?* ("Lots of flavors.") *How could we rewrite the fragment to make it a complete sentence?* (e.g., "The store has lots of flavors.") Help students identify the subject and predicate in the new sentence.

  Have students reread the letter and underline the details. Then say: *Look at the details you underlined. What do you notice?* (The straight lines and wavy lines are grouped together.) Say: *Marilyn used logical organization. She wrote all the details about her school first, and then the details about the neighborhood.*

- **Activity B:** Have students complete the activity on their own. Then have students read their revised paragraphs aloud.

Name: ______________________ **Week 2 • Day 1**

Organization Use logical organization so your writing makes sense. Group similar ideas and details together.

A. Read this friendly letter from Marilyn to Stefan. Find and circle the sentence fragment. Then:
- Use a straight line to underline the details about Marilyn's school.
- Use a wavy line to underline the details about her neighborhood.

Dear Stefan,

We have finally finished moving! Last week was my first week at my new school. I now go to Jane Addams School. My new teacher is Mr. Yi. He's nice and likes to tell jokes. I love Fridays because he lets us play soccer in the afternoon! I like my neighborhood, too. There is an ice-cream store called Mariana's. Lots of flavors. We also have a park with a playground and a baseball diamond. I miss you, but I do like my new school and neighborhood. Good luck with your soccer team this year!

Your friend,
Marilyn

B. The details in this short paragraph are not in logical order. Rewrite it so that the details about each soccer position are grouped together.

Two positions in soccer are the goalie and the sweeper. A sweeper tries to steal the ball from the other team. A goalie can touch the ball with his or her hands. A goalie blocks the other team's goal. Sweepers must be very fast.

Sample Paragraph:

Two positions in soccer are the goalie and the sweeper. A goalie blocks the other team's goal. A goalie can touch the ball with his or her hands. A sweeper tries to steal the ball from the other team. Sweepers must be very fast.

48 ORGANIZATION Daily 6-Trait Writing • EMC 6025 • © Evan-Moor Corp.

DAY 2

Read the rule aloud. Then guide students through the activities.

- **Activity A (Convention):** Read aloud the first two sentences of the description. Ask: *Which sentence is incomplete?* (the second) *What's missing?* (a subject and predicate) Show students how it can be fixed by combining it with the first sentence. Then have them read the rest of the description and correct the sentence fragments.

  Before students complete the second part of the activity, discuss how the description is organized. Point out that the writer doesn't tell us where things are and jumps between different parts of the room. Then have students draw their lines.

- **Activity B:** Say: *Imagine that you're walking through the door into the room and moving all the way around it.* Have students draw the path they would take. Then model using the words in the box to create a transition from one detail to another. For example: "**Beside** the dressers stands Neil's desk." Have students complete the activity.

Name: ______________________ **Week 2 • Day 2**

Organization When you write a description of how something looks, you can organize your details by where things are in relation to each other.

A. Look at the floor plan of Neil's room and read the description. Then:
- Use proofreading marks to fix the sentence fragments.
- Draw a line on the floor plan to show the order in which the items were presented in the description.

Neil shares a bunk bed. With his brother Wade. On Neil's desk is his microscope. It's for looking at the bugs he finds outside. The closets. Are a big mess. Sometimes when Neil and Wade clean, they just throw everything. In their closets. Through the window, they can see the backyard. There's a *Star Wars* rug on the floor. They have two dressers.

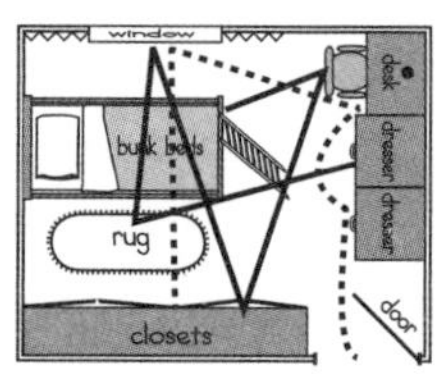

B. Look back at the line you drew. Draw another line to show a more logical order that you could follow to describe the room. Then rewrite the description. Use position words and phrases to create transitions from one detail to the next.

Position Words and Phrases				
behind	top	in front of	inside	near
on the other side	between	to the left	to the right	beside

Sample Paragraph:

Inside Neil's room, the first thing you see is two dressers to your right. Beside the dressers is Neil's desk. On top of his desk stands his microscope. It's for looking at the bugs he finds outside. To the left of the desk is the window. From the window, you can see the backyard. In the middle of the room is the bunk bed. Neil shares it with his brother Wade. A *Star Wars* rug lies between the bed and the closets, which are a big mess! Sometimes when the boys clean, they just throw everything into their closets.

© Evan-Moor Corp. • EMC 6025 • Daily 6-Trait Writing ORGANIZATION 49

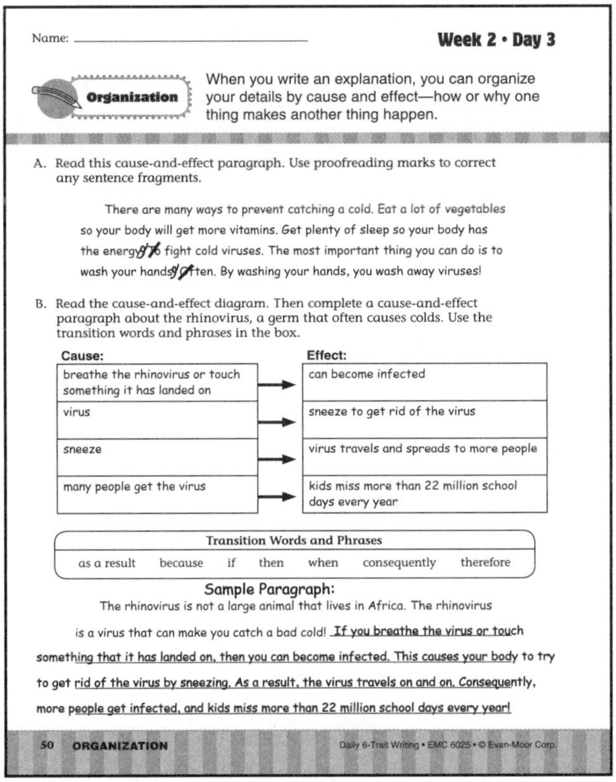

Name: ______ **Week 2 • Day 3**

Organization When you write an explanation, you can organize your details by cause and effect—how or why one thing makes another thing happen.

A. Read this cause-and-effect paragraph. Use proofreading marks to correct any sentence fragments.

There are many ways to prevent catching a cold. Eat a lot of vegetables so your body will get more vitamins. Get plenty of sleep so your body has the energy to fight cold viruses. The most important thing you can do is to wash your hands often. By washing your hands, you wash away viruses!

B. Read the cause-and-effect diagram. Then complete a cause-and-effect paragraph about the rhinovirus, a germ that often causes colds. Use the transition words and phrases in the box.

Cause:		Effect:
breathe the rhinovirus or touch something it has landed on	→	can become infected
virus	→	sneeze to get rid of the virus
sneeze	→	virus travels and spreads to more people
many people get the virus	→	kids miss more than 22 million school days every year

Transition Words and Phrases						
as a result	because	if	then	when	consequently	therefore

Sample Paragraph:
The rhinovirus is not a large animal that lives in Africa. The rhinovirus is a virus that can make you catch a bad cold! If you breathe the virus or touch something that it has landed on, then you can become infected. This causes your body to try to get rid of the virus by sneezing. As a result, the virus travels on and on. Consequently, more people get infected, and kids miss more than 22 million school days every year!

50 ORGANIZATION Daily 6-Trait Writing • EMC 6025 • © Evan-Moor Corp.

DAY 3

Read the rule aloud and guide students through the activities.

- **Activity A (Convention):** Have students read the paragraph. Then have them identify the sentence fragments. ("To fight cold viruses."; "Often.") Write the fragments on the board and have students suggest ways to make them complete sentences. (e.g., joining them with the previous sentences)
- **Activity B:** Read aloud the cause-and-effect diagram and make sure students understand how each cause results in the given effect. Then read aloud the transition words and phrases. Say: *These words and phrases show cause and effect, helping your reader make connections.*

  Have students complete the paragraph. Then have students exchange papers to check for sentence fragments and correct them. Have volunteers share their paragraphs.

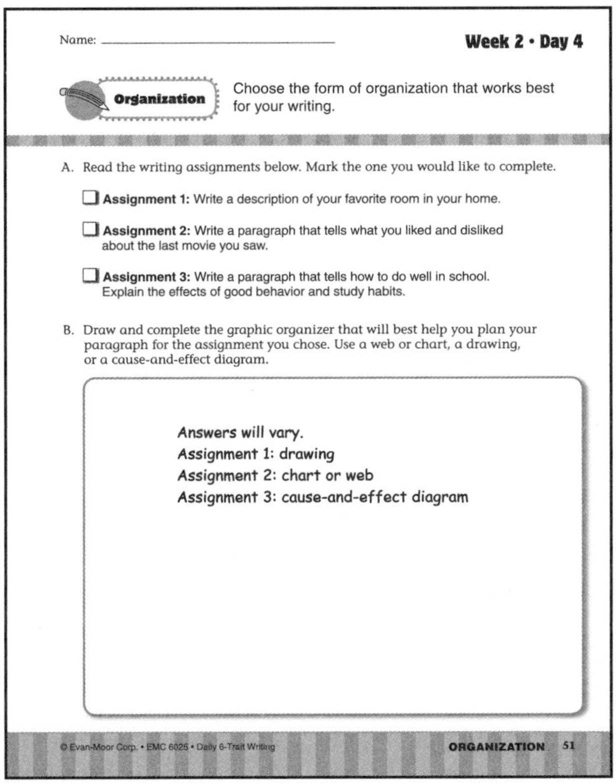

Name: ______ **Week 2 • Day 4**

Organization Choose the form of organization that works best for your writing.

A. Read the writing assignments below. Mark the one you would like to complete.

☐ **Assignment 1:** Write a description of your favorite room in your home.

☐ **Assignment 2:** Write a paragraph that tells what you liked and disliked about the last movie you saw.

☐ **Assignment 3:** Write a paragraph that tells how to do well in school. Explain the effects of good behavior and study habits.

B. Draw and complete the graphic organizer that will best help you plan your paragraph for the assignment you chose. Use a web or chart, a drawing, or a cause-and-effect diagram.

Answers will vary.
Assignment 1: drawing
Assignment 2: chart or web
Assignment 3: cause-and-effect diagram

© Evan-Moor Corp. • EMC 6025 • Daily 6-Trait Writing ORGANIZATION 51

DAY 4

Read the rule aloud. Then guide students through the activities.

- **Activity A:** Read the writing assignments aloud. For each one, ask: *What type of organization would be best for this assignment?* (1: position; 2: logical; 3: cause-and-effect) Then have students choose their assignments.
- **Activity B:** Have students identify the type of graphic organizer that would best help them plan their ideas. (1: drawing; 2: web or chart; 3: cause-and-effect diagram) Circulate to provide assistance as students complete their diagrams.

DAY 5 *Writing Prompt*

- *Write a paragraph in response to the assignment you chose on Day 4. Use the graphic organizer you completed.*
- *Have a partner check your writing for sentence fragments. Correct any that are found.*

Name: ____________________

Week 2 • Day 1

Organization

Use logical organization so your writing makes sense. Group similar ideas and details together.

A. Read this friendly letter from Marilyn to Stefan. Find and circle the sentence fragment. Then:

- Use a straight line to underline the details about Marilyn's school.
- Use a wavy line to underline the details about her neighborhood.

Dear Stefan,

We have finally finished moving! Last week was my first week at my new school. I now go to Jane Addams School. My new teacher is Mr. Yi. He's nice and likes to tell jokes. I love Fridays because he lets us play soccer in the afternoon! I like my neighborhood, too. There is an ice-cream store called Mariana's. Lots of flavors. We also have a park with a playground and a baseball diamond. I miss you, but I do like my new school and neighborhood. Good luck with your soccer team this year!

Your friend,
Marilyn

B. The details in this short paragraph are not in logical order. Rewrite it so that the details about each soccer position are grouped together.

Two positions in soccer are the goalie and the sweeper. A sweeper tries to steal the ball from the other team. A goalie can touch the ball with his or her hands. A goalie blocks the other team's goal. Sweepers must be very fast.

____

____

____

____

____

Name: ______________________

Week 2 • Day 2

Organization

When you write a description of how something looks, you can organize your details by where things are in relation to each other.

A. Look at the floor plan of Neil's room and read the description. Then:

- Use proofreading marks to fix the sentence fragments.
- Draw a line on the floor plan to show the order in which the items were presented in the description.

Neil shares a bunk bed. With his brother Wade. On Neil's desk is his microscope. It's for looking at the bugs he finds outside. The closets. Are a big mess. Sometimes when Neil and Wade clean, they just throw everything. In their closets. Through the window, they can see the backyard. There's a Star Wars rug on the floor. They have two dressers.

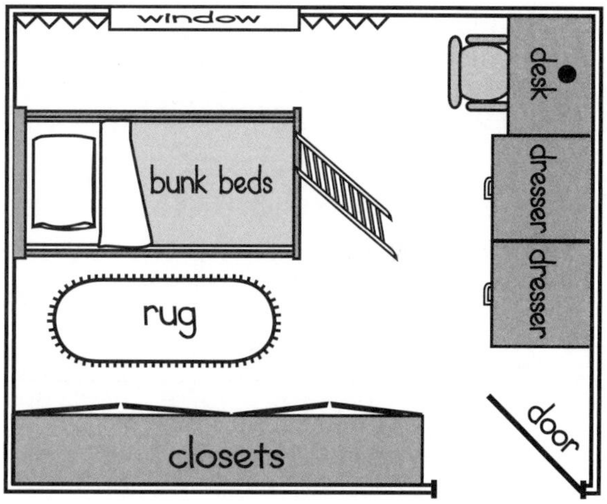

B. Look back at the line you drew. Draw another line to show a more logical order that you could follow to describe the room. Then rewrite the description. Use position words and phrases to create transitions from one detail to the next.

Position Words and Phrases				
behind	top	in front of	inside	near
on the other side	between	to the left	to the right	beside

____

____

____

____

____

____

Name: ______________________________

Week 2 • Day 3

Organization

When you write an explanation, you can organize your details by cause and effect—how or why one thing makes another thing happen.

A. Read this cause-and-effect paragraph. Use proofreading marks to correct any sentence fragments.

There are many ways to prevent catching a cold. Eat a lot of vegetables so your body will get more vitamins. Get plenty of sleep so your body has the energy. To fight cold viruses. The most important thing you can do is to wash your hands. Often. By washing your hands, you wash away viruses!

B. Read the cause-and-effect diagram. Then complete a cause-and-effect paragraph about the rhinovirus, a germ that often causes colds. Use the transition words and phrases in the box.

Cause:		Effect:
breathe the rhinovirus or touch something it has landed on	→	can become infected
virus	→	sneeze to get rid of the virus
sneeze	→	virus travels and spreads to more people
many people get the virus	→	kids miss more than 22 million school days every year

Transition Words and Phrases						
as a result	because	if	then	when	consequently	therefore

The rhinovirus is not a large animal that lives in Africa. The rhinovirus is a virus that can make you catch a bad cold! ______________________

____

____

____

Name: ____________________

Organization

Choose the form of organization that works best for your writing.

A. Read the writing assignments below. Mark the one you would like to complete.

- ☐ **Assignment 1:** Write a description of your favorite room in your home.
- ☐ **Assignment 2:** Write a paragraph that tells what you liked and disliked about the last movie you saw.
- ☐ **Assignment 3:** Write a paragraph that tells how to do well in school. Explain the effects of good behavior and study habits.

B. Draw and complete the graphic organizer that will best help you plan your paragraph for the assignment you chose. Use a web or chart, a drawing, or a cause-and-effect diagram.

ORGANIZATION

Organizing Information to Compare and Contrast

DAY 1

Say: *There are three ways to organize your writing when you compare and contrast. You can tell all about one thing and then all about the other; you can tell all of the similarities between both things and then all of the differences; or, you can compare the two things point by point, giving one similarity and difference at a time.* Read the rule aloud and guide students through the activity.

- Read the paragraph aloud. Explain that it compares the cities point by point, telling about the same aspect of each city before moving on. Then say: *We'll complete the outline according to how the sentences are organized in the paragraph. The first point is about population. What information is given after the population of Portland, Oregon?* (the population of Portland, Maine) Model adding this information to the outline. Have students complete the outline independently.
- **Convention:** Direct students to **Portland, Oregon**, in line 4 of the paragraph. Point out the commas before and after the state name. Say: *When you write the name of a city and state, always put a comma after the city. Add a comma after the state if it's in the middle of a sentence.* Have students proofread the paragraph for missing commas.

Name: ______________________ **Week 3 • Day 1**

Organization When you write to compare and contrast, you can use point-by-point order to organize your details.

Read the compare-and-contrast paragraph. Then:

- Complete the outline by filling in the missing details from the paragraph.
- Insert the missing commas.

Have you ever been to Portland? "Well, which one?" you may ask. That is a good question, because in the United States, more than ten states have cities or towns named Portland. The two largest are in Oregon and Maine. Portland, Oregon, is the largest Portland, with around 500,000 residents. Portland, Maine, has only 63,000 residents. Portland, Oregon, is known as The Rose City, because roses grow very well in the city's rainy weather. Portland, Maine, however, is known for its Italian sandwiches. They are made with soft bread, sour pickles, and oil. Portland, Maine, is on the Atlantic Coast and became a city in 1786. It was named for its large shipping port. Portland, Oregon, on the other hand, is on the Pacific Coast. It became a city in 1851 and was named after—you guessed it!—the city of Portland, Maine!

I. Population
   A. Portland, Oregon: 500,000
   B. Portland, Maine: 63,000

II. What the City Is Known For
   A. Portland, Oregon: roses
   B. Portland, Maine: Italian sandwiches

III. Location
   A. Portland, Oregon: Pacific Coast
   B. Portland, Maine: Atlantic Coast

IV. When It Became a City
   A. Portland, Oregon: 1851
   B. Portland, Maine: 1786

54 ORGANIZATION Daily 6-Trait Writing • EMC 6025 • © Evan-Moor Corp.

DAY 2

Read the rule aloud. Then guide students through the activities.

- **Activity A:** Say: *Signal words help your reader follow your ideas.* Write these words on the board under the heading **Same: both, similarly, also, alike, as well as.** Write these words under the heading **Different: unlike, however, while, on the other hand, as opposed to.** Then read aloud the first three sentences. Ask: *Which signal words did you hear?* (**different, while**) Continue the process for the rest of the paragraph.

  Convention: Point out the commas before and after **France** in the first sentence. Say: *Even though France is a country, not a state, the same rules apply.* Have students proofread the paragraph.

- **Activity B:** Have students complete the activity and share their answers.

Name: ______________________ **Week 3 • Day 2**

Organization Use signal words to tell how things are similar or different.

A. Read the paragraphs. Then:

- Circle the signal words that indicate that the cities are alike.
- Underline the signal words that indicate that the cities are different.
- Insert any missing commas.

You've probably heard of Paris, France, but did you know there is a Paris, Tennessee? These two cities are very different at first glance. For one thing, Paris, France, is in Europe, while Paris, Tennessee, is in the U.S. There are also a lot more people in Paris, France. It has a population of about 2.2 million, as opposed to only 10,000 in Paris, Tennessee. This may be partly because Paris, France, has been around for more than 2,000 years! Paris, Tennessee, on the other hand, is only about 200 years old.

However, the two cities are similar in some ways. For example, both cities are near rivers. Paris, France, lies on the Seine River, and Paris, Tennessee, lies near the West Sandy River. They even both have Eiffel Towers! The Eiffel Tower in France was built in 1889 and stands 1,063 feet tall. The one in Tennessee is a lot smaller. It's only 60 feet tall and is a copy of the original. Nonetheless, its citizens love their tower just like the French love theirs.

B. Look back at the paragraphs. List two ways in which the cities are different and two ways in which they are the same. Use commas correctly in the place names.

Sample Answers:

Different: 1. Paris, France, is in Europe, but Paris, Tennessee, is in the U.S.
2. Paris, France, is more than 2,000 years old. Paris, Tennessee, is about 200 years old.

Same: 1. Both cities lie near rivers.
2. Both cities have Eiffel Towers.

© Evan-Moor Corp. • EMC 6025 • Daily 6-Trait Writing ORGANIZATION 55

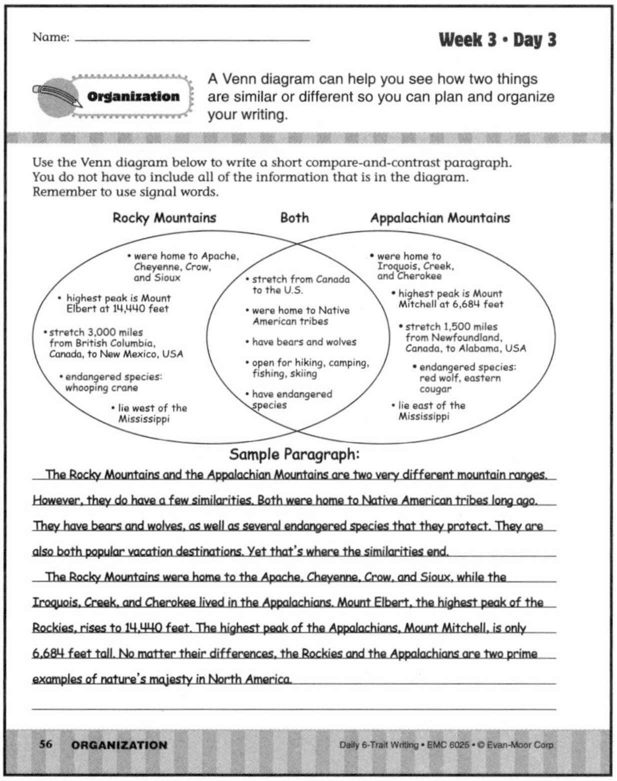
Name: ______________ **Week 3 • Day 3**

Organization A Venn diagram can help you see how two things are similar or different so you can plan and organize your writing.

Use the Venn diagram below to write a short compare-and-contrast paragraph. You do not have to include all of the information that is in the diagram. Remember to use signal words.

Sample Paragraph:

The Rocky Mountains and the Appalachian Mountains are two very different mountain ranges. However, they do have a few similarities. Both were home to Native American tribes long ago. They have bears and wolves, as well as several endangered species that they protect. They are also both popular vacation destinations. Yet that's where the similarities end.

The Rocky Mountains were home to the Apache, Cheyenne, Crow, and Sioux, while the Iroquois, Creek, and Cherokee lived in the Appalachians. Mount Elbert, the highest peak of the Rockies, rises to 14,440 feet. The highest peak of the Appalachians, Mount Mitchell, is only 6,684 feet tall. No matter their differences, the Rockies and the Appalachians are two prime examples of nature's majesty in North America.

56 ORGANIZATION Daily 6-Trait Writing • EMC 6025 • © Evan-Moor Corp.

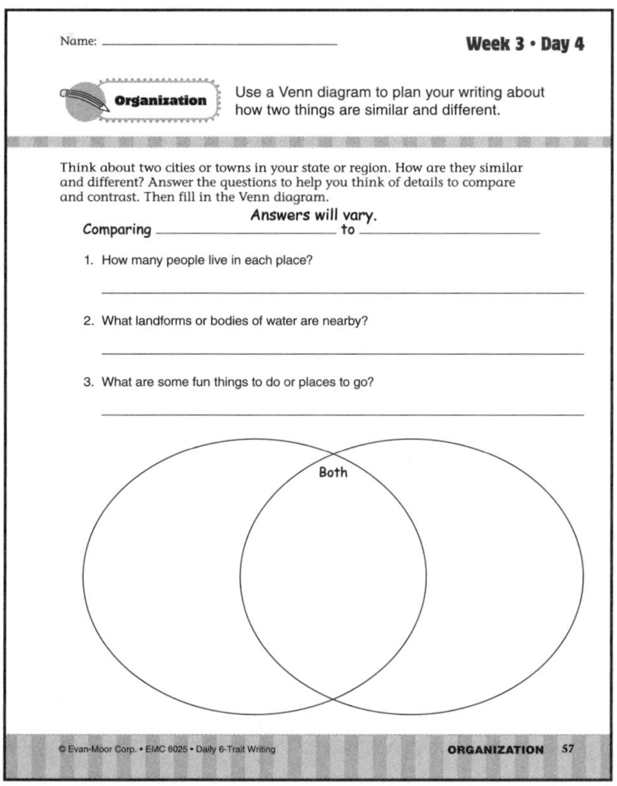
Name: ______________ **Week 3 • Day 4**

Organization Use a Venn diagram to plan your writing about how two things are similar and different.

Think about two cities or towns in your state or region. How are they similar and different? Answer the questions to help you think of details to compare and contrast. Then fill in the Venn diagram.

Answers will vary.

Comparing ______________ to ______________

1. How many people live in each place?
2. What landforms or bodies of water are nearby?
3. What are some fun things to do or places to go?

© Evan-Moor Corp. • EMC 6025 • Daily 6-Trait Writing ORGANIZATION 57

DAY 3

Read the rule aloud. Then guide students through the activity.

- Review how Venn diagrams organize information. Then ask: *What is one way that the two mountain ranges are alike?* (e.g., both start in Canada) *What is one way that they are different?* (e.g., east of Mississippi versus west)
- Model planning the paragraph. Say: *I could start by telling everything about the Rocky Mountains, and then everything about the Appalachian Mountains. Or, I could use point-by-point organization. For example: The highest peak in the Rocky Mountains stands 14,440 feet tall; however, the highest point of the Appalachian Mountains rises only 6,684 feet.* Remind students to use signal words when writing their paragraphs. Ask volunteers to share their paragraphs.

DAY 4

Read the rule aloud. Then guide students through the activity.

- Brainstorm with students different cities or towns in your area and ways they could be compared. Then have each student choose two to compare.
- **Convention:** Have students write the names of the two places in the frame provided, using commas to separate the names of the cities and states.
- Have students answer the questions and complete their diagrams. You may wish to allow time for basic research using the Internet or classroom resources. Circulate to provide assistance as necessary.

DAY 5 *Writing Prompt*

- *Use your Venn diagram from Day 4 to write a compare-and-contrast paragraph about two cities or towns. Include signal words to guide your reader.*
- *Be sure to use commas correctly between the names of the cities and states.*

Name: ____________________

Week 3 • Day 1

Organization

When you write to compare and contrast, you can use point-by-point order to organize your details.

Read the compare-and-contrast paragraph. Then:

- Complete the outline by filling in the missing details from the paragraph.
- Insert the missing commas.

Have you ever been to Portland? "Well, which one?" you may ask. That is a good question, because in the United States, more than ten states have cities or towns named Portland. The two largest are in Oregon and Maine. Portland, Oregon, is the largest Portland, with around 500,000 residents. Portland Maine, has only 63,000 residents. Portland, Oregon is known as The Rose City, because roses grow very well in the city's rainy weather. Portland, Maine, however, is known for its Italian sandwiches. They are made with soft bread, sour pickles, and oil. Portland Maine is on the Atlantic Coast and became a city in 1786. It was named for its large shipping port. Portland, Oregon on the other hand, is on the Pacific Coast. It became a city in 1851 and was named after—you guessed it!—the city of Portland Maine!

I. Population
   A. Portland, Oregon: 500,000
   B. ____________________

II. What the City Is Known For
   A. ____________________
   B. Portland, Maine: Italian sandwiches

III. Location
   A. ____________________
   B. Portland, Maine: Atlantic Coast

IV. When It Became a City
   A. ____________________
   B. Portland, Maine: 1786

Name: ______________________________

Organization Use signal words to tell how things are similar or different.

A. Read the paragraphs. Then:

- Circle the signal words that indicate that the cities are alike.
- Underline the signal words that indicate that the cities are different.
- Insert any missing commas.

You've probably heard of Paris, France, but did you know there is a Paris, Tennessee? These two cities are very different at first glance. For one thing, Paris, France is in Europe, while Paris, Tennessee is in the U.S. There are also a lot more people in Paris, France. It has a population of about 2.2 million, as opposed to only 10,000 in Paris Tennessee. This may be partly because Paris France has been around for more than 2,000 years! Paris, Tennessee on the other hand, is only about 200 years old.

However, the two cities are similar in some ways. For example, both cities are near rivers. Paris, France lies on the Seine River, and Paris, Tennessee, lies near the West Sandy River. They even both have Eiffel Towers! The Eiffel Tower in France was built in 1889 and stands 1,063 feet tall. The one in Tennessee is a lot smaller. It's only 60 feet tall and is a copy of the original. Nonetheless, its citizens love their tower just like the French love theirs.

B. Look back at the paragraphs. List two ways in which the cities are different and two ways in which they are the same. Use commas correctly in the place names.

Different: 1. ______________________________

2. ______________________________

Same: 1. ______________________________

2. ______________________________

Name: ____________________

Organization

A Venn diagram can help you see how two things are similar or different so you can plan and organize your writing.

Use the Venn diagram below to write a short compare-and-contrast paragraph. You do not have to include all of the information that is in the diagram. Remember to use signal words.

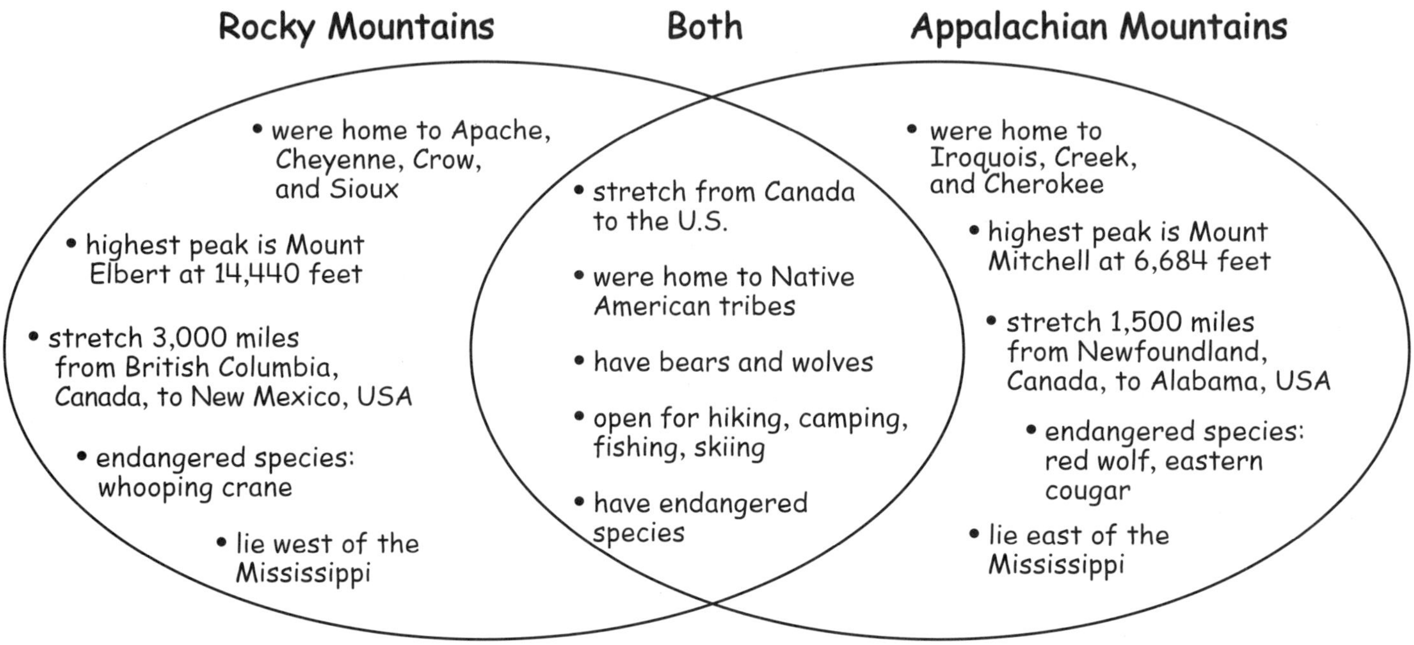

Name: ____________________

Organization

Use a Venn diagram to plan your writing about how two things are similar and different.

Think about two cities or towns in your state or region. How are they similar and different? Answer the questions to help you think of details to compare and contrast. Then fill in the Venn diagram.

Comparing ____________________ **to** ____________________

1. How many people live in each place?

   ____

2. What landforms or bodies of water are nearby?

   ____

3. What are some fun things to do or places to go?

   ____

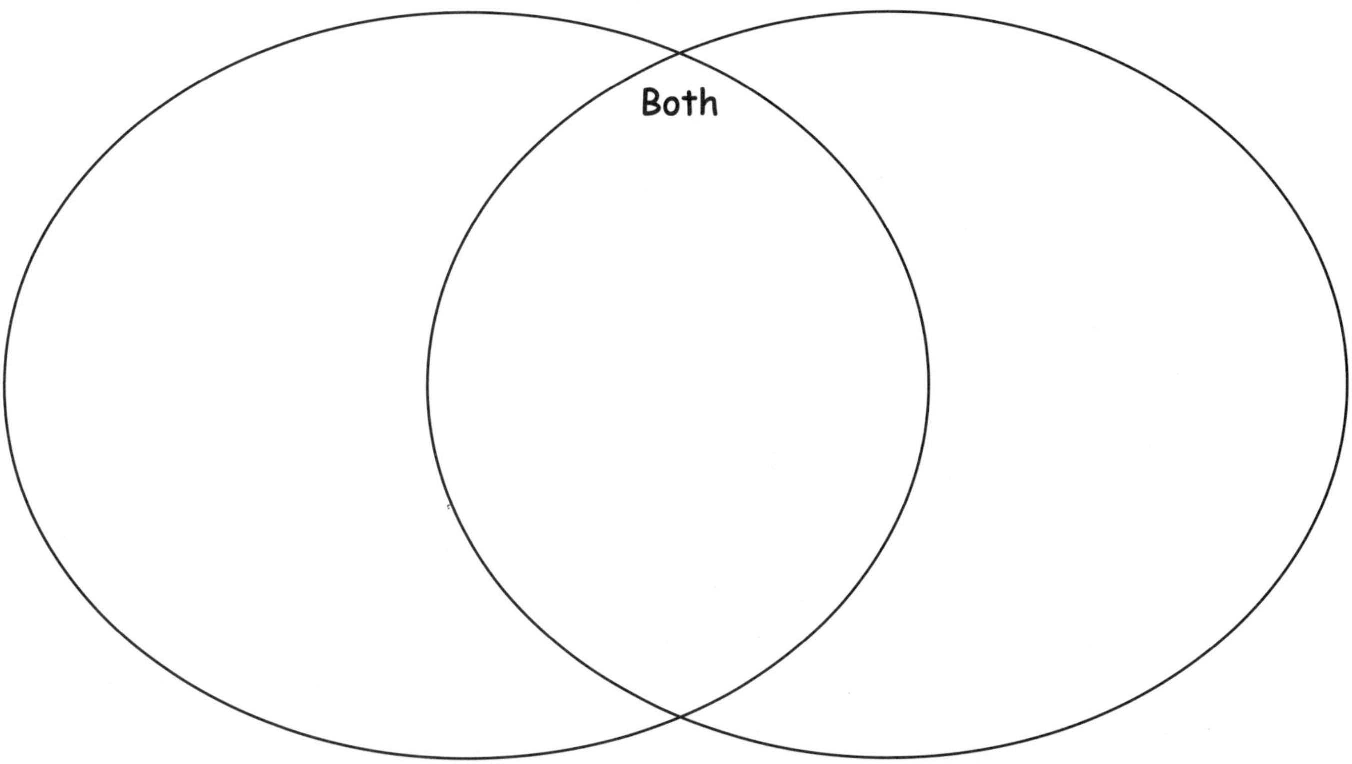

ORGANIZATION

Organizing to Persuade

DAY 1

Say: *The organization of your writing can affect how persuasive it is.* Read the rule aloud. Then guide students through the activity.

- Read the speech aloud. Direct students to the opinion diagram. Ask: *What is Cody's **opinion**?* (We should vote for him.) Model filling in the first box. Then ask: *What is Cody's first **reason**?* (He has a lot of energy to use.) Continue using the sample answers on the reduced page to guide students through Cody's reasons and examples.
- Explain that a good argument also includes possible **objections**, or reasons your audience might disagree with you, and then provides a **response** that addresses those concerns. Help students identify the objection that Cody anticipated, and how he responded to it.
- **Convention:** Direct students to the words **Hey** and **Oh** in the speech. Say: *These are interjections, or short words that show feeling. When an interjection shows strong feeling, it can be set apart from a sentence with a capital letter and an exclamation point.* (**Hey!**) *But an interjection can also be used to start a sentence, followed by a comma to show a pause.* (**Oh,...**)

DAY 2

Read the rule aloud. Say: *State your opinion in a strong, confident manner so that you get your reader's attention.* Then guide students through the activities.

- **Activity A:** Read aloud the first statement in item 1. Ask: *Is this statement very strong?* (no) Read the second statement aloud and ask: *How is this statement stronger?* (specifies **who**, **where**, and **when**; replaces "it would be nice" with "should be able to choose," a more weighty statement) Have students complete the rest of the activity independently. Review the answers as a class.
- **Activity B:** Have students read the review. Then ask: *What is the writer's main opinion?* (Ratatouille is a great movie about rats.) Have students write the opinion statement in their own words.

  Convention: Review the rules for writing interjections and have students correct the errors.

Name: ______________________ **Week 4 • Day 1**

Organization When you want to be persuasive, organize your ideas to build your argument. State your opinion, and then give reasons with supporting examples.

Read Cody's persuasive speech. Then fill in the opinion diagram to show how Cody organized his opinion, reasons, and supporting examples.

You should vote for me, Cody Walker. I'm running for class president! Most of you have seen me running before—running through the halls, in the library, and around the lunch tables! Well, I'll use my energy to improve our school. For example, I would hold a playground cleanup day. That way, we could go outside for an hour to work off some energy. Also, I spend a lot of time in the principal's office. Hey! It's a great way to stay on top of what's going on around school. Plus, I know the principal personally from chatting with her so much. Oh, you may not think I'm serious enough to be class president. But I am serious about having fun! If you want more parties, talent shows, and extra-dessert days, I'm your guy!

Cody's Opinion Statement: You should vote for me, Cody Walker.

Reason 1: I'll use my energy to improve our school.
Examples: I'll have a playground cleanup day and go outside for an hour.

Reason 2: I spend a lot of time in the principal's office.
Examples: It helps me stay on top of what's going on around school. I know the principal personally.

Possible Objection: Some people think that I am not serious enough to be class president.
Response to Objection: I am serious about having fun!

60 ORGANIZATION Daily 6-Trait Writing • EMC 6025 • © Evan-Moor Corp.

Name: ______________________ **Week 4 • Day 2**

Organization An opinion statement tells how you feel about your topic. It should be clear and specific.

A. Read these opinion statements. Mark the stronger one in each pair.

1. ☐ It would be nice to have soft drinks at school sometimes.
   ☒ Students at Old Mill Elementary should be able to choose whatever they want to drink at lunch, including soft drinks.
2. ☒ Starkey Elementary should allow fourth-grade students with musical experience to join the fifth-grade band.
   ☐ If you're in fourth grade at Starkey Elementary, I think it's OK if you play in the fifth-grade band.
3. ☐ I wish I could take my cellphone to school.
   ☒ It's important for students to be able to take their cellphones to school.

B. This movie review is missing an opinion statement. Read the review and write a strong opinion statement for it. Then fix the interjections that need correct capitalization and punctuation.

Cooking Up Fun with the Film Ratatouille

The main character is Remy, a special rat who wants to be a chef. The plot of the movie is funny because Remy helps his human friend, Linguini, cook in a fancy French restaurant. But he has to hide inside Linguini's hat! He tells Linguini what to do by pulling his hair. Ouch! The best part of Ratatouille is the end, when Remy saves Linguini's restaurant. Hooray! Some people might not want to see a movie about rats because they think rats are gross. But these rats aren't gross—they're adorable and funny! Rent Ratatouille tonight!

Sample Answer:

Opinion Statement: Ratatouille may just be the best movie ever made about rats!

© Evan-Moor Corp. • EMC 6025 • Daily 6-Trait Writing ORGANIZATION 61

Name: ____________ **Week 4 • Day 3**

Organization Use transition words and phrases to connect your opinion, reasons, and details.

Read the opinion diagram. Then use the ideas in it to write an editorial for your school newspaper about a way to help people in need. Be sure to include transition words and phrases to connect your ideas.

Opinion Statement: On our birthdays, we should tell people to donate to a charity instead of buying us presents.

Reason 1: There are other people who need the money more than we do.
Examples: Some people have lost their homes due to natural disasters or wars. Other people don't have enough food or clothing.

Reason 2: We don't need more stuff.
Examples: Your closet is probably already full.

Possible Objection: Some kids might not want to give up their presents.
Response to Objection: You can live without new toys or games more easily than people can live without food, clothing, and shelter.

Transition Words and Phrases					
also	as a result	first of all	for example	in addition	most importantly

Sample Paragraph:

This year for our birthdays, we should tell our friends and family to donate to a charity instead of buying us presents. First of all, there are people who need the money more than we do. For example, some people have lost their homes due to natural disasters or war. Other people around the world don't have enough food or clothing. In addition, do we really need more stuff? Our closets are already full! Now, I know that some kids might not want to give up their presents, and I understand. But remember that you can live without new toys or games more easily than someone can live without food, clothing, or shelter. So let's all tell our friends and family that for our birthdays this year, we want to give to others.

62 ORGANIZATION Daily 6-Trait Writing • EMC 6025 • © Evan-Moor Corp.

Name: ____________ **Week 4 • Day 4**

Organization Use an opinion diagram to plan how to persuade others about your ideas.

Plan a short editorial to persuade others to do volunteer work in your community. Fill in the opinion diagram to organize your ideas. Sample Answer:

Opinion Statement: Everyone should participate in our local park cleanup day.

Reason 1: The park is a mess.
Examples: trash is everywhere, signs need repainting, weeds, tall grass

Reason 2: could be a fun place to play if clean
Examples: could climb on jungle gym, play soccer, have picnics

Reason 3: will be fun
Examples: get to know people, spend time with friends, free food, sense of accomplishment

Possible Objection: might be yucky, hard work
Response to Objection: If we all work together, it will be easier.

© Evan-Moor Corp. • EMC 6025 • Daily 6-Trait Writing ORGANIZATION 63

DAY 3

Read the rule aloud. Say: *Certain transition words and phrases also help you make your ideas clearer and give emphasis.* Then guide students through the activity.

- Say: *An editorial is an essay in which the writer expresses an opinion about an important issue.* Read through the diagram with students, explaining that it gives specific reasons (e.g., other people need the money more) and examples (e.g., people have lost their homes to natural disasters).
- Read the transition words aloud. Explain that some, such as **also** and **in addition,** can be used to introduce more reasons; others, such as **most importantly,** give emphasis. Model using a transition word between two parts of the diagram. (e.g., "In addition to others needing the money more, we don't need anymore stuff!")
- Say: *Be sure to write a concluding sentence for your editorial in which you restate the opinion.* Ask: *What is a good restatement of the opinion for this editorial?* (e.g., "Your birthday presents might mean a lot to you, but they could mean even more to someone else.") Then have students write their editorials.

DAY 4

Read the rule aloud. Then guide students through the activity.

- Brainstorm with students various community service activities, such as visiting a senior center, working at an animal shelter, or helping at an event to solve an environmental problem.
- Have students choose a specific activity to write about. Review the opinion diagram and use the sample answers on the reduced page to model writing an opinion statement, reasons, and examples. Have students fill in their diagrams.

DAY 5 *Writing Prompt*

- *Write a short editorial persuading others to do volunteer work in your community. Use the ideas you wrote in your diagram on Day 4.*
- *Be sure to capitalize and punctuate interjections correctly.*

Name: ______________________________

Week 4 • Day 1

Organization

When you want to be persuasive, organize your ideas to build your argument. State your opinion, and then give reasons with supporting examples.

Read Cody's persuasive speech. Then fill in the opinion diagram to show how Cody organized his opinion, reasons, and supporting examples.

You should vote for me, Cody Walker. I'm running for class president! Most of you have seen me running before—running through the halls, in the library, and around the lunch tables! Well, I'll use my energy to improve our school. For example, I would hold a playground cleanup day. That way, we could go outside for an hour to work off some energy. Also, I spend a lot of time in the principal's office. Hey! It's a great way to stay on top of what's going on around school. Plus, I know the principal personally from chatting with her so much. Oh, you may not think I'm serious enough to be class president. But I am serious about having fun! If you want more parties, talent shows, and extra-dessert days, I'm your guy!

Cody's Opinion Statement:

Reason 1:

Examples:

Reason 2:

Examples:

Possible Objection:

Response to Objection:

Organization

An opinion statement tells how you feel about your topic. It should be clear and specific.

A. Read these opinion statements. Mark the stronger one in each pair.

1. ☐ It would be nice to have soft drinks at school sometimes.
   ☐ Students at Old Mill Elementary should be able to choose whatever they want to drink at lunch, including soft drinks.
2. ☐ Starkey Elementary should allow fourth-grade students with musical experience to join the fifth-grade band.
   ☐ If you're in fourth grade at Starkey Elementary, I think it's OK if you play in the fifth-grade band.
3. ☐ I wish I could take my cellphone to school.
   ☐ It's important for students to be able to take their cellphones to school.

B. This movie review is missing an opinion statement. Read the review and write a strong opinion statement for it. Then fix the interjections that need correct capitalization and punctuation.

Cooking Up Fun with the Film Ratatouille

The main character is Remy, a special rat who wants to be a chef. The plot of the movie is funny because Remy helps his human friend, Linguini, cook in a fancy French restaurant. But he has to hide inside Linguini's hat! He tells Linguini what to do by pulling his hair. Ouch The best part of Ratatouille is the end, when Remy saves Linguini's restaurant. hooray. Some people might not want to see a movie about rats because they think rats are gross. But these rats aren't *gross*—they're adorable and funny! Rent Ratatouille tonight!

Opinion Statement: ____

____

Name: ______________________________

Week 4 • Day 3

Organization

Use transition words and phrases to connect your opinion, reasons, and details.

Read the opinion diagram. Then use the ideas in it to write an editorial for your school newspaper about a way to help people in need. Be sure to include transition words and phrases to connect your ideas.

Opinion Statement: On our birthdays, we should tell people to donate to a charity instead of buying us presents.

Reason 1: There are other people who need the money more than we do.

Examples: Some people have lost their homes due to natural disasters or wars. Other people don't have enough food or clothing.

Reason 2: We don't need more stuff.

Examples: Your closet is probably already full.

Possible Objection: Some kids might not want to give up their presents.

Response to Objection: You can live without new toys or games more easily than people can live without food, clothing, and shelter.

Transition Words and Phrases					
also	as a result	first of all	for example	in addition	most importantly

____

____

____

____

____

____

____

Name: ___________________________

Organization

Use an opinion diagram to plan how to persuade others about your ideas.

Plan a short editorial to persuade others to do volunteer work in your community. Fill in the opinion diagram to organize your ideas.

Opinion Statement:

Reason 1:

Examples:

Reason 2:

Examples:

Reason 3:

Examples:

Possible Objection:

Response to Objection:

ORGANIZATION

Choosing Which Way to Organize Your Writing

DAY 1

Read the rule aloud. Say: *We've discussed many ways to organize your writing. Now, we'll talk about how to decide which type of organization to use.* Then guide students through the activities.

- Read aloud Paragraph 1. Then review each type of organization on the page. Ask: *Which type of organization did the writer of this paragraph use?* (persuasive) *How do you know?* (e.g., It gives an opinion, reasons, and examples.) Ask: *Which organizer would we use to plan a persuasive paragraph?* (the opinion diagram)
- Point out that the opinion diagram is incomplete. For example, it is missing the opinion statement. Ask: *What is the opinion statement in Paragraph 1?* ("Taylor Elementary...") Have students write it in the diagram.
- Repeat the process for each paragraph, or have students complete the activity independently.

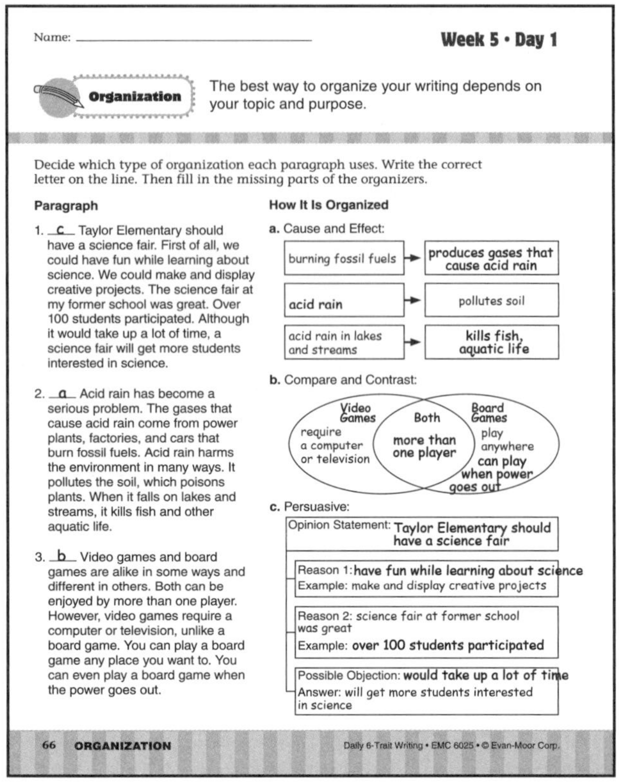

Name: ______

Week 5 • Day 1

Organization: The best way to organize your writing depends on your topic and purpose.

Decide which type of organization each paragraph uses. Write the correct letter on the line. Then fill in the missing parts of the organizers.

Paragraph

1. c Taylor Elementary should have a science fair. First of all, we could have fun while learning about science. We could make and display creative projects. The science fair at my former school was great. Over 100 students participated. Although it would take up a lot of time, a science fair will get more students interested in science.
2. a Acid rain has become a serious problem. The gases that cause acid rain come from power plants, factories, and cars that burn fossil fuels. Acid rain harms the environment in many ways. It pollutes the soil, which poisons plants. When it falls on lakes and streams, it kills fish and other aquatic life.
3. b Video games and board games are alike in some ways and different in others. Both can be enjoyed by more than one player. However, video games require a computer or television, unlike a board game. You can play a board game any place you want to. You can even play a board game when the power goes out.

How It Is Organized

a. Cause and Effect:

burning fossil fuels → produces gases that cause acid rain

acid rain → pollutes soil

acid rain in lakes and streams → kills fish, aquatic life

b. Compare and Contrast:

Video Games: require a computer or television

Both: more than one player

Board Games: play anywhere; can play when power goes out

c. Persuasive:

Opinion Statement: Taylor Elementary should have a science fair

Reason 1: have fun while learning about science
Example: make and display creative projects

Reason 2: science fair at former school was great
Example: over 100 students participated

Possible Objection: would take up a lot of time
Answer: will get more students interested in science

66 ORGANIZATION — Daily 6-Trait Writing • EMC 6025 • © Evan-Moor Corp.

DAY 2

Read the rule aloud. Then guide students through the activities.

- **Activity A:** Review the types of organization. Then read aloud Assignment 1. Say: *The words* ***compares, similar,*** *and* ***different*** *tell me that I will need to write about how the Amazon River and the Nile River are similar and different. Which type of organization should I use?* (compare and contrast) Have students complete the activity independently. Review the answers as a class.
- **Activity B (Convention):** Say: *A run-on sentence is two or more sentences that run together without proper punctuation.* Read aloud the first sentence. Then say: *This sentence has a comma where the first sentence should stop. We can change it to a period, or we can add a conjunction such as* ***and*** *after the comma.* Have students rewrite the sentence and complete item 2 on their own.

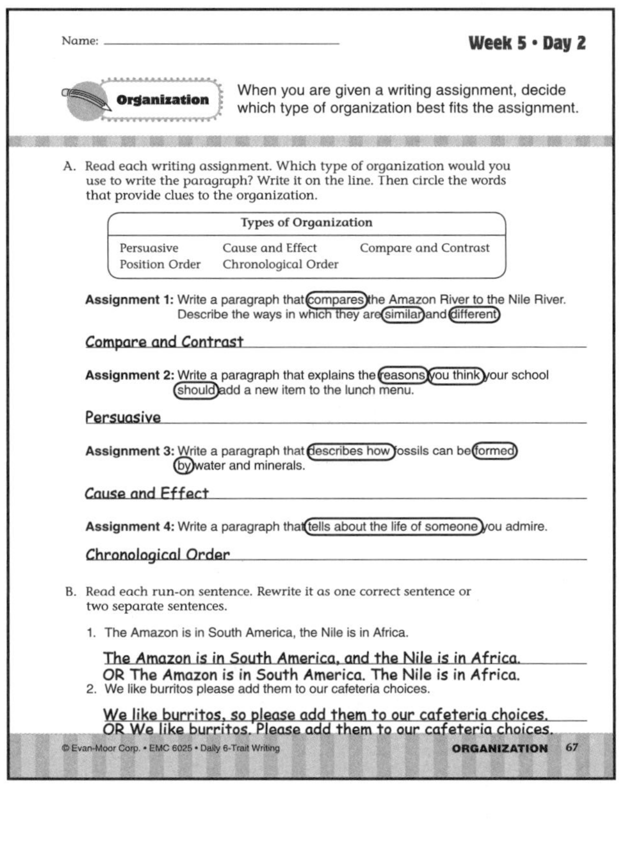

Name: ______

Week 5 • Day 2

Organization: When you are given a writing assignment, decide which type of organization best fits the assignment.

A. Read each writing assignment. Which type of organization would you use to write the paragraph? Write it on the line. Then circle the words that provide clues to the organization.

Types of Organization		
Persuasive	Cause and Effect	Compare and Contrast
Position Order	Chronological Order	

Assignment 1: Write a paragraph that compares the Amazon River to the Nile River. Describe the ways in which they are similar and different.

Compare and Contrast

Assignment 2: Write a paragraph that explains the reasons you think your school should add a new item to the lunch menu.

Persuasive

Assignment 3: Write a paragraph that describes how fossils can be formed by water and minerals.

Cause and Effect

Assignment 4: Write a paragraph that tells about the life of someone you admire.

Chronological Order

B. Read each run-on sentence. Rewrite it as one correct sentence or two separate sentences.

1. The Amazon is in South America, the Nile is in Africa.
   The Amazon is in South America, and the Nile is in Africa.
   OR The Amazon is in South America. The Nile is in Africa.
2. We like burritos please add them to our cafeteria choices.
   We like burritos, so please add them to our cafeteria choices.
   OR We like burritos. Please add them to our cafeteria choices.

© Evan-Moor Corp. • EMC 6025 • Daily 6-Trait Writing — ORGANIZATION 67

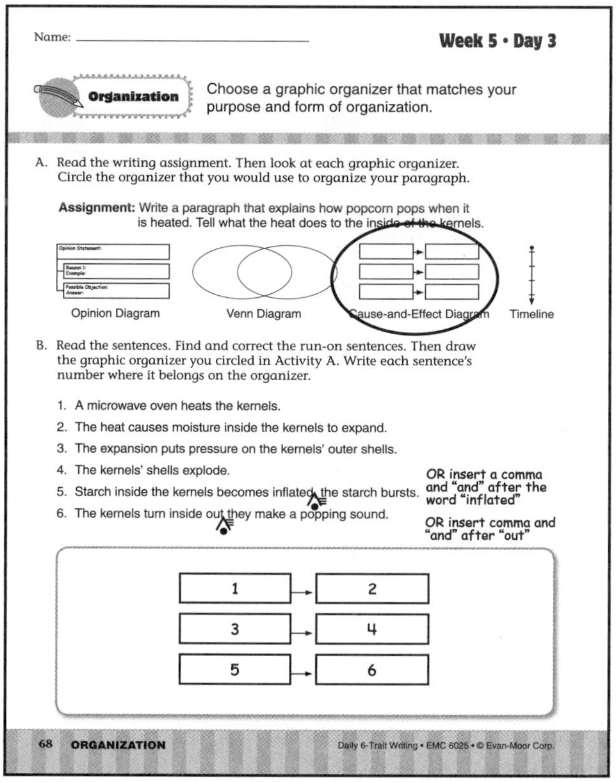

Name: ______________________ **Week 5 • Day 3**

Organization Choose a graphic organizer that matches your purpose and form of organization.

A. Read the writing assignment. Then look at each graphic organizer. Circle the organizer that you would use to organize your paragraph.

Assignment: Write a paragraph that explains how popcorn pops when it is heated. Tell what the heat does to the inside of the kernels.

B. Read the sentences. Find and correct the run-on sentences. Then draw the graphic organizer you circled in Activity A. Write each sentence's number where it belongs on the organizer.

1. A microwave oven heats the kernels.
2. The heat causes moisture inside the kernels to expand.
3. The expansion puts pressure on the kernels' outer shells.
4. The kernels' shells explode.
5. Starch inside the kernels becomes inflated. The starch bursts. OR insert a comma and "and" after the word "inflated"
6. The kernels turn inside out. They make a popping sound. OR insert comma and "and" after "out"

68 ORGANIZATION Daily 6-Trait Writing • EMC 6025 • © Evan-Moor Corp.

DAY 3

Read the rule aloud. Then guide students through the activities.

- **Activity A:** Read the assignment aloud. If necessary, review each organizer and its purpose. Then ask: *Which organizer would help you write the paragraph?* (cause-and-effect diagram) Ask: *Why?* (the assignment is to write about what causes popcorn to pop)
- **Activity B (Convention):** Read aloud the sentences. Ask: *Which ones are run-ons?* (sentences 5 and 6) Have students correct the sentences and share their answers.

  Copy the circled diagram in Activity A onto the board and have students do the same on their papers. Say: *Sentence 1 tells how a microwave heats the popcorn kernels. That is a cause, so I'll write a* ***1*** *in the first box of the "cause" column. What is the effect?* (the moisture expands) *I'll write* ***2*** *in the "effect" column.* Have students complete the remainder of the activity independently.

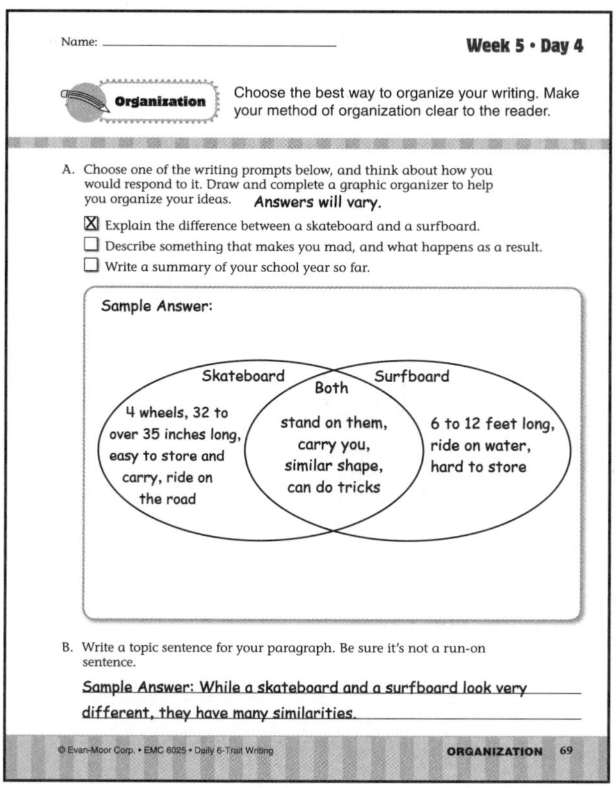

Name: ______________________ **Week 5 • Day 4**

Organization Choose the best way to organize your writing. Make your method of organization clear to the reader.

A. Choose one of the writing prompts below, and think about how you would respond to it. Draw and complete a graphic organizer to help you organize your ideas. **Answers will vary.**

- [x] Explain the difference between a skateboard and a surfboard.
- [ ] Describe something that makes you mad, and what happens as a result.
- [ ] Write a summary of your school year so far.

Sample Answer:

B. Write a topic sentence for your paragraph. Be sure it's not a run-on sentence.

Sample Answer: While a skateboard and a surfboard look very different, they have many similarities.

© Evan-Moor Corp. • EMC 6025 • Daily 6-Trait Writing ORGANIZATION 69

DAY 4

Read the rule aloud. Then guide students through the activities.

- **Activity A:** Have students read the writing prompts and discuss which graphic organizers might be used to plan each one. (Venn diagram; cause-and-effect diagram; timeline or sequence map) Then have students choose a prompt and complete an appropriate graphic organizer for it. Circulate to provide assistance as needed.
- **Activity B (Convention):** Remind students that a topic sentence states the main idea of your writing. Have students write their sentences and then trade papers with a partner to confirm that the sentences are not run-ons.

DAY 5 *Writing Prompt*

- *Write a paragraph based on the prompt you chose on Day 4. Use the diagram you completed to organize your paragraph.*
- *Trade papers with a partner to check for run-on sentences. Correct any that are found.*

Name: ______________________________

Organization

The best way to organize your writing depends on your topic and purpose.

Decide which type of organization each paragraph uses. Write the correct letter on the line. Then fill in the missing parts of the organizers.

Paragraph

1. ____ Taylor Elementary should have a science fair. First of all, we could have fun while learning about science. We could make and display creative projects. The science fair at my former school was great. Over 100 students participated. Although it would take up a lot of time, a science fair will get more students interested in science.

2. ____ Acid rain has become a serious problem. The gases that cause acid rain come from power plants, factories, and cars that burn fossil fuels. Acid rain harms the environment in many ways. It pollutes the soil, which poisons plants. When it falls on lakes and streams, it kills fish and other aquatic life.

3. ____ Video games and board games are alike in some ways and different in others. Both can be enjoyed by more than one player. However, video games require a computer or television, unlike a board game. You can play a board game any place you want to. You can even play a board game when the power goes out.

How It Is Organized

a. Cause and Effect:

Cause		Effect
burning fossil fuels	→	
	→	pollutes soil
acid rain in lakes and streams	→	

b. Compare and Contrast:

Video Games	Both	Board Games
require a computer or television		play anywhere

c. Persuasive:

Opinion Statement:

Reason 1:
Example: make and display creative projects

Reason 2: science fair at former school was great
Example:

Possible Objection:
Answer: will get more students interested in science

Name: ______________________

Organization

When you are given a writing assignment, decide which type of organization best fits the assignment.

A. Read each writing assignment. Which type of organization would you use to write the paragraph? Write it on the line. Then circle the words that provide clues to the organization.

Types of Organization		
Persuasive	Cause and Effect	Compare and Contrast
Position Order	Chronological Order	

Assignment 1: Write a paragraph that compares the Amazon River to the Nile River. Describe the ways in which they are similar and different.

____

Assignment 2: Write a paragraph that explains the reasons you think your school should add a new item to the lunch menu.

____

Assignment 3: Write a paragraph that describes how fossils can be formed by water and minerals.

____

Assignment 4: Write a paragraph that tells about the life of someone you admire.

____

B. Read each run-on sentence. Rewrite it as one correct sentence or two separate sentences.

1. The Amazon is in South America, the Nile is in Africa.

____

2. We like burritos please add them to our cafeteria choices.

____

Name: ______________________________

Week 5 • Day 3

Organization

Choose a graphic organizer that matches your purpose and form of organization.

A. Read the writing assignment. Then look at each graphic organizer. Circle the organizer that you would use to organize your paragraph.

Assignment: Write a paragraph that explains how popcorn pops when it is heated. Tell what the heat does to the inside of the kernels.

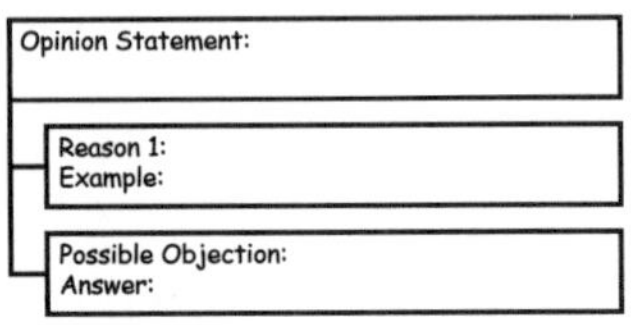

Opinion Diagram

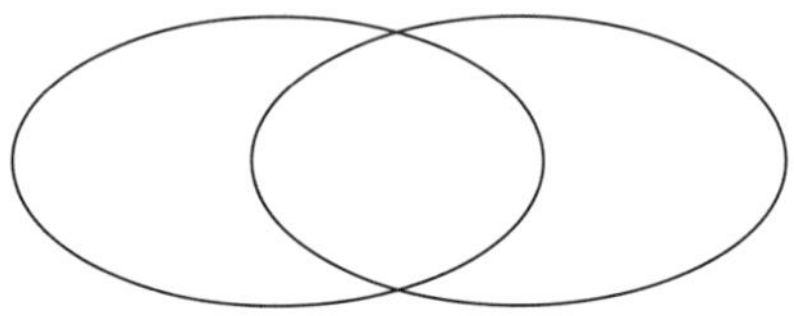

Venn Diagram

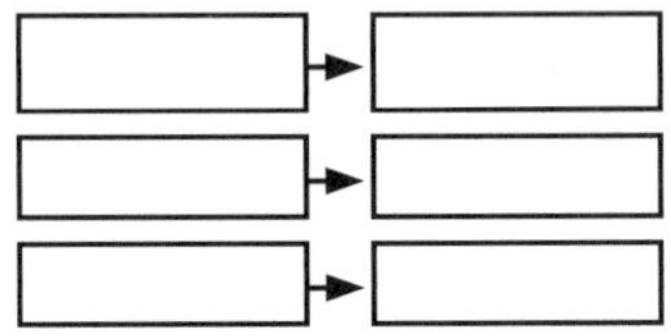

Cause-and-Effect Diagram

Timeline

B. Read the sentences. Find and correct the run-on sentences. Then draw the graphic organizer you circled in Activity A. Write each sentence's number where it belongs on the organizer.

1. A microwave oven heats the kernels.
2. The heat causes moisture inside the kernels to expand.
3. The expansion puts pressure on the kernels' outer shells.
4. The kernels' shells explode.
5. Starch inside the kernels becomes inflated, the starch bursts.
6. The kernels turn inside out they make a popping sound.

Name: ______________________________

Organization

Choose the best way to organize your writing. Make your method of organization clear to the reader.

A. Choose one of the writing prompts below, and think about how you would respond to it. Draw and complete a graphic organizer to help you organize your ideas.

- ☐ Explain the difference between a skateboard and a surfboard.
- ☐ Describe something that makes you mad, and what happens as a result.
- ☐ Write a summary of your school year so far.

B. Write a topic sentence for your paragraph. Be sure it's not a run-on sentence.

____

____

WEEK 1

WORD CHOICE

Writing About Action

Refer to pages 6 and 7 to introduce or review the writing trait.

DAY 1

Read the rule aloud. Ask: *What do you think a "tired" verb is?* (not interesting; used too much) Say: *A specific verb tells more about the action that you are describing.* Then guide students through the activities.

- **Activity A:** Have volunteers read aloud both paragraphs. Ask: *Which paragraph is a better description of what is happening? Why?* (Paragraph B—it uses stronger action verbs) Point out one stronger verb in Paragraph B, such as **whistled** (used instead of **went**). Ask: *Why is **whistled** stronger than **went**?* (It describes the speed and sound of the wind.) Have students complete the activity independently.
- **Activity B (Convention):** Say: *When you write, don't let your verbs change tense without a reason.* Read aloud the paragraph. Ask: *What tense is most of the story in?* (past tense) Reread the sentence that starts, "She quickly swings..." Say: *This is in the present tense, not the past. When you change tenses like that, the reader can get confused.* Model changing **swings** to **swung**. Then have students complete the activity.

Name: ______________________ **Week 1 • Day 1**

Word Choice Choose strong, specific verbs to show exactly what is happening. Avoid tired, overused verbs.

A. Read each paragraph. Then answer the questions. **Sample Answers:**

Paragraph A

A cold wind went through the forest, blowing the leaves of the trees. A deer ran by as owls sat on branches and called in the dark. Rain fell. Mice ran under piles of leaves to stay dry. Far in the distance, a train went by.

Paragraph B

A cold wind (whistled) through the forest, (rustling) the leaves of the trees. A deer (dashed) by as owls (perched) on branches and (hooted) to each other in the dark. Rain (pelted) the ground. Mice (scurried) under piles of leaves to (take shelter) from the rain. Far in the distance, a train (roared) by.

1. What are three examples of verbs that changed from Paragraph A to Paragraph B? Write them below.

Paragraph A	Paragraph B
went	whistled
blowing	rustling
ran	dashed

2. Circle all of the specific verbs in Paragraph B that replaced the tired verbs in Paragraph A.

B. Read the paragraph. Use proofreading marks to fix the verbs that are in the wrong tense.

Horns blared. Cars blocked the crosswalk where Talia wanted to cross the street. Suddenly, Talia caught a glimpse of a hot dog cart. She quickly ~~swings~~ swung to her left and ~~bolts~~ bolted down the crowded city street. Her stomach screamed in hunger! Luckily, she ~~finds~~ found a few dollars in her wallet. "I'll take a jumbo dog with everything on it!" Talia called.

72 WORD CHOICE Daily 6-Trait Writing • EMC 6025 • © Evan-Moor Corp.

DAY 2

Read the rule aloud. Then write the words **stroll, strut,** and **tiptoe** on the board. Say: *All of these verbs describe a way of walking, but in very different ways.* Discuss the picture each verb paints. (walking casually, walking confidently, or walking quietly) Then guide students through the activities.

- **Activity A:** Have students read the paragraph. Ask: *What is the mood of this paragraph? What feeling is the writer trying to convey?* (e.g., urgency) Then read aloud the first sentence. Say: *We can say either that **Byron crawled** or **Byron darted** out of the bushes. Which action verb conveys more of a sense of urgency?* (**darted**, because it means to move fast) Have students write the answer on the line and complete the activity independently.
- **Activity B (Convention):** Say: *This paragraph is about something that happened last weekend. Which tense should it be in?* (past) Have students read the paragraph and circle the inconsistent verbs. Model changing a verb to the past tense before having students complete the activity.

Name: ______________________ **Week 1 • Day 2**

Word Choice Choose just the right verb to convey your meaning.

A. Read the paragraph. Choose the better action verb to complete each sentence. Write the word on the line.

Byron __darted__ (darted / crawled) out of the bushes and __jumped__ (climbed / jumped) onto his bike. He __raced__ (raced / rode) home, trying to __pedal__ (go / pedal) as fast as he could. He __burst__ (burst / entered) through the door, __flew__ (climbed / flew) up the stairs, and turned on the bathtub faucet. Hearing the commotion, his mother slowly __crept__ (stepped / crept) into the bathroom. As soon as she saw Byron's legs, she __cried out__ (cried out / said), "Byron, you've got poison ivy all over you!"

"I know," Byron __moaned__ (moaned / whined). "I'm doomed!"

B. Read the paragraph. Circle the verbs that are in the wrong tense. Then rewrite those sentences, changing the verbs to the correct tense.

Last weekend, Lorena (visits) the YMCA with her parents. She participated in a gymnastics class. The teacher (comments) that Lorena (does) well. Lorena's parents signed her up for a regular class.

Last weekend, Lorena visited the YMCA with her parents.

The teacher commented that Lorena did well.

© Evan-Moor Corp. • EMC 6025 • Daily 6-Trait Writing WORD CHOICE 73

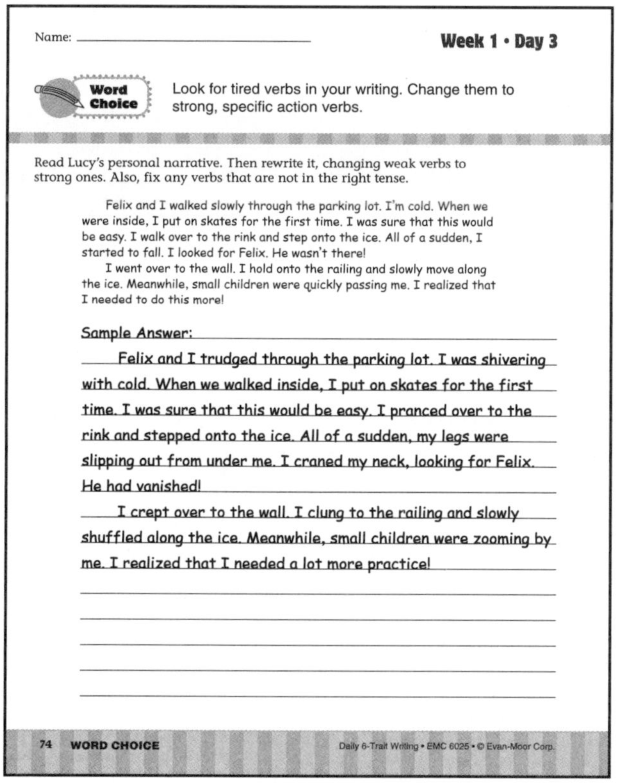

Name: ______________________ **Week 1 • Day 3**

Word Choice Look for tired verbs in your writing. Change them to strong, specific action verbs.

Read Lucy's personal narrative. Then rewrite it, changing weak verbs to strong ones. Also, fix any verbs that are not in the right tense.

Felix and I walked slowly through the parking lot. I'm cold. When we were inside, I put on skates for the first time. I was sure that this would be easy. I walk over to the rink and step onto the ice. All of a sudden, I started to fall. I looked for Felix. He wasn't there!

I went over to the wall. I hold onto the railing and slowly move along the ice. Meanwhile, small children were quickly passing me. I realized that I needed to do this more!

Sample Answer:

Felix and I trudged through the parking lot. I was shivering with cold. When we walked inside, I put on skates for the first time. I was sure that this would be easy. I pranced over to the rink and stepped onto the ice. All of a sudden, my legs were slipping out from under me. I craned my neck, looking for Felix. He had vanished!

I crept over to the wall. I clung to the railing and slowly shuffled along the ice. Meanwhile, small children were zooming by me. I realized that I needed a lot more practice!

74 WORD CHOICE Daily 6-Trait Writing • EMC 6025 • © Evan-Moor Corp.

DAY 3

Read the rule aloud. Then guide students through the activity.

- Say: *As you read Lucy's narrative, look for weak verbs that can be changed to strong action verbs.* Then read aloud the paragraph. Invite students to share the weak verbs they spot in the paragraph. (e.g., **walked, put, looked, went**)
- Model rewriting a sentence from the paragraph with stronger verbs. For example, ask: *What is a verb that means "walked slowly"?* (e.g., **trudged, lumbered**) Rewrite the sentence on the board. Then have students complete the activity in pairs or small groups, spotting weak verbs and brainstorming strong action verbs together. Allow students to use a dictionary or a thesaurus for reference. Then have students share their completed paragraphs.
- **Convention:** Have students tell which inconsistent verbs they found, and how they corrected them in their rewrites.

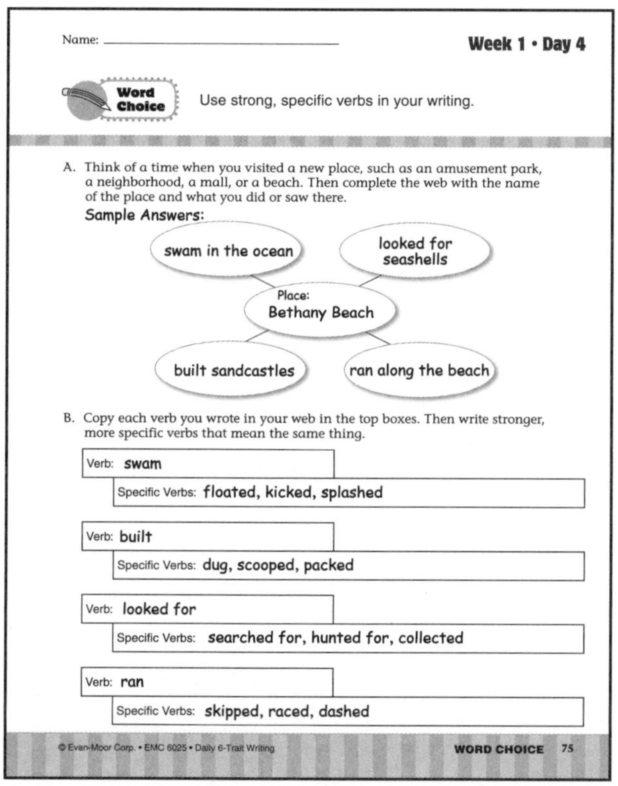

Name: ______________________ **Week 1 • Day 4**

Word Choice Use strong, specific verbs in your writing.

A. Think of a time when you visited a new place, such as an amusement park, a neighborhood, a mall, or a beach. Then complete the web with the name of the place and what you did or saw there.

Sample Answers:

B. Copy each verb you wrote in your web in the top boxes. Then write stronger, more specific verbs that mean the same thing.

Verb: swam
Specific Verbs: floated, kicked, splashed

Verb: built
Specific Verbs: dug, scooped, packed

Verb: looked for
Specific Verbs: searched for, hunted for, collected

Verb: ran
Specific Verbs: skipped, raced, dashed

© Evan-Moor Corp. • EMC 6025 • Daily 6-Trait Writing WORD CHOICE 75

DAY 4

Review the rule. Then guide students through the activities.

- **Activity A:** Help students brainstorm topics. Ask: *Have you ever been to a new place where there were a lot of things to do and see?* List a few ideas on the board. Then have students choose a topic and complete their webs.
- **Activity B:** Have a volunteer read one of the actions he or she listed in his or her web. Model generating more specific verbs for it. Then have students complete the activity.

DAY 5 *Writing Prompt*

- *Write a personal narrative about your first visit to a new place. Use the strong action verbs you wrote on Day 4.*
- *Trade papers with a partner to make sure that all of your verbs are in the past tense.*

Name: ______________________________

Week 1 • Day 1

Word Choice

Choose strong, specific verbs to show exactly what is happening. Avoid tired, overused verbs.

A. Read each paragraph. Then answer the questions.

Paragraph A

A cold wind went through the forest, blowing the leaves of the trees. A deer ran by as owls sat on branches and called in the dark. Rain fell. Mice ran under piles of leaves to stay dry. Far in the distance, a train went by.

Paragraph B

A cold wind whistled through the forest, rustling the leaves of the trees. A deer dashed by as owls perched on branches and hooted to each other in the dark. Rain pelted the ground. Mice scurried under piles of leaves to take shelter from the rain. Far in the distance, a train roared by.

1. What are three examples of verbs that changed from Paragraph A to Paragraph B? Write them below.

Paragraph A	Paragraph B
______________	______________
______________	______________
______________	______________

2. Circle all of the specific verbs in Paragraph B that replaced the tired verbs in Paragraph A.

B. Read the paragraph. Use proofreading marks to fix the verbs that are in the wrong tense.

Horns blared. Cars blocked the crosswalk where Talia wanted to cross the street. Suddenly, Talia caught a glimpse of a hot dog cart. She quickly swings to her left and bolts down the crowded city street. Her stomach screamed in hunger! Luckily, she finds a few dollars in her wallet. "I'll take a jumbo dog with everything on it!" Talia called.

Name: ______________________________

Word Choice

Choose just the right verb to convey your meaning.

A. Read the paragraph. Choose the better action verb to complete each sentence. Write the word on the line.

Byron ____________ (darted / crawled) out of the bushes and ____________ (climbed / jumped) onto his bike. He ____________ (raced / rode) home, trying to ____________ (go / pedal) as fast as he could. He ____________ (burst / entered) through the door, ____________ (climbed / flew) up the stairs, and turned on the bathtub faucet. Hearing the commotion, his mother slowly ____________ (stepped / crept) into the bathroom. As soon as she saw Byron's legs, she ____________ (cried out / said), "Byron, you've got poison ivy all over you!"

"I know," Byron ____________ (moaned / whined). "I'm doomed!"

B. Read the paragraph. Circle the verbs that are in the wrong tense. Then rewrite those sentences, changing the verbs to the correct tense.

Last weekend, Lorena visits the YMCA with her parents. She participated in a gymnastics class. The teacher comments that Lorena does well. Lorena's parents signed her up for a regular class.

____

____

____

____

Name: ___________________________

Word Choice

Look for tired verbs in your writing. Change them to strong, specific action verbs.

Read Lucy's personal narrative. Then rewrite it, changing weak verbs to strong ones. Also, fix any verbs that are not in the right tense.

Felix and I walked slowly through the parking lot. I'm cold. When we were inside, I put on skates for the first time. I was sure that this would be easy. I walk over to the rink and step onto the ice. All of a sudden, I started to fall. I looked for Felix. He wasn't there!

I went over to the wall. I hold onto the railing and slowly move along the ice. Meanwhile, small children were quickly passing me. I realized that I needed to do this more!

Name: ______________________

Word Choice

Use strong, specific verbs in your writing.

A. Think of a time when you visited a new place, such as an amusement park, a neighborhood, a mall, or a beach. Then complete the web with the name of the place and what you did or saw there.

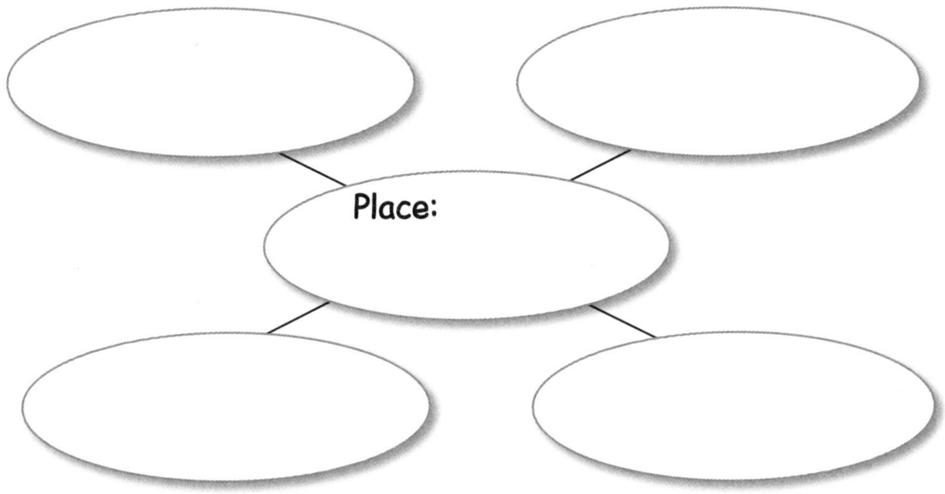

B. Copy each verb you wrote in your web in the top boxes. Then write stronger, more specific verbs that mean the same thing.

Verb:

Specific Verbs:

Verb:

Specific Verbs:

Verb:

Specific Verbs:

Verb:

Specific Verbs:

WORD CHOICE

Using Descriptive Language

DAY 1

Read the rule aloud. Say: *If you use vague, general words to describe something, your description will be weak. Use precise words and phrases to accurately describe something.* Then guide students through the activities.

- **Activity A:** Read aloud Paragraph 1. Ask: *What do you notice about the words in bold?* (e.g., They are boring, vague words.) Confirm by saying: *These words don't really tell us much about the trip.* Then read aloud Paragraph 2 and guide students to compare the two paragraphs. Ask: *What words were used in Paragraph 2 to replace **fun** in Paragraph 1?* ("full of excitement") Have students circle that phrase and continue comparing the paragraphs. Then have them answer the question.

  Convention: Point out that when "a mean dog" was changed to "an aggressive dog," the article had to be changed.

- **Activity B (Convention):** Write the words **lay** and **lie** on the board. Say: *People often confuse these words. **Lay** means "to put or place," and **lie** means "to rest or recline." You **lie** down to sleep, but **lay** your head on the pillow.* Then have students complete the activity. Review the answers.

DAY 2

Read the rule aloud. Then write a few "tired" words on the board, such as **nice**, **neat**, and **bad**. Say: *These are tired, nonspecific, overused words. Good writers avoid those words and use specific adjectives and descriptive phrases instead.* Guide students through the activities.

- **Activity A:** Read the example aloud. Say: *The writer could have just used the word **loud** or **high**, but **eardrum-shattering** is much stronger. It tells us exactly how the note sounded—painfully loud.* Then read through the words and phrases given for items 2 through 6. Discuss their meanings, and have students name the less descriptive terms that have been replaced. (e.g., **hot**, **colorful**, **smelly**, **tall**, **old**) Have students write their sentences independently. After they have finished, ask volunteers to share their sentences.

- **Activity B (Convention):** Review the rules for **lay** and **lie**. Have students complete the activity.

Name: ______________________ **Week 2 • Day 1**

Word Choice Use specific nouns and precise, descriptive language to paint a clear picture for your reader.

A. Read each paragraph. Circle the words and phrases in Paragraph 2 that replaced the bold words in Paragraph 1. Then answer the question.

Paragraph 1

Our field trip to Museum Park was **fun**. First, we ate **lunch** on the **lawn**. I decided to lie on my back and watch the **clouds in the sky**. Suddenly, I heard a dog barking **loudly**. I was worried that it might be a **mean** dog, but I looked up to see **the dog** barking at a **pretty** kite that had crashed to the ground. After cleaning up from lunch, we went inside the art museum and **looked at** the **interesting** paintings and sculptures on display.

Paragraph 2

Our trip to Museum Park was full of excitement. First, we ate gigantic submarine sandwiches on the cool, green, freshly mowed grass. I decided to lie on my back and watch the fluffy white clouds drifting through the sky. Suddenly, I heard a dog barking urgently. I was worried that it might be an aggressive dog, but I looked up to see a French poodle barking at a rainbow-colored kite that had crashed to the ground. After cleaning up from lunch, we went inside the art museum and examined the expressive paintings and carefully crafted sculptures on display.

Which paragraph does a better job of describing? Give an example to support your answer.

Sample Answer: Paragraph 2 is better because it uses more specific words and descriptive language. For example, the writer changed "fun" to "full of excitement."

B. Read each sentence. Write an *X* next to the one that uses the underlined word correctly.

___ 1. The dog lays down on the grass.
_X_ 2. The dog lies down on the grass.
_X_ 3. The girl lays her books on the table.
___ 4. The girl lies her books on the table.

78 WORD CHOICE   Daily 6-Trait Writing • EMC 6025 • © Evan-Moor Corp.

Name: ______________________ **Week 2 • Day 2**

Word Choice Use vivid adjectives to make your descriptions clear and precise.

A. Use each given word or phrase to write a strong descriptive sentence. Be as creative as possible. Remember to use *a* and *an* correctly.

Example: The audience cringed when the singer hit an **eardrum-shattering** note.

Sample Answers:

1. **eardrum-shattering:** The rooster greeted the morning with an eardrum-shattering crow.
2. **peppery:** The peppery soup made my eyes water.
3. **brightly spotted:** Her brightly spotted cheeks gave away her embarrassment.
4. **pungent:** The pungent odor of the cheese made me want to run away screaming.
5. **towering:** The towering inferno reminded us of the importance of putting out campfires.
6. **100-year-old:** The 100-year-old farmhouse stood lonely on the wind-swept hill.

B. Read the paragraph. Use *lay* or *lie* and *a* or *an* to complete each sentence.

Please _lay_ your sleeping bag in _a_ tent. But don't _lie_ down and take _a_ nap! Help me _lay_ the tablecloth on _an_ unclaimed picnic table.

© Evan-Moor Corp. • EMC 6025 • Daily 6-Trait Writing   WORD CHOICE 79

Name: ____________ **Week 2 • Day 3**

Word Choice Replace overused words with specific nouns and vivid adjectives to make your descriptions clear and precise.

A. Read the description of a painting. Then:

- Use proofreading marks to replace each word in bold with a better descriptive word or phrase. Remember to change the article before it to *a* or *an*, if necessary.
- Use proofreading marks to fix any incorrect uses of *lay* or *lie*.

Sample Answers:

My brother's friend Ismael painted an ~~interesting~~ unusual painting in his art class. The painting shows an ~~old~~ ancient cabin in the woods, with ~~old, broken~~ weather-beaten, falling down doors and windows. You can see some ~~tall~~ towering trees in the background. Their ~~colorful~~ brown, gold, and red autumn leaves lie scattered on the ground. A rusted rake ~~lays~~ lies against one wall of the cabin, and in front of the door, a peacock stands with its ~~colorful~~ flashy feathers spread wide open. Facing the peacock is a ~~little~~ scrawny 4-year-old boy on ~~an old~~ a rusted tricycle. The boy is leaning over the handlebars and staring ~~hard~~ intently at the peacock. The peacock is looking back with a ~~weird~~ quizzical look. Ismael titled this painting "Standoff." He entered it in the county fair, where it competed against many paintings and won first place!

B. Rewrite each sentence correctly.

1. There was a ugly brown snake laying across the trail.

   There was an ugly brown snake lying across the trail.

2. I saw a squirrel scurry off with an nut and lie it in a hole.

   I saw a squirrel scurry off with a nut and lay it in a hole.

80 WORD CHOICE Daily 6-Trait Writing • EMC 6025 • © Evan-Moor Corp.

DAY 3

Read the rule aloud and remind students: *It's important not to use the same words over and over again to describe things.* Then guide students through the activities.

- **Activity A:** Read the paragraph aloud. Then return to the word **interesting**. Say: ***Interesting*** *is a word we use too often that really doesn't tell us much. In what way could the painting be interesting?* (e.g., unusual, brightly colored, surreal)

  Convention: Point out the article (**an**) before **interesting**. Say: *Be sure to change* ***an*** *to* ***a*** *if you replace* ***interesting*** *with a word that begins with a consonant.* Then review the difference between **lay** and **lie**, pointing out that nonliving objects can also rest against something.

  Have students complete the activity. Then have volunteers read aloud their revised paragraphs.

- **Activity B (Convention):** Have students complete the activity independently. Then have them trade papers to check each other's work.

Name: ____________ **Week 2 • Day 4**

Word Choice Use precise nouns and adjectives to write a strong description.

A. If you were going to write a description of the picture below, what could you say? Write eight strong descriptive phrases to describe the truck, the kids, or other things in the picture.

Sample Answers:

vintage pickup	palm trees swishing in the wind
tassled dress	turned-up collar
pillbox hat	wide-brimmed sombrero
fur collar	leather boots

B. Write one sentence you could use in your description. Remember to use *a* and *an* correctly.

Sample Answer: A boy in cuffed jeans and a black leather jacket lies in front of a hulking vintage truck.

© Evan-Moor Corp. • EMC 6025 • Daily 6-Trait Writing WORD CHOICE 81

DAY 4

Read the rule aloud. Guide students through the activities.

- **Activity A:** Have students examine the picture. Ask questions to elicit ideas about what's happening in the picture. For example, ask: *Why are the kids in costume? How would you describe their costumes? What historical eras might they represent?*

  Brainstorm strong descriptive words and phrases. Ask: *What could you say about the trees? How would you describe the shape of the truck? The kids in costumes?* Then circulate to check for understanding as students complete the activity.

- **Activity B (Convention):** Review the rules for **a** and **an**, as well as **lay** and **lie** before having students write their sentences.

DAY 5 *Writing Prompt*

- *Use precise, descriptive language to write a description of the picture on Day 4.*
- *Be sure to use the articles* ***a*** *and* ***an*** *correctly, as well as the verbs* ***lie*** *and* ***lay****.*

Name: ___________________________

Word Choice Use specific nouns and precise, descriptive language to paint a clear picture for your reader.

A. Read each paragraph. Circle the words and phrases in Paragraph 2 that replaced the bold words in Paragraph 1. Then answer the question.

Paragraph 1

Our field trip to Museum Park was **fun**. First, we ate **lunch** on the **lawn**. I decided to lie on my back and watch the **clouds in the sky**. Suddenly, I heard a dog barking **loudly**. I was worried that it might be a **mean** dog, but I looked up to see **the dog** barking at a **pretty** kite that had crashed to the ground. After cleaning up from lunch, we went inside the art museum and **looked at** the **interesting** paintings and sculptures on display.

Paragraph 2

Our trip to Museum Park was full of excitement. First, we ate gigantic submarine sandwiches on the cool, green, freshly mowed grass. I decided to lie on my back and watch the fluffy white clouds drifting through the sky. Suddenly, I heard a dog barking urgently. I was worried that it might be an aggressive dog, but I looked up to see a French poodle barking at a rainbow-colored kite that had crashed to the ground. After cleaning up from lunch, we went inside the art museum and examined the expressive paintings and carefully crafted sculptures on display.

Which paragraph does a better job of describing? Give an example to support your answer.

____

____

B. Read each sentence. Write an *X* next to the one that uses the underlined word correctly.

____ 1. The dog lays down on the grass.

____ 2. The dog lies down on the grass.

____ 3. The girl lays her books on the table.

____ 4. The girl lies her books on the table.

Name: ______________________________

Word Choice

Use vivid adjectives to make your descriptions clear and precise.

A. Use each given word or phrase to write a strong descriptive sentence. Be as creative as possible. Remember to use *a* and *an* correctly.

Example: The audience cringed when the singer hit an **eardrum-shattering** note.

1. **eardrum-shattering:** ______________________________
2. **peppery:** ______________________________
3. **brightly spotted:** ______________________________
4. **pungent:** ______________________________
5. **towering:** ______________________________
6. **100-year-old:** ______________________________

B. Read the paragraph. Use *lay* or *lie* and *a* or *an* to complete each sentence.

Please __________ your sleeping bag in __________ tent. But don't __________ down and take __________ nap! Help me __________ the tablecloth on __________ unclaimed picnic table.

Name: ______________________________

Word Choice

Replace overused words with specific nouns and vivid adjectives to make your descriptions clear and precise.

A. Read the description of a painting. Then:

- Use proofreading marks to replace each word in bold with a better descriptive word or phrase. Remember to change the article before it to *a* or *an,* if necessary.
- Use proofreading marks to fix any incorrect uses of *lay* or *lie.*

My brother's friend Ismael painted an **interesting** painting in his art class. The painting shows an **old** cabin in the woods, with **old, broken** doors and windows. You can see some **tall** trees in the background. Their **colorful** autumn leaves lie scattered on the ground. A rusted rake lays against one wall of the cabin, and in front of the door, a peacock stands with its **colorful** feathers spread wide open. Facing the peacock is a **little** boy on an **old** tricycle. The boy is leaning over the handlebars and staring **hard** at the peacock. The peacock is looking back with a **weird** look. Ismael titled this painting "Standoff." He entered it in the county fair, where it competed against many paintings and won first place!

B. Rewrite each sentence correctly.

1. There was a ugly brown snake laying across the trail.

____

2. I saw a squirrel scurry off with an nut and lie it in a hole.

____

Name: ______________________________

Word Choice

Use precise nouns and adjectives to write a strong description.

A. If you were going to write a description of the picture below, what could you say? Write eight strong descriptive phrases to describe the truck, the kids, or other things in the picture.

______________________________ ______________________________

______________________________ ______________________________

______________________________ ______________________________

______________________________ ______________________________

B. Write one sentence you could use in your description. Remember to use *a* and *an* correctly.

____

____

WORD CHOICE

Using Similes, Metaphors, and Personification

DAY 1

Read the rule aloud. Say: *Similes and metaphors are tools that writers use to compare things. They create more interesting images.* Then guide students through the activities.

- **Activity A:** Read the poem aloud. Say: *The first line uses the word **like** to compare leaves and cornflakes, so it is a simile. What does the next line compare **cheeks** to?* (red roses) Say: *That comparison doesn't use **like** or **as**, so it is a metaphor.* Have students complete the activity.
- **Activity B:** Read aloud the simile for Subject 1. Say: *This simile describes the shape of the diamond in an unusual way. What other things could the diamond be?* (e.g., battlefield, stage) Model turning one idea into a metaphor: *The diamond-shaped battlefield awaits soldiers armed with bats and gloves.* Have students complete the activity.

  Convention: Remind students that the subject of a sentence and its verb must "agree." Point out the verb **are** in the fourth line of the poem. Say: *The verb is plural because the subject, "Jen and Grandma Josie," is plural—it's two people.* Have students check their similes and metaphors for subject-verb agreement.

DAY 2

Read the rule aloud. Then guide students through the activities.

- **Activity A:** Read aloud the description. Ask: *Does the moon really "hide"?* (no, that's a human action) Say: *It just changes position, so we can see only the parts that are lit up by the sun. The writer **personified** this action.* Have students underline **hides** and complete the activity independently.

  Convention: Read the sentence "Some nights you sees her..." Ask: *Is this verb correct?* (no) Explain that even though **you** can be singular or plural, it must always have a plural verb. Have students correct the other incorrect verbs.
- **Activity B:** Read aloud the example. Then have students complete the activity on their own or in pairs. Have students share what they wrote, and discuss the characteristics that were personified.

Name: ____________________ **Week 3 • Day 1**

Word Choice Using similes and metaphors makes your writing richer. A simile compares two things using *like* or *as*. A metaphor does not use *like* or *as*.

A. Read the free-verse poem. Underline each simile, and circle each metaphor.

Autumn Night

Golden leaves crunch under my feet like cornflakes at breakfast.
My cheeks are red roses in bloom.
Cotton balls of smoke puff out of chimneys, and
Jen and Grandma Josie are cozy cats in their blankets.
I'm as warm as a mug of cocoa,
Falling like leaves, falling asleep.

B. Pretend you are writing about a baseball game. For each subject below, read the simile or the metaphor that has been written about it. Then write your own simile or metaphor.

Sample Answers:

1. **Subject:** baseball diamond before a game
   Simile: The empty diamond is like a kite lying on the ground, waiting for the wind.
   Metaphor: The baseball diamond is a battlefield ready for two armies to clash.
2. **Subject:** the pitcher throwing a fastball
   Simile: The pitcher's arm is like a cannon exploding.
   Metaphor: The pitcher shoots a white bullet into the catcher's glove.
3. **Subject:** the umpire making a call
   Simile: The umpire watches the ball like an eagle eyeing its prey.
   Metaphor: The umpire is the principal breaking up a scuffle on the playground.
4. **Subject:** runner stealing a base
   Simile: The runner sprints as fast as a hungry cheetah.
   Metaphor: The runner is on fire, burning toward second base.

84 WORD CHOICE Daily 6-Trait Writing • EMC 6025 • © Evan-Moor Corp.

Name: ____________________ **Week 3 • Day 2**

Word Choice Using personification, or giving nonliving things human form or characteristics, brings your writing to life.

A. Read the description of the moon. Underline the words or phrases that make the moon seem human. Then use proofreading marks to correct any errors in subject-verb agreement.

The moon is fickle. She's always changing her mind. Some nights you sees her, some nights you don't. Sometimes she smile down on you with her moonbeams. Other nights she hides in the dark. Dogs howls at the moon. Maybe they want her to slow down so they can catch her. But she keep strolling across the sky, never stopping in one place for too long.

B. Pretend you're writing about a street scene. Describe each subject below by writing a sentence that includes personification.

Example:

Subject: stop sign
Description: The stop sign stands there sternly, waiting to command "Stop!"

Sample Answers:

1. **Subject:** traffic light
   Description: The traffic light's eyes blink from green to yellow to red.
2. **Subject:** bus shelter
   Description: The bus shelter wraps a warm hug around the waiting passengers.
3. **Subject:** mailbox
   Description: The mailbox opens its huge jaws and gobbles up people's letters.

© Evan-Moor Corp. • EMC 6025 • Daily 6-Trait Writing WORD CHOICE 85

Name: ______________________ **Week 3 • Day 3**

Word Choice Use similes, metaphors, and personification to make your descriptions memorable.

Read Jack's description of his first roller coaster ride. Then:
- Help him finish some of the similes, metaphors, and personification by filling in the blanks.
- Use proofreading marks to correct any errors in subject-verb agreement.

"Who's up for the Mountain of Mayhem?" asked Sam. That ~~were~~ was the LAST ride I wanted to go on, but I couldn't show my fear in front of my friends. So I put on a brave face, like a pirate walking the plank.

This coaster was as high as a Sample Answers: mountain. Every time I looked at it, my stomach became a pancake flipping in a frying pan. As we moved closer to the front of the line, I began trembling like a tiny chihuahua in the snow.

When it ~~were~~ was our turn, I listened carefully to the safety instructions. I pulled the harness as tight as it would go and clung to the safety bar like glue.

Suddenly, the train was a rocket, shooting away from the platform. The track tossed us around as if it was juggling baseballs. Then we roared into a tunnel. The darkness gobbled me up, and the car slowly started to climb up, and up, and up.

Finally, we ~~was~~ were at the top. The car hung suspended for a moment, like the calm before a storm. Then I was a kite without a string, hanging in midair as I rose out of my seat. All I remember is screaming like a baby.

As we exited the ride, my legs ~~was~~ were two ropes of wobbly licorice.

"Want to go again?" Sam asked.

"Maybe later," I whispered, running for the bathroom.

86 WORD CHOICE Daily 6-Trait Writing • EMC 6025 • © Evan-Moor Corp.

DAY 3

Read the rule aloud. Then guide students through the activity.

- Read aloud the description. Say: *Jack did a great job of describing how he felt about the ride.* Call students' attention to the simile "like a pirate walking the plank." Say: *"Like a pirate walking the plank" describes Jack's false face of bravery. He wasn't really feeling brave, but he pretended to be.*
- Ask: *What are some other similes, metaphors, and personifications we can add to the description?* Read the beginning of the second paragraph aloud and help students brainstorm things that the height of the coaster could be compared to. (e.g., mountain, Eiffel Tower)
- Guide students through the rest of the description, or have them complete the activity independently or in pairs.
- **Convention:** Review subject-verb agreement. Have students identify the errors and explain how they corrected them.

Name: ______________________ **Week 3 • Day 4**

Word Choice Use similes, metaphors, and personification to develop your ideas for a description.

A. Think of the first time you did something. Plan a description of that event. Answer the questions to help you.

The First Time I Went Snow Skiing

1. How did you feel before the event? Sample Answers:
   nervous, excited
2. Write a simile that describes how you felt.
   I felt like a kid on her birthday, wondering what's inside the biggest present.
3. How did you feel during the event?
   a little scared, uncoordinated
4. Write a metaphor that describes how you felt.
   I was a baby learning how to walk, falling for no reason!
5. What verbs could describe the event or how you felt?
   zoom, crash, fall
6. What adjectives could you use to describe the event?
   cold, dangerous, thrilling
7. Write an example of personification that describes the event or how you felt.
   One leg wanted to go right, but the other insisted on going left.

B. Have a partner check your answers for errors in subject-verb agreement. Fix any that are found.

© Evan-Moor Corp. • EMC 6025 • Daily 6-Trait Writing WORD CHOICE 87

DAY 4

Read the rule aloud. Then guide students through the activities.

- **Activity A:** Help students brainstorm "first" events in their lives. (e.g., losing their first tooth, first day at a new school, riding a bike, giving a performance) Then discuss the feelings evoked by the event.

  Have students complete the activity independently. Circulate to help students as necessary.
- **Activity B (Convention):** Have students exchange papers to proofread for errors in subject-verb agreement.

DAY 5 *Writing Prompt*

- *Write a description of the first time you did something exciting or scary. Include similes, metaphors, and personification. You may use the ones you wrote on Day 4.*
- *Be sure that subjects and verbs agree with each other.*

Name: ______________________

Word Choice

Using similes and metaphors makes your writing richer. A simile compares two things using *like* or *as*. A metaphor does not use *like* or *as*.

A. Read the free-verse poem. Underline each simile, and circle each metaphor.

Autumn Night

Golden leaves crunch under my feet like cornflakes at breakfast.
My cheeks are red roses in bloom.
Cotton balls of smoke puff out of chimneys, and
Jen and Grandma Josie are cozy cats in their blankets.
I'm as warm as a mug of cocoa,
Falling like leaves, falling asleep.

B. Pretend you are writing about a baseball game. For each subject below, read the simile or the metaphor that has been written about it. Then write your own simile or metaphor.

1. **Subject:** baseball diamond before a game

   Simile: The empty diamond is like a kite lying on the ground, waiting for the wind.

   Metaphor: ______________________

2. **Subject:** the pitcher throwing a fastball

   Simile: ______________________

   Metaphor: The pitcher shoots a white bullet into the catcher's glove.

3. **Subject:** the umpire making a call

   Simile: The umpire watches the ball like an eagle eyeing its prey.

   Metaphor: ______________________

4. **Subject:** runner stealing a base

   Simile: ______________________

   Metaphor: The runner is on fire, burning toward second base.

Word Choice

Using personification, or giving nonliving things human form or characteristics, brings your writing to life.

A. Read the description of the moon. Underline the words or phrases that make the moon seem human. Then use proofreading marks to correct any errors in subject-verb agreement.

The moon is fickle. She's always changing her mind. Some nights you sees her, some nights you don't. Sometimes she smile down on you with her moonbeams. Other nights she hides in the dark. Dogs howls at the moon. Maybe they want her to slow down so they can catch her. But she keep strolling across the sky, never stopping in one place for too long.

B. Pretend you're writing about a street scene. Describe each subject below by writing a sentence that includes personification.

Example:

Subject: stop sign

Description: The stop sign stands there sternly, waiting to command "Stop!"

1. **Subject:** traffic light

   Description: ______________________

   ____

2. **Subject:** bus shelter

   Description: ______________________

   ____

3. **Subject:** mailbox

   Description: ______________________

   ____

Name: ______________________________

Week 3 • Day 3

Word Choice

Use similes, metaphors, and personification to make your descriptions memorable.

Read Jack's description of his first roller coaster ride. Then:

- Help him finish some of the similes, metaphors, and personification by filling in the blanks.
- Use proofreading marks to correct any errors in subject-verb agreement.

"Who's up for the Mountain of Mayhem?" asked Sam. That were the LAST ride I wanted to go on, but I couldn't show my fear in front of my friends. So I put on a brave face, like a pirate walking the plank.

This coaster was **as high as a** ______________________. Every time I looked at it, my stomach became a pancake flipping in a frying pan. As we moved closer to the front of the line, I began trembling **like a** ______________________.

When it were our turn, I listened carefully to the safety instructions. I pulled the harness as tight as it would go and clung to the safety bar **like** ______________________.

Suddenly, the train was a ______________________, shooting away from the platform. The track tossed us around **as if it** ______________________. Then we roared into a tunnel. The darkness gobbled me up, and the car slowly started to climb up, and up, and up.

Finally, we was at the top. The car hung suspended for a moment, like the calm before a storm. Then I was ______________________, hanging in midair as I rose out of my seat. All I remember is screaming **like a** ______________________.

As we exited the ride, my legs was ______________________.

"Want to go again?" Sam asked.

"Maybe later," I whispered, running for the bathroom.

Word Choice

Use similes, metaphors, and personification to develop your ideas for a description.

A. Think of the first time you did something. Plan a description of that event. Answer the questions to help you.

The First Time I ______________________

1. How did you feel before the event?

____

2. Write a simile that describes how you felt.

____

3. How did you feel during the event?

____

4. Write a metaphor that describes how you felt.

____

5. What verbs could describe the event or how you felt?

____

6. What adjectives could you use to describe the event?

____

7. Write an example of personification that describes the event or how you felt.

____

B. Have a partner check your answers for errors in subject-verb agreement. Fix any that are found.

WORD CHOICE
Choosing Words for Your Audience

DAY 1

Read the rule aloud. Review the definitions of formal and informal language. Then say: *There are certain forms of writing for which it is especially important to keep your audience in mind. Letters are one of those, as you are usually writing to someone very specific.* Guide students through the activities.

- **Activity A:** Read aloud each letter. Confirm that the audience of the first one is a member of the bike club, and the audience of the second one is Mr. Armstrong's manager. Model comparing the language of the two letters. For example, say: *The first letter says "get the guy who...," while the second letter says "request that the man who..."* Have students complete the activity.

- **Activity B (Convention):** Write these sentences on the board: *I don't know* ***who's*** *using this pen. I don't know* ***whose*** *pen this is.* Circle **who's** and **whose** and say: *These words are often confused.* ***Who's*** *is a contraction for* ***who is. Whose*** *shows ownership.* Have students complete the activity.

Name: ______________________ **Week 4 • Day 1**

Word Choice When you write to someone you know well, it's OK to use informal language. Use formal language for anyone else.

A. Read each letter. Underline the words in the formal letter that replaced the bolded words in the informal letter.

Informal

Hey Luiz,

I'd love to get the **guy** who just won the **bike** race, Mr. Armstrong, to come **talk** to our bike club. We could **set up a time that would work for him** to come out here. I bet he'd have some tips he could give us for our next **few** races. **What do you think?** How cool would that be? I think that our members would be **totally psyched** to have someone like him **give us an edge** over the other bike clubs in the upcoming races.

Formal

Dear Sir:

I am writing to request that the man who won the recent bicycle race, Mr. Armstrong, come give a presentation to our bicycle club. We would schedule the meeting at a convenient time for Mr. Armstrong. He could discuss skills that would help us in our future races. Do you think this would be possible? Our club would be honored to have someone like Mr. Armstrong advise us on how to win races.

B. Complete each sentence with the word *who's* or *whose.*

1. Who's going on the bicycle ride tomorrow?
2. Whose bicycle was left in front of the door?
3. Do you know whose helmet this is?

90 WORD CHOICE Daily 6-Trait Writing • EMC 6025 • © Evan-Moor Corp.

DAY 2

Read the rule aloud. Then guide students through the activities.

- **Activity A:** Say: *A journal entry is meant to be read by you, so you don't need to use formal language.* Have students complete the activity and share their answers.

- **Activity B (Convention):** Read the paragraph aloud. Then write these sentences on the board: *The mother nursed* ***its*** *kitten.* ***It's*** *a hungry kitten.* Say: ***Its*** *means "belongs to it."* ***It's*** *is a contraction for* ***it is***. Have students find **its** and **it's** in the paragraph and correct them.

  Next, ask: *Would a 6-year-old understand this paragraph?* (no) *Why not?* (uses too many hard words) Reread the first sentence and have students brainstorm simpler words for **alarm** (**bell**), **activates** (**rings, goes off**), and **frightened** (**scared, worried**). Then guide students in rewriting the sentence. Continue going through the paragraph as a class, or have students write their own versions.

Name: ______________________ **Week 4 • Day 2**

Word Choice Choose words that fit your audience. When you write informally or for younger children, use simpler words.

A. Read the journal entry. Choose the word or phrase below each line that sounds more informal. Write it on the line.

November 7

Today, we had a long (long / lengthy) talk (talk / presentation) about school safety in the gym (gymnasium / gym). All students had to go (attend / go). One of my BFFs (BFFs / friends) asked some funny (amusing / funny) questions!

After everyone spoke, we went (went / proceeded) to the cafeteria to stuff our faces (stuff our faces / dine). We talked about (discussed / talked about) what the speakers had said.

B. Read this paragraph about a school's safety plan. Use proofreading marks to correct any incorrect usage of *its* or *it's*. Then rewrite the paragraph in simpler language so a first-grade student could understand it.

When the alarm activates, there's no need to be frightened. Simply line up behind your teacher in an orderly fashion. You may then leave the classroom and proceed to the rear door of the school. Its critical that you maintain a calm, quiet composure. Remain outside until the emergency personnel can ensure the safety of the building and it's classrooms.

Sample Paragraph:
When the bell rings, don't be scared. Just line up calmly with your teacher. Then leave your room and walk to the back door of the school. It's important to be quiet and not goof around. Stay outside until the firefighters make sure the building and its classrooms are safe.

© Evan-Moor Corp. • EMC 6025 • Daily 6-Trait Writing WORD CHOICE 91

Name: ______________________ **Week 4 • Day 3**

Word Choice When your audience is someone important or someone you don't know well, use formal language. Choose serious-sounding words.

Susan wrote a letter to a judge, but she did not use formal enough language. She also made mistakes with *whose* and *its*. Rewrite her letter, correcting the mistakes and using formal language. Use the words in the box to give you ideas.

Hey Judge Lee,

In our class, we've been learning all about trials, lawyers, judges, and other legal things. We've learned about who does what, and we even had a pretend trial. Also, some old judge came to our classroom. He told us about the law and it's history, but now we wanna meet a judge whose still in court. We also want to check out your courtroom. We could see your robe and your gavel, and everything. And some of us want to be lawyers when we grow up, so you could tell us what to do and stuff. That would be totally cool! Thanks!

TTYL,
Susan Zack

Dear	understanding	features	consider	system	request
experience	appreciate	thank you	Sincerely	explain	process

Sample Answer:

Dear Judge Lee,

Our class has been studying the legal system. We've learned the roles of everyone involved, and even held a mock trial. Also, a former judge visited our classroom. He told us about the law and its history, but we would like to speak with a judge who's still in court. We would also like to visit a real courtroom. We know it would be a good experience. We could see all of the features of a courtroom. In addition, some of us would like to be lawyers some day, so we would greatly appreciate any advice you have. Thank you.

Sincerely,
Susan Zack

92 WORD CHOICE Daily 6-Trait Writing • EMC 6025 • © Evan-Moor Corp.

DAY 3

Read the rule aloud. Then guide students through the activity.

- Invite a student to read aloud the letter. Then say: *This letter is to a judge. A judge is usually a powerful, respected person. Should you use informal words such as* **hey** *and* **stuff***?* (no) Say: *In addition, when you are writing to ask somebody for something, especially an adult, you should use formal language.*
- Guide students in identifying examples of informal language in the letter. For example, point out the phrase "who does what" in the second sentence. Ask: *What are some formal words we could use that mean* **job***?* (**role, duty**) Model rephrasing the sentence. (e.g., *We've learned about the role of each person.*) Then read aloud the words in the box. Say: *These are some other formal words that you could use when revising the letter.*
- You may want students to rewrite the letter in small groups. Circulate to offer suggestions. Invite students to share their completed letters.

Name: ______________________ **Week 4 • Day 4**

Word Choice Choose words that fit your audience. Think about whom you're writing to. Ask yourself what type of writing he or she would best respond to.

A. Think about someone whom you would like to visit your classroom. Write a letter in which you ask that person to visit. Complete the chart to plan your ideas.

Sample Answers:

Whom would you like to visit?	an astronaut
What would you like this person to do, show you, or tell you about?	show us photos from space, help us conduct an experiment, tell us what it's like to go up into space
Why do you want this person to visit?	I want to be an astronaut. I think outer space is really interesting. Everyone wants to know more about astronauts.
When would you like this person to visit?	maybe during our science fair
How would you convince this person to visit?	I would make a video to send to an astronaut. I would explain how much I love space, and show him or her all of my science projects.

B. Fill in the blanks to complete each sentence with the correct word. Use *whose, who's, it's,* or *its.*

1. I want to meet somebody __whose__ job is to protect wild animals.
2. Donnie wants to talk with someone __who's__ involved with computers.
3. Malik thinks __it's__ fun to talk about our future careers.
4. Wendy wants to go to State University and be on __its__ basketball team.

© Evan-Moor Corp. • EMC 6025 • Daily 6-Trait Writing WORD CHOICE 93

DAY 4

Read the rule aloud. Guide students through the activities.

- **Activity A:** List students' ideas of people they would like to visit on the board. Point out two diverse people, such as an astronaut and a wrestler. Ask: *Would you use the same language and words when writing to an astronaut as you would a wrestler?* (probably not) *Why?* (They work in different fields. An astronaut is professional, but a wrestler provides entertainment.) Have students complete the chart.
- **Activity B:** Have students complete the sentences. Review the answers as a class.

DAY 5 *Writing Prompt*

- *Use your ideas from Day 4 to write a letter inviting someone to visit your classroom. Use the type of language most appropriate for the recipient.*
- *Be sure to spell* **whose, who's, it's,** *and* **its** *correctly.*

Name: ________________________________

Word Choice

When you write to someone you know well, it's OK to use informal language. Use formal language for anyone else.

A. Read each letter. Underline the words in the formal letter that replaced the bolded words in the informal letter.

Informal

Hey Luiz,

I'd love to get the **guy** who just won the **bike** race, Mr. Armstrong, to come **talk** to our bike club. We could **set up a time that would work for him** to come out here. I bet he'd have some tips he could give us for our next **few** races. **What do you think?** How cool would that be? I think that our members would be **totally psyched** to have someone like him **give us an edge** over the other bike clubs in the upcoming races.

Formal

Dear Sir:

I am writing to request that the man who won the recent bicycle race, Mr. Armstrong, come give a presentation to our bicycle club. We would schedule the meeting at a convenient time for Mr. Armstrong. He could discuss skills that would help us in our future races. Do you think this would be possible? Our club would be honored to have someone like Mr. Armstrong advise us on how to win races.

B. Complete each sentence with the word *who's* or *whose.*

1. __________ going on the bicycle ride tomorrow?

2. __________ bicycle was left in front of the door?

3. Do you know __________ helmet this is?

Name: ______________________________

Word Choice

Choose words that fit your audience. When you write informally or for younger children, use simpler words.

A. Read the journal entry. Choose the word or phrase below each line that sounds more informal. Write it on the line.

November 7

Today, we had a ________ (long / lengthy) ________ (talk / presentation) about school safety in the ________ (gymnasium / gym). All students had to ________ (attend / go). One of my ________ (BFFs / friends) asked some ________ (amusing / funny) questions!

After everyone spoke, we ________ (went / proceeded) to the cafeteria to ________ (stuff our faces / dine). We ________ (discussed / talked about) what the speakers had said.

B. Read this paragraph about a school's safety plan. Use proofreading marks to correct any incorrect usage of *its* or *it's*. Then rewrite the paragraph in simpler language so a first-grade student could understand it.

When the alarm activates, there's no need to be frightened. Simply line up behind your teacher in an orderly fashion. You may then leave the classroom and proceed to the rear door of the school. Its critical that you maintain a calm, quiet composure. Remain outside until the emergency personnel can ensure the safety of the building and it's classrooms.

____

____

____

____

____

Name: ______________________________

Word Choice

When your audience is someone important or someone you don't know well, use formal language. Choose serious-sounding words.

Susan wrote a letter to a judge, but she did not use formal enough language. She also made mistakes with *whose* and *its*. Rewrite her letter, correcting the mistakes and using formal language. Use the words in the box to give you ideas.

Hey Judge Lee,

In our class, we've been learning all about trials, lawyers, judges, and other legal things. We've learned about who does what, and we even had a pretend trial. Also, some old judge came to our classroom. He told us about the law and it's history, but now we wanna meet a judge whose still in court. We also want to check out your courtroom. We could see your robe and your gavel, and everything. And some of us want to be lawyers when we grow up, so you could tell us what to do and stuff. That would be totally cool! Thanks!

TTYL,
Susan Zack

Dear	understanding	features	consider	system	request
experience	appreciate	thank you	Sincerely	explain	process

Name: ________________________________

Word Choice

Choose words that fit your audience. Think about whom you're writing to. Ask yourself what type of writing he or she would best respond to.

A. Think about someone whom you would like to visit your classroom. Write a letter in which you ask that person to visit. Complete the chart to plan your ideas.

Whom would you like to visit?	
What would you like this person to do, show you, or tell you about?	
Why do you want this person to visit?	
When would you like this person to visit?	
How would you convince this person to visit?	

B. Fill in the blanks to complete each sentence with the correct word. Use *whose, who's, it's,* or *its.*

1. I want to meet somebody __________ job is to protect wild animals.

2. Donnie wants to talk with someone __________ involved with computers.

3. Malik thinks __________ fun to talk about our future careers.

4. Wendy wants to go to State University and be on __________ basketball team.

WORD CHOICE
Getting the Reader's Attention

DAY 1

Read the rule aloud. Say: *Use everything you've learned about word choice—vivid verbs, descriptive language, similes, metaphors, and personification—to craft openings that make your readers want to read more.* Guide students through the activities.

- **Activity A:** Read aloud the two openings, and guide students in comparing them. For example, say: *The first word in Opening 1 is* ***Money****. The first phrase in Opening 2 is "Millions of dollars." Which is more specific and descriptive?* ("Millions of dollars") Have students continue to compare the openings, circling the more specific words and phrases. Then ask: *Which opening is more powerful?* (Opening 2)
- **Activity B:** Read aloud the first sentence. Ask: *Which is stronger and more precise,* ***broken*** *or* ***trampled****?* (**trampled**) Have students complete the rest of the activity, then review the answers.
- **Convention:** Write these words on the board: **owner, dollar, sculptor.** Say: *All of these words end with the /er/ sound. This sound can be spelled* ***er, ar,*** *or* ***or****. Use a dictionary to check your spelling of words ending with /er/.* Then have students look for these and other words with the /er/ ending in Activities A and B.

DAY 2

Read the rule aloud. Then guide students through the activities.

- **Activity A:** Say: *It's important to be able to grab a reader's interest in a sentence or two.* Read the first pair of openings. Then say: *In the second opening, the phrase* ***nice place*** *doesn't tell us much. Also, the word* ***might*** *is not very strong.* Discuss what makes the first opening stronger. (e.g., makes you feel "there"; uses the word **beautiful**) Repeat the process for each pair of openings.

  Convention: Allow students to use dictionaries to correct the misspelled words.

- **Activity B:** Read the opening aloud. Ask: *What could we do to make this opening more exciting?* (e.g., use confident language; name specific flavors) Have students rewrite the opening independently.

Name: ______________________ **Week 5 • Day 1**

Word Choice To write a strong opening and get your reader's attention, use powerful, precise language.

A. Read each opening for a persuasive essay. Circle the precise word or phrase in Opening 2 that replaces each boldface word in Opening 1.

Opening 1

Money is often **taken** from **musicians**. It happens because musicians own their music, just as store owners own their **stuff**. When people **copy** music for free, they're **taking** the money from musicians.

Opening 2

(Millions of dollars) are (stolen) from (musicians' pockets every day.) How does it happen? Just as a store owner owns the (items on his or her shelves,) musical artists own their music. When people (download) music without paying for it, they are (stealing.) And every dollar adds up!

B. Read this opening paragraph for a story. Complete the sentences by writing the words or phrases that are more likely to grab the reader's attention.

The fact that Dan's science fair entry was __trampled__ (broken / trampled) by his darling __German shepherd__ (German shepherd / dog) would certainly have __thrown__ (put / thrown) any other boy into __hysterics__ (hysterics / a mood). However, Dan was different from all the other boys. He had __a secret weapon__ (a secret weapon / help)—his mom! She just happened to be an expert __sculptor__ (artist / sculptor), who could put his clay volcano model back together __lickety-split__ (lickety-split / quickly).

96 WORD CHOICE Daily 6-Trait Writing • EMC 6025 • © Evan-Moor Corp.

Name: ______________________ **Week 5 • Day 2**

Word Choice Review and revise your opening to make it stronger. Use words and phrases that will get your reader's attention.

A. Read each pair of opening sentences. Write an *X* next to the opening that gets your attention more. Then use proofreading marks to fix any misspelled words ending in *or, er,* or *ar.*

1. X You've got the whole day ahead of you. Where do you go to pass the time? You hit the road and head to beautiful Lake Romana.
   ___ If you are looking for a nice place to spend the day, you might ~~consider~~ consider going to Lake Romana.
2. ___ Helen Tarrosa is a great doctor who is known around town for helping others.
   X Everyone in town is ~~familier~~ familiar with Dr. Helen Tarrosa, who has helped hundreds of people in need.
3. X The T-shirt Factory sells any T-shirt you could ever want! In fact, it sells shirts in more than 60 different ~~colers~~ colors and styles.
   ___ The T-shirt Factory sells many kinds of T-shirts.
4. X Imagine waking up on a farm, surrounded by quiet cows, cheerful chickens, cozy cats, and one very happy hound.
   ___ At Old Farm Inn, you can ~~wandor~~ wander all around a real farm.

B. Read this opening for a restaurant ad. Then rewrite it, using more powerful, precise language.

Think about having dinner at Pete's Pizza. His interesting flavors will probably surprise you.

Sample Answer: Have you ever tried peanut butter, carrots, and mangoes on pizza? If not, you must take a trip to Pete's Pizza!

© Evan-Moor Corp. • EMC 6025 • Daily 6-Trait Writing WORD CHOICE 97

Name: ______________________ **Week 5 • Day 3**

Word Choice Use powerful, precise language to make your reader want to keep reading.

A. Read this interview. Use a dictionary to check the spellings of words ending in *or, er,* or *ar,* and use proofreading marks to fix any that are misspelled.

~~Reportor~~ Reporter: What happened?

Mayor Ruiz: There was a small fire in Public Square on Tuesday night.

Reporter: How did it start?

~~Mayer~~ Mayor Ruiz: A small ~~tremer~~ tremor caused a huge, tall light to fall over. It landed on a movie camera and knocked it to the ground. There were sparks, which started a small fire.

Reporter: Who was involved at the fire?

Mayor Ruiz: The ~~acters~~ actors, ~~directer~~ director, and film crew, who were in town to make a movie.

Reporter: How did they react?

Mayor Ruiz: The most ~~populer~~ popular actor ran from the scene. A crew member knocked over the food table. Some of the food fell into the fire, and it smelled like a skunk!

Reporter: How was the fire put out?

Mayor Ruiz: ~~Firefightors~~ Firefighters arrived and put out the fire. Thankfully, no one was hurt.

B. Use the interview above to write a short article describing what happened in Public Square. Be sure to write a beginning that grabs the reader's attention. Sample Answer:

The popular actor Jason Star was caught running in panic from the scene when a fire broke out in Public Square on Tuesday night. The fire was started by a light that had fallen when a small tremor shook the area. The light was owned by a film crew who was shooting a movie in the square. While the mayor later confirmed that no one was hurt, the stench of burned food was detected throughout surrounding neighborhoods for hours.

98 WORD CHOICE Daily 6-Trait Writing • EMC 6025 • © Evan-Moor Corp.

Name: ______________________ **Week 5 • Day 4**

Word Choice Use powerful, precise language to write a strong opening that makes your reader want to read more.

Imagine that you're a reporter on the scene of one of the events listed in the box below. Complete the chart with information about the event. Use words that will grab your reader's attention.

- A bear is found wandering through a shopping mall.
- School bus drivers compete in a bus race.
- Famous actors come to town for the premier of a new movie.

Sample Answers:

Event: Bear at the Mall

Who was there?	A young brown bear, mall security guards, animal control officers
What happened?	found wandering around and looking confused
Where did it happen?	Willow Creek Mall on Forest Road
When did it happen?	last Saturday morning, just before opening
Why did it happen?	The Animal Control Department said that the poor bear had lost its mother and wandered out of Ryan State Forest. It was probably searching for food.
How did it happen?	The bear entered through a door left open by an employee.

© Evan-Moor Corp. • EMC 6025 • Daily 6-Trait Writing WORD CHOICE 99

DAY 3

Read the rule aloud. Say: *Newspaper reporters grab their readers' attention by writing strong, precise openings that tell all of the basic information up front.* Then guide students through the activities.

- **Activity A (Convention):** Have two students read the interview, taking the roles of the reporter and the mayor. Then have students work in pairs to look up the misspelled words and correct them. Review the answers as a class.
- **Activity B:** Brainstorm words and phrases students could use in their articles. Ask: *What strong adjectives, nouns, and verbs could you use to tell about the fire?* (e.g., **fiery**, **panic**, **running**, **stench**, **scorched**) Read aloud the sample article on the reduced page as an example. Then have students write their articles independently or in pairs.

DAY 4

Review the rule. Guide students through the activity.

- Read the list of events aloud and have students discuss what might happen at each one. Then have each student choose an event to write about.
- Read through the questions on the chart and say: *Reporters try to answer the questions* ***who, what, where, when, why,*** *and* ***how*** *in every newspaper article. Try to answer each one in the chart.*
- Have students complete the chart, using powerful, precise language to describe the details. Circulate to assist as needed.

DAY 5 *Writing Prompt*

- *Use your chart from Day 4 to write a newspaper article about the event you chose. Get your reader's attention by using powerful, precise language.*
- *Be sure to spell words ending in* ***or***, ***er***, *or* ***ar*** *correctly.*

Name: ______________________________

Week 5 • Day 1

Word Choice

To write a strong opening and get your reader's attention, use powerful, precise language.

A. Read each opening for a persuasive essay. Circle the precise word or phrase in Opening 2 that replaces each boldface word in Opening 1.

Opening 1

Money is often **taken** from **musicians**. It happens because musicians own their music, just as store owners own their **stuff**. When people **copy** music for free, they're **taking** the money from musicians.

Opening 2

Millions of dollars are stolen from musicians' pockets every day! How does it happen? Just as a store owner owns the items on his or her shelves, musical artists own their music. When people download music without paying for it, they are stealing. And every dollar adds up!

B. Read this opening paragraph for a story. Complete the sentences by writing the words or phrases that are more likely to grab the reader's attention.

The fact that Dan's science fair entry was ______________________ (broken / trampled) by his darling ______________________ (German shepherd / dog) would certainly have ______________________ (put / thrown) any other boy into ______________________ (hysterics / a mood). However, Dan was different from all the other boys. He had ______________________ (a secret weapon / help)—his mom! She just happened to be an expert ______________________ (artist / sculptor), who could put his clay volcano model back together ______________________ (lickety-split / quickly).

Word Choice

Review and revise your opening to make it stronger. Use words and phrases that will get your reader's attention.

A. Read each pair of opening sentences. Write an *X* next to the opening that gets your attention more. Then use proofreading marks to fix any misspelled words ending in *or, er,* or *ar.*

1. ___ You've got the whole day ahead of you. Where do you go to pass the time? You hit the road and head to beautiful Lake Romana.

   ___ If you are looking for a nice place to spend the day, you might considor going to Lake Romana.

2. ___ Helen Tarrosa is a great doctor who is known around town for helping others.

   ___ Everyone in town is familier with Dr. Helen Tarrosa, who has helped hundreds of people in need.

3. ___ The T-shirt Factory sells any T-shirt you could ever want! In fact, it sells shirts in more than 60 different colers and styles.

   ___ The T-shirt Factory sells many kinds of T-shirts.

4. ___ Imagine waking up on a farm, surrounded by quiet cows, cheerful chickens, cozy cats, and one very happy hound.

   ___ At Old Farm Inn, you can wandor all around a real farm.

B. Read this opening for a restaurant ad. Then rewrite it, using more powerful, precise language.

Think about having dinner at Pete's Pizza. His interesting flavors will probably surprise you.

____

____

____

____

Word Choice

Use powerful, precise language to make your reader want to keep reading.

A. Read this interview. Use a dictionary to check the spellings of words ending in *or, er,* or *ar,* and use proofreading marks to fix any that are misspelled.

Reportor: What happened?

Mayor Ruiz: There was a small fire in Public Square on Tuesday night.

Reporter: How did it start?

Mayar Ruiz: A small tremer caused a huge, tall light to fall over. It landed on a movie camera and knocked it to the ground. There were sparks, which started a small fire.

Reporter: Who was involved at the fire?

Mayor Ruiz: The acters, directar, and film crew, who were in town to make a movie.

Reporter: How did they react?

Mayor Ruiz: The most populor actor ran from the scene. A crew member knocked over the food table. Some of the food fell into the fire, and it smelled like a skunk!

Reporter: How was the fire put out?

Mayor Ruiz: Firefightors arrived and put out the fire. Thankfully, no one was hurt.

B. Use the interview above to write a short article describing what happened in Public Square. Be sure to write a beginning that grabs the reader's attention.

Name: ____

Word Choice

Use powerful, precise language to write a strong opening that makes your reader want to read more.

Imagine that you're a reporter on the scene of one of the events listed in the box below. Complete the chart with information about the event. Use words that will grab your reader's attention.

- A bear is found wandering through a shopping mall.
- School bus drivers compete in a bus race.
- Famous actors come to town for the premier of a new movie.

Event:

Who was there?	
What happened?	
Where did it happen?	
When did it happen?	
Why did it happen?	
How did it happen?	

WEEK 1

SENTENCE FLUENCY

Combining Sentences with Conjunctions

Refer to pages 6 and 7 to introduce or review the writing trait.

DAY 1

Read the rule aloud and review the definition of a compound sentence. (two complete sentences joined by a comma and a conjunction) Then guide students through the activities.

- **Activity A:** Read the paragraph aloud. Then direct students back to the third sentence. Say: *This sentence combines two related ideas into one sentence that flows naturally, using the conjunction* ***but***. Have students identify the two sentences within the compound sentence. Then have them complete the activity on their own.

- **Activity B:** Read the paragraph aloud, emphasizing its choppiness. Say: *When you have short, complete sentences that contain related information, you can join them into compound sentences to make your writing less choppy. For example, the sentences "They have old phones" and "They have new ones" are short, and both are about types of phones, so they could be combined.* Model combining the sentences into "They have old phones, and they have new ones."

  Convention: Point out the comma you wrote after **phones**, as well as the commas in all of the compound sentences in Activity A. Say: *When you write a compound sentence, always remember to use a comma before the conjunction.* Then have students complete the activity.

DAY 2

Read the rule aloud. Say: *A rambling sentence is several sentences strung together with too many coordinating conjunctions.* Guide students through the activities.

- **Activity A:** Read aloud the first sentence. Say: *This sentence has too many ideas for just one sentence.* Model breaking the sentence into two separate sentences, emphasizing that one of them can still be a compound sentence. Then have students rewrite the paragraph. Ask volunteers to read aloud their revisions and explain how they corrected the rambling sentences.

- **Activity B (Convention):** Use students' paragraphs to review the use of commas in compound sentences.

Name: ______________________ **Week 1 • Day 1**

Sentence Fluency Make your writing flow by combining short, choppy sentences into compound sentences. Use conjunctions (*and*, *but*, *or*, and *so*) to make compound sentences.

A. Read this description. Underline each compound sentence, and circle its conjunction.

Have you ever been to the Bug Museum? This museum is dedicated to helping kids know more about the many roles that bugs play on Earth. You may not love bugs, but this museum will help you understand why they're so important! You can discover how bees communicate, and you can learn how ladybugs help farmers. You can touch some live beetles, and you can crawl around in a giant ant farm. The museum offers tours, or you can explore on your own. There is even a place to have lunch. Just remember that the museum is crowded on weekends, so it's better to go during the week.

B. Read this description. Underline the short, choppy sentences that could be combined. Then combine them to write three compound sentences, using a comma and a conjunction.

The Museum of Communication has collected telephones for the past century. They have old phones. They have new ones. Many phones are antiques. Some still work. My favorite phone is the one with an earpiece that you hold to your ear while talking into a box on the wall. It reminds me of old movies. I tried using an old phone. It was hard to hear. I had to talk loudly. My friend and I pretended to be living when people used those phones. People had less privacy then. You couldn't move or carry around the phone. The closest thing to text messaging was the telegraph machine.

Sample Answers:

1. They have old phones, and they have new ones.
2. Many phones are antiques, but some still work.
3. I tried using an old phone, but it was hard to hear.
   OR It was hard to hear, so I had to talk loudly.

102 SENTENCE FLUENCY Daily 6-Trait Writing • EMC 6025 • © Evan-Moor Corp.

Name: ______________________ **Week 1 • Day 2**

Sentence Fluency When you combine sentences to make your writing flow, be careful not to form rambling sentences.

A. Underline the rambling sentences in this paragraph. Then rewrite the paragraph, changing the rambling sentences to compound or simple sentences.

Most creatures have some sort of way to protect themselves from predators, but there are some creatures that have very unusual defense mechanisms, and some animals use toxic chemicals to protect themselves. For example, the poison dart frog has many poison glands all over its body, and the fire salamander squirts poison at its enemies from glands on its back, but other animals use camouflage to hide from their enemies. For instance, the chameleon changes its color to match its surroundings, and so do some octopuses, but one type of octopus, the mimic octopus, even changes its shape to look like other animals, so it just goes to show that animals will do anything to keep from being eaten!

Sample Paragraph:

Most creatures have some sort of way to protect themselves from predators, but there are some creatures that have very unusual defense mechanisms. Some animals use toxic chemicals to protect themselves. For example, the poison dart frog has many poison glands all over its body, and the fire salamander squirts poison at its enemies from glands on its back. Other animals use camouflage to hide from their enemies. For instance, the chameleon changes its color to match its surroundings, and so do some octopuses. One type of octopus, the mimic octopus, even changes its shape to look like other animals. It just goes to show that animals will do anything to keep from being eaten!

B. Look back at the paragraph you wrote. Check to make sure you used commas correctly. Circle the commas, and add them if necessary.

© Evan-Moor Corp. • EMC 6025 • Daily 6-Trait Writing SENTENCE FLUENCY 103

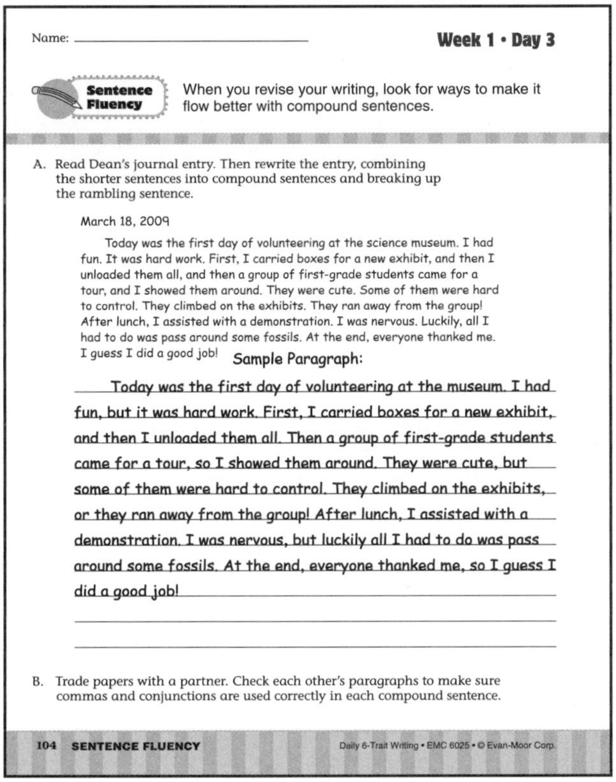

Name: ______________ **Week 1 • Day 3**

Sentence Fluency When you revise your writing, look for ways to make it flow better with compound sentences.

A. Read Dean's journal entry. Then rewrite the entry, combining the shorter sentences into compound sentences and breaking up the rambling sentence.

March 18, 2009

Today was the first day of volunteering at the science museum. I had fun. It was hard work. First, I carried boxes for a new exhibit, and then I unloaded them all, and then a group of first-grade students came for a tour, and I showed them around. They were cute. Some of them were hard to control. They climbed on the exhibits. They ran away from the group! After lunch, I assisted with a demonstration. I was nervous. Luckily, all I had to do was pass around some fossils. At the end, everyone thanked me. I guess I did a good job!

Sample Paragraph:

Today was the first day of volunteering at the museum. I had fun, but it was hard work. First, I carried boxes for a new exhibit, and then I unloaded them all. Then a group of first-grade students came for a tour, so I showed them around. They were cute, but some of them were hard to control. They climbed on the exhibits, or they ran away from the group! After lunch, I assisted with a demonstration. I was nervous, but luckily all I had to do was pass around some fossils. At the end, everyone thanked me, so I guess I did a good job!

B. Trade papers with a partner. Check each other's paragraphs to make sure commas and conjunctions are used correctly in each compound sentence.

104 SENTENCE FLUENCY Daily 6-Trait Writing • EMC 6025 • © Evan-Moor Corp.

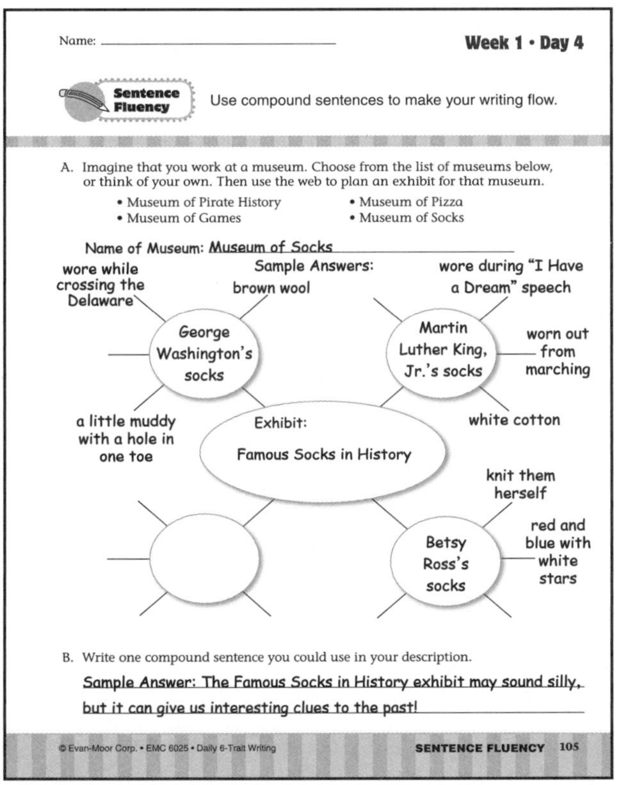

Name: ______________ **Week 1 • Day 4**

Sentence Fluency Use compound sentences to make your writing flow.

A. Imagine that you work at a museum. Choose from the list of museums below, or think of your own. Then use the web to plan an exhibit for that museum.

- Museum of Pirate History
- Museum of Pizza
- Museum of Games
- Museum of Socks

Name of Museum: Museum of Socks

B. Write one compound sentence you could use in your description.

Sample Answer: The Famous Socks in History exhibit may sound silly, but it can give us interesting clues to the past!

© Evan-Moor Corp. • EMC 6025 • Daily 6-Trait Writing SENTENCE FLUENCY 105

DAY 3

Read the rule aloud. Remind students that a compound sentence can be formed with **and, but, or,** or **so**. Then guide students through the activities.

- **Activity A:** Read aloud the journal entry, emphasizing its choppiness. Then draw students' attention to the second and third sentences. Ask: *What conjunction could we use to connect these two thoughts?* (**but**) Write the sentences on the board and model combining them into a compound sentence. Then have students complete the activity.
- **Activity B (Convention):** Have students exchange papers and check each other's work. Circulate to offer help and clarification.

DAY 4

Review the rule. Then guide students through the activities.

- **Activity A:** Read the list of museums aloud. Invite students to brainstorm other interesting museums that might be fun to work at. Then discuss what types of exhibits might be found in these museums. (e.g., eye patch collection; board games from other cultures; photos of famous people eating pizza; socks from around the world) Have students choose their favorite exhibit to complete the web.
- **Activity B (Convention):** Use a student's web to model forming a compound sentence about the exhibit. Review the correct placement of the comma. Then have students write their own sentences. Circulate to check for skill acquisition.

DAY 5 *Writing Prompt*

- *Use your web from Day 4 to write a description of an exhibit in your museum. Make sure your writing flows smoothly.*
- *Be sure to use commas in compound sentences correctly, and avoid writing rambling sentences.*

Name: ___________________________________

Sentence Fluency

Make your writing flow by combining short, choppy sentences into compound sentences. Use conjunctions (*and, but, or,* and *so*) to make compound sentences.

A. Read this description. Underline each compound sentence, and circle its conjunction.

Have you ever been to the Bug Museum? This museum is dedicated to helping kids know more about the many roles that bugs play on Earth. You may not love bugs, but this museum will help you understand why they're so important! You can discover how bees communicate, and you can learn how ladybugs help farmers. You can touch some live beetles, and you can crawl around in a giant ant farm. The museum offers tours, or you can explore on your own. There is even a place to have lunch. Just remember that the museum is crowded on weekends, so it's better to go during the week.

B. Read this description. Underline the short, choppy sentences that could be combined. Then combine them to write three compound sentences, using a comma and a conjunction.

The Museum of Communication has collected telephones for the past century. They have old phones. They have new ones. Many phones are antiques. Some still work. My favorite phone is the one with an earpiece that you hold to your ear while talking into a box on the wall. It reminds me of old movies. I tried using an old phone. It was hard to hear. I had to talk loudly. My friend and I pretended to be living when people used those phones. People had less privacy then. You couldn't move or carry around the phone. The closest thing to text messaging was the telegraph machine.

1. ___________________________________

2. ___________________________________

3. ___________________________________

Name: ______________________________

Sentence Fluency

When you combine sentences to make your writing flow, be careful not to form rambling sentences.

A. Underline the rambling sentences in this paragraph. Then rewrite the paragraph, changing the rambling sentences to compound or simple sentences.

Most creatures have some sort of way to protect themselves from predators, but there are some creatures that have very unusual defense mechanisms, and some animals use toxic chemicals to protect themselves. For example, the poison dart frog has many poison glands all over its body, and the fire salamander squirts poison at its enemies from glands on its back, but other animals use camouflage to hide from their enemies. For instance, the chameleon changes its color to match its surroundings, and so do some octopuses, but one type of octopus, the mimic octopus, even changes its shape to look like other animals, so it just goes to show that animals will do anything to keep from being eaten!

____

____

____

____

____

____

____

____

____

____

____

B. Look back at the paragraph you wrote. Check to make sure you used commas correctly. Circle the commas, and add them if necessary.

Name: ______________________________

Sentence Fluency

When you revise your writing, look for ways to make it flow better with compound sentences.

A. Read Dean's journal entry. Then rewrite the entry, combining the shorter sentences into compound sentences and breaking up the rambling sentence.

March 18, 2009

Today was the first day of volunteering at the science museum. I had fun. It was hard work. First, I carried boxes for a new exhibit, and then I unloaded them all, and then a group of first-grade students came for a tour, and I showed them around. They were cute. Some of them were hard to control. They climbed on the exhibits. They ran away from the group! After lunch, I assisted with a demonstration. I was nervous. Luckily, all I had to do was pass around some fossils. At the end, everyone thanked me. I guess I did a good job!

____

____

____

____

____

____

____

____

____

____

____

B. Trade papers with a partner. Check each other's paragraphs to make sure commas and conjunctions are used correctly in each compound sentence.

Name: ______________________________

Week 1 • Day 4

Sentence Fluency Use compound sentences to make your writing flow.

A. Imagine that you work at a museum. Choose from the list of museums below, or think of your own. Then use the web to plan an exhibit for that museum.

- Museum of Pirate History
- Museum of Games
- Museum of Pizza
- Museum of Socks

Name of Museum: ______________________________

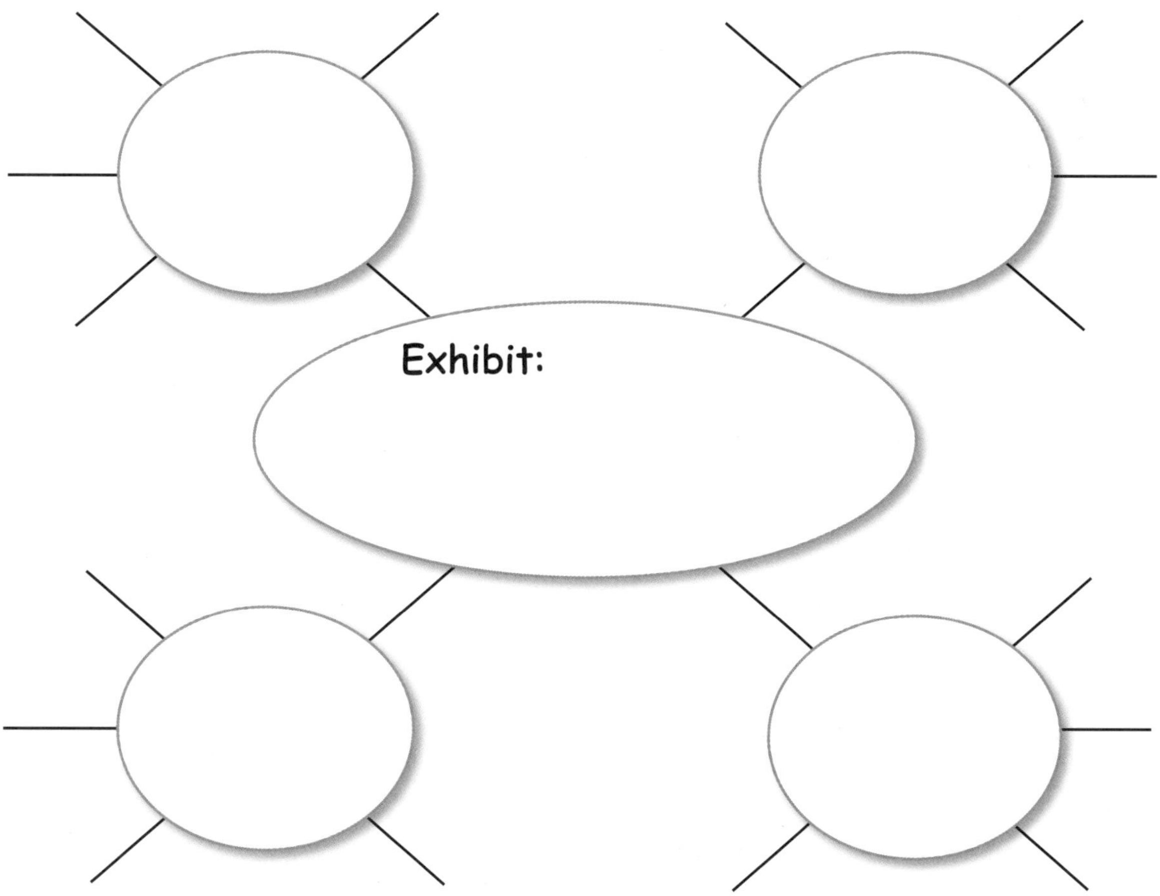

B. Write one compound sentence you could use in your description.

____

____

SENTENCE FLUENCY

Writing Complex Sentences

DAY 1

Read the rule aloud. Say: *Just as you can combine short, related sentences into compound sentences, you can use complex sentences to combine your ideas.* Write this sentence on the board: *I will read some great books before the summer is over.* Underline "I will read some great books" and say: *This is an **independent clause**, or a group of words that can stand alone as a complete sentence.* Then underline "before the summer is over" and say: *This is a **dependent clause**, or a group of words that cannot stand alone as a complete sentence. It starts with a **subordinating conjunction**.* Circle **before** and say: *This is a subordinating conjunction.* Discuss other examples, such as **while, until**, etc.

Convention: Rewrite the above sentence as: *Before the summer is over, I will read some great books.* Say: *Sometimes the sentence sounds better if you put the dependent clause first, beginning with the conjunction. When the dependent clause comes first, write a comma after it.* Then guide students through the activities.

- **Activity A:** Read aloud the words in the box. Say: *In compound sentences, we use conjunctions such as **and, but**, and **or**. But in complex sentences, we use conjunctions like these.* Read the paragraph aloud and have students complete the activity.
- **Activity B (Convention):** Say: *You must decide if a complex sentence sounds better with its dependent clause first or last. If it comes first, write a comma after it.* Model writing sentence 1 on the board. Have students complete sentences 2 and 3.

DAY 2

Read the rule aloud. Then guide students through the activities.

- **Activity A:** Read each clause aloud. Point out the ones that begin with **once** and **although** to introduce these conjunctions. Then model choosing two clauses to form a sentence. Write it with the dependent clause first, and then write it the other way around. Have students discuss which way sounds better or makes more sense. Then have students complete the activity.
- **Activity B (Convention):** Have students trade papers and check each other's work.

Name: ____________________ **Week 2 • Day 1**

Sentence Fluency Complex sentences help your writing flow. A complex sentence is an independent clause and a dependent clause joined by a subordinating conjunction.

A. Underline the complex sentences in this paragraph. Then, for each sentence you underlined:
- Circle the subordinating conjunction.
- Draw a second line under the independent clause.

Subordinating Conjunctions				
after	because	when	while	until

On Saturday, I helped my mom get ready to open her new bookstore. My job was to straighten all the bookshelves while Mom prepared the cash register. We were expecting a lot of customers because Mom had put a big ad in the paper. Finally, Mom was ready to open the store, but there was a problem. When she tried to open the door from the inside, it was stuck! She had to call a locksmith. He said he couldn't get there until he finished another job. Mom was frantic! While we waited nervously, customers started gathering outside. After twenty minutes, the locksmith finally arrived. He fixed the door and let everyone in. We all cheered, especially Mom!

B. Combine each pair of sentences to write a complex sentence, using the conjunction in parentheses. Remember, the conjunction can come at the beginning or in the middle of the sentence.

1. Rafael writes the story. Jessie will draw the pictures. *(if)*
   If Rafael writes the story, Jessie will draw the pictures.
2. Please help me think of plot ideas. I have to start writing. *(before)*
   Please help me think of plot ideas before I have to start writing.
3. I revised my story. Yuki liked it better. *(after)*
   After I revised my story, Yuki liked it better.

108 SENTENCE FLUENCY Daily 6-Trait Writing • EMC 6025 • © Evan-Moor Corp.

Name: ____________________ **Week 2 • Day 2**

Sentence Fluency When you write a complex sentence, you can start with either the dependent clause or the independent clause. Choose the way that sounds the most natural.

A. Read the clauses. Match each dependent clause to an independent clause to write six complex sentences. Be sure to think about which way the sentence makes more sense—with the dependent clause or the independent clause first.

Dependent Clause	Independent Clause
once he has finished his homework	he writes in his reading journal
when Eli has time	Eli's mom built him a bookcase
while he reads	Eli is also interested in historical fiction
before his little sister goes to bed	he reads her a story
although he likes fantasy novels	Eli will read his book
because he has so many books	Eli always makes a snack to eat

1. Eli will read his book once he has finished his homework. OR Once he has finished his homework, Eli will read his book.
2. When Eli has time, he writes in his reading journal.
3. Eli always makes a snack to eat while he reads.
4. Before his little sister goes to bed, he reads her a story.
5. Although he likes fantasy novels, Eli is also interested in historical fiction.
6. Eli's mom built him a bookcase because he has so many books.

B. Exchange papers with a partner. Check to make sure commas are used correctly in the sentences that begin with a dependent clause. Circle the commas, or add them if necessary.

© Evan-Moor Corp. • EMC 6025 • Daily 6-Trait Writing SENTENCE FLUENCY 109

Name: ______________________ **Week 2 • Day 3**

Sentence Fluency Use complex sentences to help your writing flow smoothly.

A. Rewrite this book review to make it flow more smoothly. Combine some sentences into complex sentences, using any of the conjunctions in the box.

A Wrinkle in Time

I don't normally enjoy reading fantasy books. I really liked the fantasy A Wrinkle in Time by Madeleine L'Engle. The story is about a brother and sister. They have to work hard to save their father. He is trapped on another planet. They journey through time and space to reach him. They find out more about themselves. They realize that the power of love is stronger than evil. They return home—with their father. This book had me hooked. I couldn't stop reading. I finally got to the end. You will love this book. You'll finish reading it. You'll want to read it again!

Subordinating Conjunctions				
after	because	if	unless	when
although	before	once	until	while

Sample Answer:

Although I don't normally enjoy reading fantasy books, I really liked the fantasy A Wrinkle in Time by Madeleine L'Engle. The story is about a brother and sister. They have to work hard to save their father because he is trapped on another planet. While they journey through time and space to reach him, they find out more about themselves. Once they realize that the power of love is stronger than evil, they return home—with their father. This book had me hooked. I couldn't stop reading until I finally got to the end! You will love this book. After you finish reading it, you'll want to read it again!

B. Exchange papers with another student. Underline each complex sentence in the rewritten review. Check to make sure commas have been used correctly.

110 SENTENCE FLUENCY Daily 6-Trait Writing • EMC 6025 • © Evan-Moor Corp.

Name: ______________________ **Week 2 • Day 4**

Sentence Fluency Use complex sentences to help your writing flow smoothly.

Think of a book you have read that you could write a review about. Then complete the items. Sample Answers:

1. What is the name of the book? Remember to underline the title.
   The Invention of Hugo Cabret
2. Who is the author?
   Brian Selznick
3. What happens in the book? Write a few sentences to summarize the plot. Use subordinating conjunctions such as *before, after,* or *while* in your answer.
   Hugo lives with his uncle in a train station. After his uncle disappears, Hugo does his uncle's job. Hugo hides while he lives in the station. One day, he makes friends with a girl whose grandfather knows a big secret.
4. Did you like or dislike the book? Why? Use the word *because* in your answer. Write at least one complex sentence.
   I like the book because it is full of detailed drawings. The drawings tell most of the story. It is a big book, but it does not take a long time to read.
5. Who would like or dislike this book? Answer the question using a complex sentence.
   If you like to draw, you will love this book.

© Evan-Moor Corp. • EMC 6025 • Daily 6-Trait Writing SENTENCE FLUENCY 111

DAY 3

Read the rule aloud. Then guide students through the activities.

- **Activity A:** Invite students who have read A Wrinkle in Time to summarize the plot and describe some of their favorite parts of it.

  Read aloud the book review. Say: *This paragraph sounds too choppy. It would flow better if we combined some of the sentences.* Reread the first two sentences. Say: *The first sentence says that the writer doesn't normally like to read fantasy stories. But the second says that he or she liked this story. A good conjunction to link those ideas is* ***although:*** *"Although I don't normally enjoy reading fantasy books, I really liked* A Wrinkle in Time*."* Write the sentence on the board, using it to briefly review dependent and independent clauses. Invite students to suggest other sentences that can be combined. Then have students complete the activity.

- **Activity B (Convention):** Review commas in complex sentences. Then have students exchange papers and check each other's sentences for correct comma usage.

DAY 4

Review the rule. Guide students through the activity.

- Remind students: *In a book review, you give your opinion. You explain why you would or would not recommend the book to others.* Then use a book that the class is familiar with to model completing the questionnaire.
- Have students complete the activity. Circulate to monitor progress and assist as necessary.

DAY 5 *Writing Prompt*

- *Use your answers to the questionnaire on Day 4 to write a book review. Explain what you thought of the book and who would or would not like it. Include complex sentences to help your writing flow smoothly.*
- *Be sure to use commas correctly.*

Name: ______________________________

Week 2 • Day 1

Sentence Fluency

Complex sentences help your writing flow. A complex sentence is an independent clause and a dependent clause joined by a subordinating conjunction.

A. Underline the complex sentences in this paragraph. Then, for each sentence you underlined:
- Circle the subordinating conjunction.
- Draw a second line under the independent clause.

Subordinating Conjunctions				
after	because	when	while	until

On Saturday, I helped my mom get ready to open her new bookstore. My job was to straighten all the bookshelves while Mom prepared the cash register. We were expecting a lot of customers because Mom had put a big ad in the paper. Finally, Mom was ready to open the store, but there was a problem. When she tried to open the door from the inside, it was stuck! She had to call a locksmith. He said he couldn't get there until he finished another job. Mom was frantic! While we waited nervously, customers started gathering outside. After twenty minutes, the locksmith finally arrived. He fixed the door and let everyone in. We all cheered, especially Mom!

B. Combine each pair of sentences to write a complex sentence, using the conjunction in parentheses. Remember, the conjunction can come at the beginning or in the middle of the sentence.

1. Rafael writes the story. Jessie will draw the pictures. *(if)*

____

2. Please help me think of plot ideas. I have to start writing. *(before)*

____

3. I revised my story. Yuki liked it better. *(after)*

____

Name: ______________________

Sentence Fluency

When you write a complex sentence, you can start with either the dependent clause or the independent clause. Choose the way that sounds the most natural.

A. Read the clauses. Match each dependent clause to an independent clause to write six complex sentences. Be sure to think about which way the sentence makes more sense—with the dependent clause or the independent clause first.

Dependent Clause	Independent Clause
once he has finished his homework	he writes in his reading journal
when Eli has time	Eli's mom built him a bookcase
while he reads	Eli is also interested in historical fiction
before his little sister goes to bed	he reads her a story
although he likes fantasy novels	Eli will read his book
because he has so many books	Eli always makes a snack to eat

1. ______________________
2. ______________________
3. ______________________
4. ______________________
5. ______________________
6. ______________________

B. Exchange papers with a partner. Check to make sure commas are used correctly in the sentences that begin with a dependent clause. Circle the commas, or add them if necessary.

Name: ______________________________

Sentence Fluency Use complex sentences to help your writing flow smoothly.

A. Rewrite this book review to make it flow more smoothly. Combine some sentences into complex sentences, using any of the conjunctions in the box.

A Wrinkle in Time

I don't normally enjoy reading fantasy books. I really liked the fantasy A Wrinkle in Time by Madeleine L'Engle. The story is about a brother and sister. They have to work hard to save their father. He is trapped on another planet. They journey through time and space to reach him. They find out more about themselves. They realize that the power of love is stronger than evil. They return home—with their father. This book had me hooked. I couldn't stop reading. I finally got to the end. You will love this book. You'll finish reading it. You'll want to read it again!

Subordinating Conjunctions				
after	because	if	unless	when
although	before	once	until	while

____

____

____

____

____

____

____

____

B. Exchange papers with another student. Underline each complex sentence in the rewritten review. Check to make sure commas have been used correctly.

Name: ______________________________

Sentence Fluency

Use complex sentences to help your writing flow smoothly.

Think of a book you have read that you could write a review about. Then complete the items.

1. What is the name of the book? Remember to underline the title.

____

2. Who is the author?

____

3. What happens in the book? Write a few sentences to summarize the plot. Use subordinating conjunctions such as *before, after,* or *while* in your answer.

____

____

____

____

4. Did you like or dislike the book? Why? Use the word *because* in your answer. Write at least one complex sentence.

____

____

____

5. Who would like or dislike this book? Answer the question using a complex sentence.

____

____

WEEK 3

SENTENCE FLUENCY

Parallel Structure Within a Sentence

DAY 1

Read the rule aloud. Then guide students through the activities.

- **Activity A:** Write **swim**, **swimming**, and **to swim** on the board. Say: *These verbs mean the same thing. They are just in different forms.* Write **laughing** and **splashing** under **swimming**. Say: *When you write verbs in a series, keep them in the same form. That is known as staying **parallel**.* Read aloud both fragments in item 1. Ask: *Which fragment is correct?* (the second) Say: *The first one is not parallel, because **hiking** does not match the forms of the other verbs.*

  Guide students through the remaining items, explaining the other ways in which words or phrases must stay parallel. (e.g., using articles or other words in front of nouns consistently; in a series of verb phrases, using a verb before each object consistently)

- **Activity B (Convention):** Review the difference between subject pronouns (**I**, **he**, **she**, **we**, **they**) and object pronouns (**me**, **him**, **her**, **us**, **them**). Read aloud sentence 1. Ask: *Which pronoun is correct?* (**I**) *Why?* (It's part of the subject of the sentence.) Have students complete the activity.

Name: ______________________ **Week 3 • Day 1**

Sentence Fluency Use parallel structure in your writing. Keep lists of words or phrases in the same form.

A. Read each pair of sentence fragments. In each pair:
- Make a check next to the fragment in which all three words or phrases are parallel.
- Write an *X* next to the fragment whose words or phrases are not parallel. Circle the word or phrase that does not match.

1. X to walk, to climb, and (hiking)
   ✓ to walk, to climb, and to hike
2. ✓ my sneakers, my baseball bat, and my mitt
   X my sneakers, (baseball bat) and my mitt
3. ✓ two flies, a beetle, a grasshopper, and an ant
   X two flies, a beetle, (grasshopper) and an ant
4. X sweep the floor, do the laundry, and (the dishes)
   ✓ sweep the floor, do the laundry, and wash the dishes

B. Write the correct pronoun to complete each sentence.

1. My sister Dara and __I__ (I / me) are taking karate lessons this year.
2. __We__ (We / Us) are learning how to kick, how to block, and how to punch.
3. Dad takes __her and me__ (her and me / she and I) to the gym on Tuesdays, Thursdays, and Saturdays.
4. A lot of my friends want to take karate now. __They__ (Them / They) have heard how fun it is!
5. They always ask __me__ (I / me) to demonstrate kicks.

114 SENTENCE FLUENCY Daily 6-Trait Writing • EMC 6025 • © Evan-Moor Corp.

DAY 2

Read the rule aloud. Then guide students through the activities.

- **Activity A:** Read aloud sentence 1 twice: once with answer a, and once with answer b. Ask: *Which is correct?* (answer b) Then have students complete the activities, and review the answers.
- **Activity B:** Model answering question 1 on the board. (e.g., I will visit family, grade papers, and ride my bike.) Then have students complete the activity and share their sentences.
- **Activity C (Convention):** Begin reading the paragraph aloud. Have students raise their hands when they hear the first error. (**Him** and **me**) Ask: *Why is "Him and me" wrong?* (They are object pronouns, not subject pronouns.) Then have students complete the activity. Read aloud the edited paragraph.

Name: ______________________ **Week 3 • Day 2**

Sentence Fluency When you write a series of words or phrases in a sentence, be sure to use parallel structure.

A. Complete each sentence with the word or phrase that keeps the sentence parallel.

1. Kira needs to perform twenty sit-ups, __do ten push-ups__, and run a mile.
   a. ten push-ups b. do ten push-ups
2. To make a fruit shake, you need some milk, several strawberries, a banana, and __a blender__.
   a. blender b. a blender
3. Mr. Milos likes running in races, swimming laps, and __playing basketball__.
   a. playing basketball b. basketball

B. Write a complete sentence with parallel structure to answer each question. Sample Answers:

1. What are three things you will do this weekend?
   I will go to soccer practice, clean my room, and do my homework.
2. What are three things you need to make your favorite sandwich?
   I need bread, turkey, and Swiss cheese.

C. Use proofreading marks to fix the incorrect pronouns in this paragraph.

Jay is my best friend. ~~Him~~ He and ~~me~~ I go everywhere together. Our parents are friends, too. ~~Them~~ They go to football games together. Jay's dad taught us how to play football. Next year, ~~me~~ Jay and ~~Jay~~ I will try out for the team.

© Evan-Moor Corp. • EMC 6025 • Daily 6-Trait Writing SENTENCE FLUENCY 115

Name: ______________________ **Week 3 • Day 3**

Sentence Fluency When you revise your writing, check to make sure you have used parallel structure in each sentence.

Read this compare-and-contrast paragraph. Then:

- Circle the incorrect pronouns.
- Underline the sentences that do not have parallel structure.
- Rewrite the paragraph correctly.

Two of the hardest athletic events are marathons and triathlons. These competitions aren't for regular people like you and (I). They are only for really good athletes. A marathon is a running race. A triathlon is a race with three parts. First, you run, then you swim, and riding a bike. For a marathon, athletes need a running outfit and comfortable shoes. For a triathlon, (them) also need a swimsuit, a bicycle, and they need a helmet. In a marathon, an athlete runs 26 miles. (Him or her) might take a few hours to finish. In a triathlon, an athlete swims 2 miles, bikes 4 miles, and runs 26. This can take ten hours or more to complete! So you can see why both marathons and triathlons require special training, incredible endurance, and you have to work hard.

Sample Paragraph:

Two of the hardest athletic events are marathons and triathlons. These competitions aren't for regular people like you and me. They are only for really good athletes. A marathon is a running race. A triathlon is a race with three parts. First you run, then you swim, and then you ride a bike. For a marathon, athletes need a running outfit and a comfortable pair of shoes. For a triathlon, they also need a swimsuit, a bicycle, and a helmet. In a marathon, an athlete runs 26 miles. He or she might take a few hours to finish. In a triathlon, an athlete swims 2 miles, bikes 4 miles, and runs 26 miles. This can take ten hours or more to complete! So you can see why both marathons and triathlons require special training, incredible endurance, and hard work.

116 SENTENCE FLUENCY Daily 6-Trait Writing • EMC 6025 • © Evan-Moor Corp.

DAY 3

Read the rule aloud. Then guide students through the activity.

- **Convention:** Have a student read the paragraph aloud. Then reread the second sentence. Say: *The pronouns **you** and **I** are the objects of the phrase "for regular people like." So are they correct?* (No, **I** should be **me**.) Help students find and circle the other incorrect pronouns in the paragraph.
- Return to the sentence beginning "First, you run..." Ask: *Which verbs are being used in a series?* (**run, swim, riding**) *Are they parallel?* (no) Model rewriting the sentence. Say: *The first two verbs are in the simple form with the subject **you**, so I need to change **riding** to **you ride**.*
- Have students complete the activity independently. Then ask a volunteer to read aloud his or her paragraph.

Name: ______________________ **Week 3 • Day 4**

Sentence Fluency Use parallel structure in your writing. Keep series of words or phrases in the same form.

Think of two sports you like to watch or play. Complete the chart below to plan a compare-and-contrast paragraph. Remember to use parallel structure in your answers. Sample Answers:

Sport 1: Basketball	Sport 2: Volleyball
Name three actions you do while playing it. running, dribbling, and throwing	Name three actions you do while playing it. jumping up, running to the net, hitting the ball
Name three things you need to play it. a basketball, a net, and a court	Name three things you need to play it. a volleyball, a net, some kneepads
Name three things you need to do well in order to win. shoot baskets, guard players, get rebounds	Name three things you need to do well in order to win. serve the ball to your opponents, spike the ball over the net, pass the ball to your teammates

© Evan-Moor Corp. • EMC 6025 • Daily 6-Trait Writing SENTENCE FLUENCY 117

DAY 4

Review the rule. Then guide students through the activity.

- Remind students that to compare and contrast is to tell how things are alike and different. Then help students brainstorm sports they are familiar enough with to write about. (e.g., soccer, dancing, cheerleading, gymnastics, skateboarding)
- Model answering the first item for Sport 1. For example, say: *For basketball, there's running and dribbling. You also have to pass the ball to other players. So, I'll write **running, dribbling,** and **passing**.* Write the verbs on the board, pointing out their parallel forms. Then have students complete the activity independently. Ask volunteers to share their ideas.

DAY 5 *Writing Prompt*

- *Write a compare-and-contrast paragraph about two sports. Use the lists you created on Day 4 to write sentences that have parallel structure.*
- *Be sure to use pronouns correctly.*

Name: ____________________________________

Week 3 • Day 1

Sentence Fluency

Use parallel structure in your writing.
Keep lists of words or phrases in the same form.

A. Read each pair of sentence fragments. In each pair:

- Make a check next to the fragment in which all three words or phrases are parallel.
- Write an *X* next to the fragment whose words or phrases are not parallel. Circle the word or phrase that does not match.

1. ____ to walk, to climb, and hiking

   ____ to walk, to climb, and to hike

2. ____ my sneakers, my baseball bat, and my mitt

   ____ my sneakers, baseball bat, and my mitt

3. ____ two flies, a beetle, a grasshopper, and an ant

   ____ two flies, a beetle, grasshopper, and an ant

4. ____ sweep the floor, do the laundry, and the dishes

   ____ sweep the floor, do the laundry, and wash the dishes

B. Write the correct pronoun to complete each sentence.

1. My sister Dara and ____________ (I / me) are taking karate lessons this year.
2. ____________ (We / Us) are learning how to kick, how to block, and how to punch.
3. Dad takes ____________ (her and me / she and I) to the gym on Tuesdays, Thursdays, and Saturdays.
4. A lot of my friends want to take karate now. ____________ (Them / They) have heard how fun it is!
5. They always ask ____________ (I / me) to demonstrate kicks.

Name: ______________________________

Sentence Fluency

When you write a series of words or phrases in a sentence, be sure to use parallel structure.

A. Complete each sentence with the word or phrase that keeps the sentence parallel.

1. Kira needs to perform twenty sit-ups, ____________________, and run a mile.

   a. ten push-ups b. do ten push-ups

2. To make a fruit shake, you need some milk, several strawberries, a banana, and ________________.

   a. blender b. a blender

3. Mr. Milos likes running in races, swimming laps, and ____________________.

   a. playing basketball b. basketball

B. Write a complete sentence with parallel structure to answer each question.

1. What are three things you will do this weekend?

   ____

2. What are three things you need to make your favorite sandwich?

   ____

C. Use proofreading marks to fix the incorrect pronouns in this paragraph.

Jay is my best friend. Him and me go everywhere together. Our parents are friends, too. Them go to football games together. Jay's dad taught us how to play football. Next year, me and Jay will try out for the team.

Name: ______________________________

Sentence Fluency

When you revise your writing, check to make sure you have used parallel structure in each sentence.

Read this compare-and-contrast paragraph. Then:

- Circle the incorrect pronouns.
- Underline the sentences that do not have parallel structure.
- Rewrite the paragraph correctly.

Two of the hardest athletic events are marathons and triathlons. These competitions aren't for regular people like you and I. They are only for really good athletes. A marathon is a running race. A triathlon is a race with three parts. First, you run, then you swim, and riding a bike. For a marathon, athletes need a running outfit and comfortable shoes. For a triathlon, them also need a swimsuit, a bicycle, and they need a helmet. In a marathon, an athlete runs 26 miles. Him or her might take a few hours to finish. In a triathlon, an athlete swims 2 miles, bikes 4 miles, and runs 26. This can take ten hours or more to complete! So you can see why both marathons and triathlons require special training, incredible endurance, and you have to work hard.

____

____

____

____

____

____

____

____

____

Name: ______________________________

Sentence Fluency

Use parallel structure in your writing.
Keep series of words or phrases in the same form.

Think of two sports you like to watch or play. Complete the chart below to plan a compare-and-contrast paragraph. Remember to use parallel structure in your answers.

Sport 1:	Sport 2:
Name three actions you do while playing it.	Name three actions you do while playing it.
Name three things you need to play it.	Name three things you need to play it.
Name three things you need to do well in order to win.	Name three things you need to do well in order to win.

SENTENCE FLUENCY
Beginning Sentences in Different Ways

DAY 1

Read the rule aloud. Then guide students through the activities.

- **Activity A:** Have students read both narratives and circle the first word in each sentence. Then have them say which one they think is better. Say: *Both narratives have the same information, but the first one contains many sentences that begin with* ***I*** *or* ***We.*** *The second one has more of a variety.*

  Ask: *How is "I wondered where she was" different from "Where was she?"* (The question puts you in the writer's head; **shows** rather than **tells.**) Say: *Beginning the sentence with a question word adds variety and makes the writing more interesting.* Then have students identify other improvements.

- **Activity B (Convention):** Review: *When you write dialogue, write the exact words that someone said, with quotation marks around those words.* Have students find the dialogue in both narratives. Ask: *What is the difference between the sentences?* (One starts by telling who is speaking; the other starts with the exclamation.) Then say: *When an exclamation or question comes before the phrase that tells who's speaking, you don't need a comma after the dialogue.* Have students complete the activity.

DAY 2

Read the rule aloud. Remind students: *You can begin sentences not only with nouns and articles, but with verbs, adverbs, interjections, introductory words and phrases, and subordinating conjunctions.* Guide students through the activities.

- **Activity A:** Read aloud the example. Ask: *What do the first two sentences begin with?* (**I** followed by a verb) *What does the rewritten sentence begin with?* ("**Following...**") Read the first two sentences again, replacing the underlined one with the rewritten one. Have students discuss how this changes the rhythm and makes it sound less repetitive. Then have students complete the activity and share their rewritten sentences.

- **Activity B (Convention):** Review the use of quotation marks and commas in dialogue. Then have students complete the activity.

Name: ______________________ **Week 4 • Day 1**

Sentence Fluency If you begin your sentences in different ways, your writing will sound more interesting.

A. Read each personal narrative. Circle the first word in each sentence. Draw a star next to the narrative that has more variety in the way the sentences begin.

Narrative 1

(I) looked for Aunt Linda as I stepped off the train. (I) wondered where she was. (I) saw her standing outside the station. (I) was so happy! (I) raced over to her, and we hugged.

(Aunt) Linda exclaimed, "You're growing like a weed!" (We) walked to the parking lot and climbed into her car. (We) talked about all sorts of things as we drove. (I) looked out the window at all the tall buildings.

(We) pulled up in front of my aunt's apartment building. (I) carefully climbed the stairs to her apartment. (I) didn't want to fall. (I) was so tired! (I) knew I needed a nap.

Narrative 2

★ (As) I stepped off the train, I looked for Aunt Linda. (Where) was she? (Finally,) I saw her standing outside the station. (It) was so good to see her! (We) raced toward each other and hugged.

"(You're) growing like a weed!" Aunt Linda exclaimed. (Then) we walked to the parking lot and climbed into her car. (We) talked about all sorts of things. (I) asked her about the tall buildings we were passing, and she told me their names.

(Soon) my aunt pulled the car up in front of her building. (Carefully,) I climbed the stairs to her apartment. (The) last thing I needed was to fall! (Boy,) was I tired. (A) nap was certainly in store for me.

B. Make a check next to the sentences that are punctuated correctly.

- ☑ Rita cried, "Oh no, the elevator is broken! We'll have to take the stairs!"
- ☐ "How many floors does this building have?", Jeffrey asked nervously.
- ☑ "There are ten floors!" exclaimed Rita.
- ☐ Jeffrey said "Well, I guess we'd better start climbing!"
- ☑ "How long do you think it will take us?" wondered Rita.

120 SENTENCE FLUENCY Daily 6-Trait Writing • EMC 6025 • © Evan-Moor Corp.

Name: ______________________ **Week 4 • Day 2**

Sentence Fluency Begin sentences in different ways. Use different types of words and phrases to add variety to your writing.

A. Read each pair of sentences. Rewrite the underlined sentence so it begins in a different way.

Example: I left the playground. I followed the muddy tracks that headed into the forest.

Following the muddy tracks, I headed into the forest.

1. I heard strange high-pitched noises coming from the bushes. I trembled in my boots!

   Sample Answers:

   Strange high-pitched noises were coming from the bushes.

2. I saw a tiny raccoon suddenly rocket past me. I felt silly for being scared.

   Boy, did I feel silly for being scared!

3. I returned to my house and immediately called my best friend. I told her what had happened.

   The first thing I did when I got home was call my best friend.

B. Read each sentence. Use proofreading marks to add punctuation to the dialogue.

1. "What's up?" Tiana asked.
2. Arthur replied, "I just saw a raccoon in the forest!"
3. "I see raccoons all the time," Tiana said.
4. "That high-pitched noise is weird!" Arthur exclaimed.
5. "It's just the raccoon complaining that you're too close," explained Tiana.

© Evan-Moor Corp. • EMC 6025 • Daily 6-Trait Writing SENTENCE FLUENCY 121

Name: ______________________ **Week 4 • Day 3**

Sentence Fluency Look for sentences that begin the same way. Revise them so they begin differently.

Read this personal narrative. Then:

- Correct the punctuation errors in the dialogue.
- Underline at least five sentences that could be revised to begin differently.
- Rewrite the narrative, changing the sentences you underlined.

We had all gathered at Auntie Giselle's house by 6 o'clock for Grandpa's surprise party. She had invited him to dinner at 6:15. We had parked around the corner so Grandpa wouldn't see our cars. Then Auntie Giselle got a phone call while we were waiting for Grandpa to arrive. He was calling to say he wasn't coming! He wanted to stay home and watch the ballgame. She convinced him that they could watch it together at her house. She saved the party!

Grandpa finally rang the doorbell at 6:30. We darted behind the furniture. Auntie Giselle threw open the door. We yelled, "Surprise!"

Grandpa gasped. "I was not expecting this," he said, in a daze.

Sample Answer:

By six o'clock, we had all gathered at Auntie Giselle's house for Grandpa's surprise party. She had invited him to dinner at 6:15. We had made sure to park around the corner so Grandpa wouldn't see our cars. While we waited for him to arrive, the phone rang. Grandpa was calling to say he wasn't coming! There was a ballgame on TV that he wanted to watch. Luckily, Auntie Giselle was able to convince him that they could watch it together at her house. The party was saved!

Finally, at 6:30, the doorbell rang. It was Grandpa! We all darted behind the furniture. As Auntie Giselle threw open the door, we yelled, "Surprise!"

Grandpa gasped. "I was not expecting this," he said, in a daze.

122 SENTENCE FLUENCY Daily 6-Trait Writing • EMC 6025 • © Evan-Moor Corp.

Name: ______________________ **Week 4 • Day 4**

Sentence Fluency Begin your sentences in different ways to keep your reader interested.

A. Think about a time when something surprising or unexpected happened to you. Then complete the chart to plan a personal narrative about that event. Sample Answers:

Event: I won a computer in the PTA raffle.	
What I saw:	the shiny black laptop up on the auditorium stage
What I heard:	my family cheering excitedly as our ticket number was announced
What I smelled:	the popcorn that the PTA was selling in the lobby
What I felt:	my cheeks burning from excitement
What I tasted:	the salty, buttery popcorn we ate to celebrate our win

B. Write a sentence that describes something that happened during the event. Then rewrite the sentence, using a different beginning.

Sample Answers:

1. As soon as I heard the announcer call our ticket number, my feet were up and off the ground.
2. My feet were up off the ground as soon as I heard those numbers come from the announcer's mouth.

C. Write something you said or heard someone else say. Use correct punctuation.

Sample Answer: My mom screamed, "Woo hoo!"

© Evan-Moor Corp. • EMC 6025 • Daily 6-Trait Writing SENTENCE FLUENCY 123

DAY 3

Read the rule aloud. Then guide students through the activity.

- **Convention:** Have students read the narrative and correct the punctuation on their own. Then review the answers together.
- Read aloud the narrative, emphasizing the boring, repetitive rhythm of the phrasing. Point out that most of the sentences begin with a pronoun or a name followed by a verb. Call students' attention to the first sentence and say: *We can rearrange this sentence so it begins differently. We can move the phrase "by 6 o'clock" to the beginning.* Write the new sentence on the board.
- Have students complete the activity. Then have them read their rewritten narratives aloud.

DAY 4

Read the rule aloud. Then guide students through the activities.

- **Activity A:** Help students brainstorm events to write about. For example, ask: *Have you ever won anything? Has someone ever paid you a surprise visit? Have you ever been caught in a sudden storm?* Model completing the chart, using the sample answers on the reduced page to the left. Remind students of the importance of sensory details in their writing. Then have students complete the chart.
- **Activity B:** Use the sample answers to model writing and then rewriting a sentence. Then have students write their own sentences.
- **Activity C (Convention):** If necessary, use the sample sentence to the left to model writing dialogue correctly.

DAY 5 *Writing Prompt*

- *Use your completed chart from Day 4 to write a personal narrative of a time when something unexpected happened to you. Be sure to begin your sentences in different ways.*
- *Include dialogue in your narrative. Be sure to punctuate the dialogue correctly.*

Name: ______________________________

Sentence Fluency If you begin your sentences in different ways, your writing will sound more interesting.

A. Read each personal narrative. Circle the first word in each sentence. Draw a star next to the narrative that has more variety in the way the sentences begin.

Narrative 1

I looked for Aunt Linda as I stepped off the train. I wondered where she was. I saw her standing outside the station. I was so happy! I raced over to her, and we hugged.

Aunt Linda exclaimed, "You're growing like a weed!" We walked to the parking lot and climbed into her car. We talked about all sorts of things as we drove. I looked out the window at all the tall buildings.

We pulled up in front of my aunt's apartment building. I carefully climbed the stairs to her apartment. I didn't want to fall. I was so tired! I knew I needed a nap.

Narrative 2

As I stepped off the train, I looked for Aunt Linda. Where was she? Finally, I saw her standing outside the station. It was so good to see her! We raced toward each other and hugged.

"You're growing like a weed!" Aunt Linda exclaimed. Then we walked to the parking lot and climbed into her car. We talked about all sorts of things. I asked her about the tall buildings we were passing, and she told me their names.

Soon, my aunt pulled the car up in front of her building. Carefully, I climbed the stairs to her apartment. The last thing I needed was to fall! Boy, was I tired. A nap was certainly in store for me.

B. Make a check next to the sentences that are punctuated correctly.

- ☐ Rita cried, "Oh no, the elevator is broken! We'll have to take the stairs!"
- ☐ "How many floors does this building have?", Jeffrey asked nervously.
- ☐ "There are ten floors!" exclaimed Rita.
- ☐ Jeffrey said "Well, I guess we'd better start climbing!"
- ☐ "How long do you think it will take us?" wondered Rita.

Name: ______________________________

Sentence Fluency

Begin sentences in different ways. Use different types of words and phrases to add variety to your writing.

A. Read each pair of sentences. Rewrite the underlined sentence so it begins in a different way.

Example: I left the playground. I followed the muddy tracks that headed into the forest.

Following the muddy tracks, I headed into the forest.

1. I heard strange high-pitched noises coming from the bushes. I trembled in my boots!

   ____

2. I saw a tiny raccoon suddenly rocket past me. I felt silly for being scared.

   ____

3. I returned to my house and immediately called my best friend. I told her what had happened.

   ____

B. Read each sentence. Use proofreading marks to add punctuation to the dialogue.

1. What's up? Tiana asked.
2. Arthur replied I just saw a raccoon in the forest!
3. I see raccoons all the time Tiana said.
4. That high-pitched noise is weird! Arthur exclaimed.
5. It's just the raccoon complaining that you're too close explained Tiana.

Name: ____________________

Sentence Fluency

Look for sentences that begin the same way. Revise them so they begin differently.

Read this personal narrative. Then:

- Correct the punctuation errors in the dialogue.
- Underline at least five sentences that could be revised to begin differently.
- Rewrite the narrative, changing the sentences you underlined.

We had all gathered at Auntie Giselle's house by 6 o'clock for Grandpa's surprise party. She had invited him to dinner at 6:15. We had parked around the corner so Grandpa wouldn't see our cars. Then Auntie Giselle got a phone call while we were waiting for Grandpa to arrive. He was calling to say he wasn't coming! He wanted to stay home and watch the ballgame. She convinced him that they could watch it together at her house. She saved the party!

Grandpa finally rang the doorbell at 6:30. We darted behind the furniture. Auntie Giselle threw open the door. We yelled "Surprise!"

Grandpa gasped. "I was not expecting this he said, in a daze.

____

____

____

____

____

____

____

____

____

____

Name: ______________________________

Sentence Fluency

Begin your sentences in different ways to keep your reader interested.

A. Think about a time when something surprising or unexpected happened to you. Then complete the chart to plan a personal narrative about that event.

Event:	
What I saw:	
What I heard:	
What I smelled:	
What I felt:	
What I tasted:	

B. Write a sentence that describes something that happened during the event. Then rewrite the sentence, using a different beginning.

1. ______________________________

____

2. ______________________________

____

C. Write something you said or heard someone else say. Use correct punctuation.

____

SENTENCE FLUENCY
Writing a Smooth Paragraph

DAY 1

Say: *We've learned many ways to make our sentences flow smoothly. This week, we'll put these skills together to write smooth paragraphs.* Read the rule aloud. Guide students through the activities.

- **Activity A:** Review the definitions of compound and complex sentences. Then read aloud the first three sentences of Larry's autobiography. Ask: *What kind of sentence is the second sentence?* (compound) *How about the third?* (complex)

  Have students read each autobiography and complete the underlining independently. Then review the answers as a class. Ask: *Which autobiography sounds better?* (Larry's) *Why? It has a better mix of compound, complex, and simple sentences.*

- **Activity B:** Say: *Renee's autobiography has many short, choppy sentences that could be combined to improve the flow of her writing.* If necessary, model the activity, using the sample answers on the reduced page to the right. Then have students complete the activity independently.

Name: ______________________ **Week 5 • Day 1**

Sentence Fluency To write a smooth paragraph, vary the types of sentences you use. Include simple, compound, and complex sentences.

A. Read each student's autobiography. Then:
- Use a straight line to underline each compound sentence.
- Use a wavy line to underline each complex sentence.

Larry Alvarez

On December 1, 1997, I was born in Las Vegas. I already had a brother, but my sister wasn't born yet. She didn't arrive until I was two years old. When I was three, we adopted a puppy. We named him Racer, and he sure lived up to his name! We also moved from an apartment to a house that year. This was important because Racer really needed a yard to run in. When I was eight, I joined City League Sports and Recreation. Unfortunately, I could only pick one team to be on. I could play soccer, or I could swim. I chose soccer, and the rest is history!

Renee Narcizo

I was born on January 27, 1998. I was born in Chicago. I don't remember much about it. In 2002, we moved to Alabama. We moved to Florida two years later. My dad is in the military, so we have moved a lot. I don't mind. I have made some great friends. We have visited friends and family in a lot of places! I have a baby brother. I have a baby sister. Their names are Damon and Valeria. They are twins. They were born when I was seven. They are fun to watch.

B. Choose two pairs of short sentences in Renee's autobiography. Combine them to write compound or complex sentences. **Sample Answers:**

1. I was born in Chicago, but I don't remember much about it.
2. I don't mind because I have made some great friends.

126 SENTENCE FLUENCY Daily 6-Trait Writing • EMC 6025 • © Evan-Moor Corp.

DAY 2

Read the rule aloud. Say: *Transition words and phrases help your writing flow smoothly by connecting your sentences.* Then guide students through the activities.

- **Activity A:** Read the paragraph aloud, without the transition words. Say: *This paragraph makes sense, but it would sound better and be easier to follow if the ideas were connected with transitions.* Read the words and phrases in the box. Then have students complete the activity.

- **Activity B (Convention):** Remind students that a complete sentence must have a subject and a predicate. Otherwise, it is a sentence fragment. Then read the paragraph aloud. Point out the fragment "When we ride our bikes" and explain: *This is not a sentence. It is a dependent clause that begins with a subordinating conjunction. It cannot stand on its own as a sentence. It needs to be combined with an independent clause to form a complex sentence.* Have students complete the activity and share their revisions.

Name: ______________________ **Week 5 • Day 2**

Sentence Fluency Use transition words and phrases to improve the flow of your sentences.

A. Read the paragraph. Use the words and phrases in the box to fill in the blanks.

Transition Words and Phrases		
as a result	in fact	furthermore
for example	of course	

Accidents happen all the time, so all kids should have a basic knowledge of first aid. For example, do you know what to do if your friend falls and cuts his arm? Of course, you should seek an adult's help. But what if there are no adults around and your friend needs immediate attention? You may not have time to wait for help. Furthermore, you wouldn't want to just stand there doing nothing while your friend is in pain. So ask your parents to sign you up for a first-aid class. There is a free one, in fact, being offered at the community center next week. You'll learn some simple things that even kids can do if someone is bleeding, choking, or injured. As a result, you will know what to do in an emergency.

B. Underline the sentence fragments in this short paragraph. Then rewrite the paragraph, using complete sentences.

We've lived next door to Mr. Green for a long time. Like forever. He's very nice. When we ride our bikes. Lets us cut through his yard. To thank him, we take him cookies. Chocolate chip! His favorite.

Sample Answer: We've lived next door to Mr. Green for so long, it feels like forever. He's very nice. When we ride our bikes, he lets us cut through his yard. To thank him, we take him chocolate chip cookies. They're his favorite!

© Evan-Moor Corp. • EMC 6025 • Daily 6-Trait Writing SENTENCE FLUENCY 127

Name: ______________________ **Week 5 • Day 3**

Sentence Fluency Include different kinds of sentences for a smooth-sounding paragraph.

Read this persuasive letter. Look for sentences that can be revised or improved. Then rewrite the body of the letter by:

- Correcting any sentence fragments.
- Combining simple sentences into compound or complex sentences.
- Beginning sentences in different ways.
- Using parallel structure.
- Adding transition words and phrases.

Dear Mayor,

Tia Shin deserves an award. The Best Neighbor Award. She is kind, friendly, and she cares. She treats us like family. Although she is just a neighbor. Once we were sick. She took care of us. My mom had to go to work. Nobody else could take us to the doctor. Tia did.

She watches out for all the kids on our street. She will flag a driver down. If she sees a car speeding down our street. She will tell the driver to slow down. Children play around here. Best neighbor in the city.

Sincerely,
Zane Childers

Sample Answer:

My neighbor, Tia Shin, deserves the Best Neighbor Award. She is kind, friendly, and caring. Although she is just a neighbor, she treats us like family. Once when we were sick, she took care of us. My mom had to go to work, and nobody else could take us to the doctor. Tia did.

In fact, Tia watches out for all the kids on our street. If she sees a car speeding down our street, she will flag the driver down. She will tell the driver to slow down because children play around here! Tia is definitely the best neighbor in our great city.

128 SENTENCE FLUENCY Daily 6-Trait Writing • EMC 6025 • © Evan-Moor Corp.

Name: ______________________ **Week 5 • Day 4**

Sentence Fluency Include different kinds of sentences for a smooth-sounding paragraph.

Think of an adult you know. Is there an award you think he or she should win, such as Best Coach or Greatest Custodian? What would you tell someone about the person you chose? Use the questionnaire below to plan a letter recommending this person for the award.

Sample Answers:

1. Whom will you write about?
   Custodian Craig Cano
2. What kind of award should this person win?
   Best Custodian in the School District
3. What does your favorite person do that is so great? Write your answer as a **compound sentence.**
   He fixes doors and windows, and he makes sure that the classrooms are always clean.
4. Give a specific example of a time when your favorite person helped others. Write your answer as a **complex sentence.**
   Although it's not his job, he fixed our computer when we needed it for a class project.
5. Write a sentence that tells three things about what your favorite person looks like. Use **parallel structure** in your sentence.
   He wears a brown jacket, a baseball hat, and a blue name badge every day.
6. What else would you want to say about this person?
   He knows every student by name.

© Evan-Moor Corp. • EMC 6025 • Daily 6-Trait Writing SENTENCE FLUENCY 129

DAY 3

Read the rule aloud. Then guide students through the activity.

- Invite a volunteer to read the letter aloud. Then ask: *What's wrong with this letter?* (sounds choppy, doesn't flow, has sentence fragments) Ask: *How can we fix the problems?* Review the list of ways to improve sentences.
- Choose one or two sentences to model correcting. For example, say: *"Although she is just a neighbor" isn't a complete sentence. But "Although" is a subordinating conjunction, so it's a dependent clause. What sentence could I combine it with to make a complex sentence?* ("She treats us like family.") Write the new sentence on the board. ("Although she is just a neighbor, she treats us like family.") Point out the comma between the dependent and independent clauses. Then have students complete the activity.
- **Convention:** Have students trade papers with a partner to check for sentence fragments and correct any that are found. Then have students read their partner's letters to the class.

DAY 4

Review the rule. Guide students through the activity.

- Help students brainstorm adults they could write about. For example, ask: *Who always helps you? Who has done something special for you? Whom do you admire?* (e.g., teacher, coach, neighbor, dance instructor, choir director)
- If necessary, use the sample answers on the reduced page to model completing the items. Then travel the room and assist students as they complete the activity.

DAY 5 *Writing Prompt*

- *Write a persuasive letter, recommending an adult you know for an award. Use the sentences you wrote on Day 4 to make your letter flow smoothly.*
- *Exchange papers with a partner to check for sentence fragments. Correct any that are found.*

Name: ______________________________ **Week 5 • Day 1**

Sentence Fluency

To write a smooth paragraph, vary the types of sentences you use. Include simple, compound, and complex sentences.

A. Read each student's autobiography. Then:

- Use a straight line to underline each compound sentence.
- Use a wavy line to underline each complex sentence.

Larry Alvarez

On December 1, 1997, I was born in Las Vegas. I already had a brother, but my sister wasn't born yet. She didn't arrive until I was two years old. When I was three, we adopted a puppy. We named him Racer, and he sure lived up to his name! We also moved from an apartment to a house that year. This was important because Racer really needed a yard to run in. When I was eight, I joined City League Sports and Recreation. Unfortunately, I could only pick one team to be on. I could play soccer, or I could swim. I chose soccer, and the rest is history!

Renee Narcizo

I was born on January 27, 1998. I was born in Chicago. I don't remember much about it. In 2002, we moved to Alabama. We moved to Florida two years later. My dad is in the military, so we have moved a lot. I don't mind. I have made some great friends. We have visited friends and family in a lot of places! I have a baby brother. I have a baby sister. Their names are Damon and Valeria. They are twins. They were born when I was seven. They are fun to watch.

B. Choose two pairs of short sentences in Renee's autobiography. Combine them to write compound or complex sentences.

1. ______________________________

2. ______________________________

Name: ______________________________

Sentence Fluency

Use transition words and phrases to improve the flow of your sentences.

A. Read the paragraph. Use the words and phrases in the box to fill in the blanks.

Transition Words and Phrases		
as a result	in fact	furthermore
for example	of course	

Accidents happen all the time, so all kids should have a basic knowledge of first aid. ______________, do you know what to do if your friend falls and cuts his arm? ______________, you should seek an adult's help. But what if there are no adults around and your friend needs immediate attention? You may not have time to wait for help. ______________, you wouldn't want to just stand there doing nothing while your friend is in pain. So ask your parents to sign you up for a first-aid class. There is a free one, ______________, being offered at the community center next week. You'll learn some simple things that even kids can do if someone is bleeding, choking, or injured. ______________, you will know what to do in an emergency.

B. Underline the sentence fragments in this short paragraph. Then rewrite the paragraph, using complete sentences.

We've lived next door to Mr. Green for a long time. Like forever. He's very nice. When we ride our bikes. Lets us cut through his yard. To thank him, we take him cookies. Chocolate chip! His favorite.

____

____

____

____

Name: ____________________

Sentence Fluency

Include different kinds of sentences for a smooth-sounding paragraph.

Read this persuasive letter. Look for sentences that can be revised or improved. Then rewrite the body of the letter by:

- Correcting any sentence fragments.
- Combining simple sentences into compound or complex sentences.
- Beginning sentences in different ways.
- Using parallel structure.
- Adding transition words and phrases.

Dear Mayor,

Tia Shin deserves an award. The Best Neighbor Award. She is kind, friendly, and she cares. She treats us like family. Although she is just a neighbor. Once we were sick. She took care of us. My mom had to go to work. Nobody else could take us to the doctor. Tia did.

She watches out for all the kids on our street. She will flag a driver down. If she sees a car speeding down our street. She will tell the driver to slow down. Children play around here. Best neighbor in the city.

Sincerely,
Zane Childers

Name: ______________________________

Sentence Fluency

Include different kinds of sentences for a smooth-sounding paragraph.

Think of an adult you know. Is there an award you think he or she should win, such as Best Coach or Greatest Custodian? What would you tell someone about the person you chose? Use the questionnaire below to plan a letter recommending this person for the award.

1. Whom will you write about?

   ____

2. What kind of award should this person win?

   ____

3. What does your favorite person do that is so great? Write your answer as a **compound sentence**.

   ____

   ____

4. Give a specific example of a time when your favorite person helped others. Write your answer as a **complex sentence**.

   ____

   ____

5. Write a sentence that tells three things about what your favorite person looks like. Use **parallel structure** in your sentence.

   ____

6. What else would you want to say about this person?

   ____

   ____

WEEK 1

VOICE

Examining Different Writing Voices

Refer to pages 6 and 7 to introduce or review the writing trait.

DAY 1

Say: ***Voice** is the way a writer's personality, or style, comes through in writing. It's shaped by the writer's purpose for writing, as well as the audience.* Then read the rule aloud. Say: *One type of voice is the kind you use to sound mysterious.* Write these sentences on the board: *1) The ball couldn't be found. 2) No one knew how the ball had disappeared.* Ask: *Which is more mysterious?* (Sentence 2) *Why?* (the words **No one knew** and **disappeared**) Then guide students through the activities.

- **Activity A:** Have students fill in the paragraph on their own. Then have a student read aloud the completed paragraph. Ask: *Which words and ideas give this writing a mysterious sound?* (e.g., **startled, screamed, thoroughly mystified, theories**)
- **Activity B (Convention):** Say: *A series is a list of three or more items in a sentence. Use a comma after each item in a series.* Write the following sentence on the board: *The teacher gave us pencils rulers paper and a test booklet.* Ask: *Where should commas be placed in this sentence?* (after **pencils, rulers,** and **paper**) Have students complete the activity.
- **Activity C:** Encourage students to use words that express feeling and create a sense of mystery. Have volunteers share their sentences.

Name: ______________________ **Week 1 • Day 1**

Voice Your voice can come through your writing in a variety of ways. For example, you can write with a mysterious voice.

A. Read Ms. West's narrative about a strange event that happened in her classroom. Fill in the words and phrases that help make it mysterious.

startled	flew through the window	no one
theories	thoroughly mystified	we still don't know
screamed	phantom offender	erupted into confusion

A Real "Whodunit"

This morning, as I was about to give my students a math test, something odd happened. Just as I was giving directions, a soccer ball __flew through the window__ and bounced off my desk! Naturally, this __startled__ everyone. A few students __screamed__. The class __erupted into confusion__. A student ran to the window, but there was __no one__ in sight. We were all __thoroughly mystified__. The students came up with various __theories__ about who might have been the __phantom offender__. Some thought it was a student in another class. Other kids wondered if it was the gym teacher, the custodian, or someone from the house across the street. The true scary part is that __we still don't know__ who did it—or why!

B. Commas are used to separate words in a series. Underline the sentence in Ms. West's story that contains a series. Circle the commas.

C. Imagine you are a student in Ms. West's class. How would you have told the story? Rewrite the beginning, using your own mysterious voice.

Sample Answer: There I was, dreading the math test I was about to take, when all of a sudden the strangest thing happened. Out of nowhere, a soccer ball came flying into the room!

132 VOICE Daily 6-Trait Writing • EMC 6025 • © Evan-Moor Corp.

DAY 2

Read the rule aloud. Say: *Writers sometimes play with language to have fun with their readers.* Guide students through the activities.

- **Activity A (Convention):** Have students read the paragraph and insert the commas independently. Review the answers as a class.
- **Activity B:** Say: *Sam did several things to make his writing fun. For example, he used **alliteration**. That is the use of words placed close together that have the same beginning sounds.* Read the title of the story aloud and ask: *What beginning sound is repeated?* (/f/) Then say: *Sam also used fun words and informal language.* Help students find examples of both in the first two sentences. (informal language: **You won't believe**; fun words: **zoomed**) Then have students complete the activity.

Name: ______________________ **Week 1 • Day 2**

Voice Some writers use a playful voice that makes their writing fun to read.

A. Read Sam's funny narrative. Underline the sentences that contain a series. Add commas where they are needed.

Fascinating Fifth-Grade Flying Soccer Ball Mystery

You won't believe what happened in math class today! We were getting ready to take a test when a soccer ball zoomed through the window! It just missed bopping Ms. West on the head and bounced off her desk instead. Then it whacked the wall, the whiteboard, and the wastebasket. I jumped to my feet and hotfooted it to the window. I looked left, right, up, and down, but there was no one to be seen. I did hear one teeny-tiny thing, however. The back door to Mr. Ventura's classroom clicked shut. Was he playing a joke on us? You're probably wondering why in the world I'd suspect a teacher! Well, guess who once turned all the maps upside down when we were studying the fifty states. Guess who once filled the closet with crumpled newspaper. I concluded that the phantom soccer player was the marvelous, mischievous Mr. Ventura!

B. How did Sam make his writing fun to read? Write two examples of each way listed below.

1. Alliteration: Fascinating Fifth-Grade Flying; whacked, wall, whiteboard, wastebasket; wondering why in the world; marvelous, mischievous Mr.
2. Amusing Words and Phrases: E.g., zoomed, bopping, whacked, hotfooted it to the window, teeny-tiny, phantom soccer player
3. Informal Language: You won't believe; You're probably wondering; Well,

© Evan-Moor Corp. • EMC 6025 • Daily 6-Trait Writing VOICE 133

Name: ______________________ **Week 1 • Day 3**

Voice Sometimes it's important to write with a formal, serious-sounding voice.

A. Read this letter of apology. The writer used formal language to match her purpose, and she used facts to explain what happened. Underline the facts and circle examples of formal language.

> Dear Ms. West and Class,
>
> My sincere apologies to you for disturbing your class yesterday. I am a college student who hopes to be a professional soccer player one day. So, I was using the grassy area in front of your school to practice my dribbling. However, I got carried away imagining that I was a soccer star and tried a banana kick. Unfortunately, the ball curved in a different direction than I planned. When I realized that it was flying through your window, I panicked and ran. I am terribly embarrassed by my carelessness, rudeness, and improper behavior. Please accept my apology.
>
> Yours sincerely,
> Becky Beckham

B. Pretend you are Ms. West. Write three sentences to Becky, accepting her apology and offering the ball back. Use a formal style.

Sample Answer: Our class appreciates and accepts your apology. These things happen sometimes. Please do not be too distressed, because we enjoyed the mystery! You are welcome to come to our classroom anytime to pick up your soccer ball.

C. Insert commas where they belong in these sentences.

1. To be a good soccer player, you must know how to dribble, pass, and kick.
2. The goalie, fullback, halfback, and forward are four different positions in soccer.

134 VOICE Daily 6-Trait Writing • EMC 6025 • © Evan-Moor Corp.

Name: ______________________ **Week 1 • Day 4**

Voice When you plan your writing, think about the voice you will use. For instance, it can be mysterious, playful, or serious.

A. Plan a story about something that mysteriously disappears from your school. Fill in the events in this flowchart. Then choose which voice you want to use for your story.

Sample Answers:

Event 1: One day, the kids from Room 9 come back from recess to find scraps of paper scattered all over the classroom.

Event 2: The next day, there's a page missing from the teacher's grade book, and the paper towels are on the floor beneath the dispenser.

Event 3: The kids take turns staking out the classroom during recess. They discover a mouse chewing off pieces of paper to build a nest. They find the nest in the supply closet.

Event 4: The next day, the kids ask the custodian to remove the nest and place it under a bush just outside the classroom window.

Writing Voice: ☒ mysterious ☐ playful ☐ serious

B. Write a sentence with a series that you could use in your story. Use commas correctly.

Sample Answer: Pages were missing from textbooks, novels, and the teacher's grade book.

© Evan-Moor Corp. • EMC 6025 • Daily 6-Trait Writing VOICE 135

DAY 3

Read the rule aloud. Ask: *When is it important to use a more serious voice?* (e.g., research report, business letter) *Using formal language and including important, concrete facts in your writing will give it a serious-sounding voice.* Guide students through the activities.

- **Activity A:** Read the letter aloud. Then point out the phrase "My sincere apologies" and ask: *If the writer had just said, "I'm sorry," would she have sounded as serious?* (no) Have students find the fact stated in the second sentence. ("I am a college student") Say: *Being clear and direct like this also helps her sound serious. Why is this appropriate for her audience and purpose?* (When you apologize, you should sound serious.) Have students complete the activity.
- **Activity B:** Ask: *Why would it be appropriate for Ms. West to also write in a serious voice?* (to show Becky that she took her apology seriously) Have students write their sentences and then read aloud what they wrote.
- **Activity C (Convention):** Have students complete the activity and trade papers with a partner to check each other's work.

DAY 4

Read the rule aloud. Review the types of voices covered this week. Then guide students through the activities.

- **Activity A:** To help students brainstorm plots, ask: *What would you notice missing from a classroom or other place in school? Who or what might take it? Why?* Have students write a description of each event that happens in their story. Then have them choose the best voice for their story.
- **Activity B (Convention):** Circulate to help students think of sentences they might write, and also check for proper use of commas.

DAY 5 *Writing Prompt*

- *Write a story about something that mysteriously disappears from school. Use your ideas from Day 4, and write in a mysterious, serious, or playful voice.*
- *Be sure to use commas in a series correctly.*

Name: ______________________________

Voice Your voice can come through your writing in a variety of ways. For example, you can write with a mysterious voice.

A. Read Ms. West's narrative about a strange event that happened in her classroom. Fill in the words and phrases that help make it mysterious.

startled	flew through the window	no one
theories	thoroughly mystified	we still don't know
screamed	phantom offender	erupted into confusion

A Real "Whodunit"

This morning, as I was about to give my students a math test, something odd happened. Just as I was giving directions, a soccer ball ______________ and bounced off my desk! Naturally, this ______________ everyone. A few students ______________. The class ______________. A student ran to the window, but there was ______________ in sight. We were all ______________. The students came up with various ______________ about who might have been the ______________. Some thought it was a student in another class. Other kids wondered if it was the gym teacher, the custodian, or someone from the house across the street. The true scary part is that ______________ who did it—or why!

B. Commas are used to separate words in a series. Underline the sentence in Ms. West's story that contains a series. Circle the commas.

C. Imagine you are a student in Ms. West's class. How would you have told the story? Rewrite the beginning, using your own mysterious voice.

____

____

Name: ______________________________

Voice

Some writers use a playful voice that makes their writing fun to read.

A. Read Sam's funny narrative. Underline the sentences that contain a series. Add commas where they are needed.

Fascinating Fifth-Grade Flying Soccer Ball Mystery

You won't believe what happened in math class today! We were getting ready to take a test when a soccer ball zoomed through the window! It just missed bopping Ms. West on the head and bounced off her desk instead. Then it whacked the wall the whiteboard and the wastebasket. I jumped to my feet and hotfooted it to the window. I looked left right up and down, but there was no one to be seen. I did hear one teeny-tiny thing, however. The back door to Mr. Ventura's classroom clicked shut. Was he playing a joke on us? You're probably wondering why in the world I'd suspect a teacher! Well, guess who once turned all the maps upside down when we were studying the fifty states. Guess who once filled the closet with crumpled newspaper. I concluded that the phantom soccer player was the marvelous, mischievous Mr. Ventura!

B. How did Sam make his writing fun to read? Write two examples of each way listed below.

1. Alliteration: ______________________________

____

2. Amusing Words and Phrases: ______________________________

____

3. Informal Language: ______________________________

____

Name: ______________________________

Voice Sometimes it's important to write with a formal, serious-sounding voice.

A. Read this letter of apology. The writer used formal language to match her purpose, and she used facts to explain what happened. Underline the facts and circle examples of formal language.

Dear Ms. West and Class,

My sincere apologies to you for disturbing your class yesterday. I am a college student who hopes to be a professional soccer player one day. So, I was using the grassy area in front of your school to practice my dribbling. However, I got carried away imagining that I was a soccer star and tried a banana kick. Unfortunately, the ball curved in a different direction than I planned. When I realized that it was flying through your window, I panicked and ran. I am terribly embarrassed by my carelessness, rudeness, and improper behavior. Please accept my apology.

Yours sincerely,
Becky Beckham

B. Pretend you are Ms. West. Write three sentences to Becky, accepting her apology and offering the ball back. Use a formal style.

____

____

____

____

C. Insert commas where they belong in these sentences.

1. To be a good soccer player, you must know how to dribble pass and kick.
2. The goalie fullback halfback and forward are four different positions in soccer.

Voice

When you plan your writing, think about the voice you will use. For instance, it can be mysterious, playful, or serious.

A. Plan a story about something that mysteriously disappears from your school. Fill in the events in this flowchart. Then choose which voice you want to use for your story.

Event 1

↓

Event 2

↓

Event 3

↓

Event 4

Writing Voice: ☐ mysterious ☐ playful ☐ serious

B. Write a sentence with a series that you could use in your story. Use commas correctly.

____

____

VOICE
Using Different Voices for Different Purposes

DAY 1

Read the rule aloud. Review what it means to persuade. (to convince someone to do something) Say: *When you write to persuade, your voice should be persuasive.* Guide students through the activities.

- **Activity A:** Read the letter aloud. Then say: *Not only did Dani give good reasons why Ellie should come, but she wrote with an exciting, enthusiastic voice. She used strong words that appeal to Ellie's emotions.* Have students find an example of a strong adjective in the third sentence. (**amazing**) Then have students complete the activity independently. Afterward, discuss the activities and emotional words students identified and why these things might convince Ellie.
- **Activity B:** Read the final sentence again. Ask: *What words make Dani's voice sound not as strong or convincing as the rest of the letter?* (e.g., **sometime, probably, kind of soon**) Have students rewrite the sentence and share what they wrote.
- **Activity C (Convention):** Remind students that a possessive noun tells to whom or what something belongs, and that a singular possessive noun ends with an apostrophe and **s**. Write the phrase "the girl's cousin" on the board and say: ***Girl's** is another way of saying "of the girl"—as in "the cousin of the girl."* Then have students complete the activity.

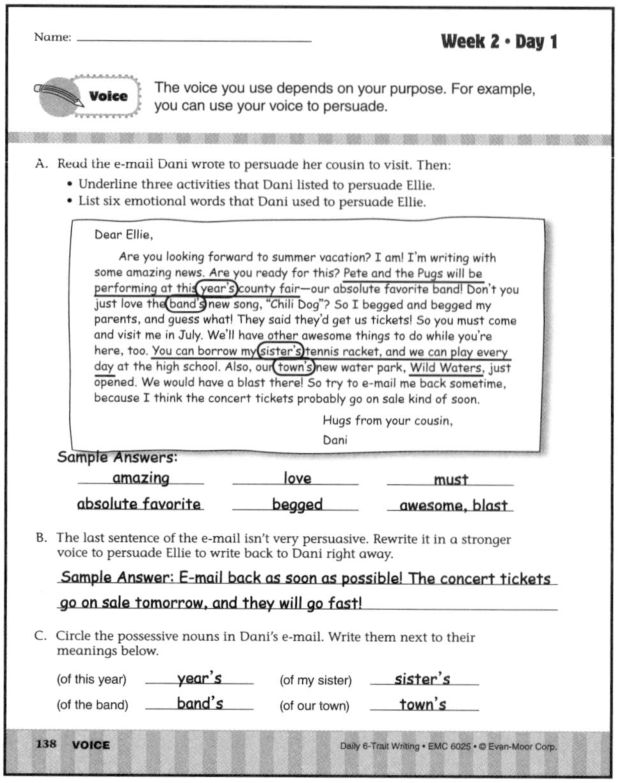

Name: ______________________ **Week 2 • Day 1**

Voice The voice you use depends on your purpose. For example, you can use your voice to persuade.

A. Read the e-mail Dani wrote to persuade her cousin to visit. Then:
- Underline three activities that Dani listed to persuade Ellie.
- List six emotional words that Dani used to persuade Ellie.

Dear Ellie,

Are you looking forward to summer vacation? I am! I'm writing with some amazing news. Are you ready for this? Pete and the Pugs will be performing at this year's county fair—our absolute favorite band! Don't you just love the band's new song, "Chili Dog"? So I begged and begged my parents, and guess what! They said they'd get us tickets! So you must come and visit me in July. We'll have other awesome things to do while you're here, too. You can borrow my sister's tennis racket, and we can play every day at the high school. Also, our town's new water park, Wild Waters, just opened. We would have a blast there! So try to e-mail me back sometime, because I think the concert tickets probably go on sale kind of soon.

Hugs from your cousin,
Dani

Sample Answers:

amazing	love	must
absolute favorite	begged	awesome, blast

B. The last sentence of the e-mail isn't very persuasive. Rewrite it in a stronger voice to persuade Ellie to write back to Dani right away.

Sample Answer: E-mail back as soon as possible! The concert tickets go on sale tomorrow, and they will go fast!

C. Circle the possessive nouns in Dani's e-mail. Write them next to their meanings below.

(of this year) year's (of my sister) sister's
(of the band) band's (of our town) town's

138 VOICE Daily 6-Trait Writing • EMC 6025 • © Evan-Moor Corp.

DAY 2

Read the rule aloud. Say: *When you write to entertain, your voice should be funny and exciting.* Then guide students through the activities.

- **Activity A:** Read Ethan's paragraph aloud. Point out the word **flavorful** in the first sentence. Say: *There's nothing wrong with this word; it's just not very exciting. Which word in the box could we replace it with?* (**mouthwatering**) Repeat the process for the rest of the boldface words and phrases. Have a volunteer read the revised paragraph aloud.
- **Activity B (Convention):** Point out the word **customers'** in the second sentence of Ethan's paragraph. Say: *When you write the possessive form of a plural noun, the apostrophe comes after the* **s**. Have students complete the activity.

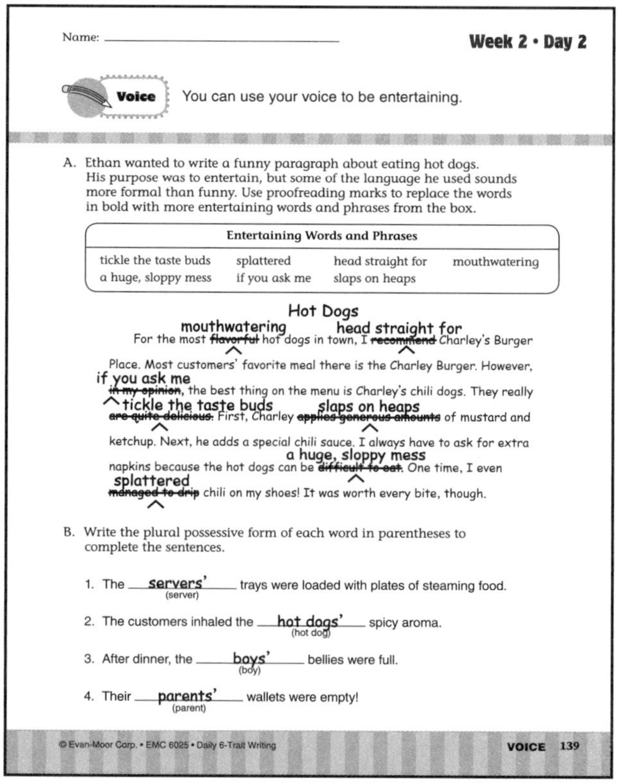

Name: ______________________ **Week 2 • Day 2**

Voice You can use your voice to be entertaining.

A. Ethan wanted to write a funny paragraph about eating hot dogs. His purpose was to entertain, but some of the language he used sounds more formal than funny. Use proofreading marks to replace the words in bold with more entertaining words and phrases from the box.

Entertaining Words and Phrases			
tickle the taste buds	splattered	head straight for	mouthwatering
a huge, sloppy mess	if you ask me	slaps on heaps	

Hot Dogs

For the most ~~flavorful~~ mouthwatering hot dogs in town, I ~~recommend~~ head straight for Charley's Burger Place. Most customers' favorite meal there is the Charley Burger. However, ~~in my opinion~~ if you ask me, the best thing on the menu is Charley's chili dogs. They really ~~are quite delicious~~ tickle the taste buds. First, Charley ~~applies generous amounts~~ slaps on heaps of mustard and ketchup. Next, he adds a special chili sauce. I always have to ask for extra napkins because the hot dogs can be ~~difficult to eat~~ a huge, sloppy mess. One time, I even ~~managed to drip~~ splattered chili on my shoes! It was worth every bite, though.

B. Write the plural possessive form of each word in parentheses to complete the sentences.

1. The servers' (server) trays were loaded with plates of steaming food.
2. The customers inhaled the hot dogs' (hot dog) spicy aroma.
3. After dinner, the boys' (boy) bellies were full.
4. Their parents' (parent) wallets were empty!

© Evan-Moor Corp. • EMC 6025 • Daily 6-Trait Writing VOICE 139

Name: ____________________ **Week 2 • Day 3**

Voice Be sure your voice matches your purpose.

A. Kim's assignment was to write an exciting description. However, she didn't use a very exciting voice. Read what Kim wrote. Rewrite the paragraph in a more exciting voice. Use the words in the box to help you.

Exciting Words						
amazing	colossal	dare	dark	deep	hottest	longest
plunge	roaring	soar	splash	thrilling	wild	zoom

A Day at the Water Park

A trip to Wild Waters on a hot day is a lot of fun. You will like the park's Turbo Slide. The slide has twists and turns through a tunnel. At the tunnel's end is a pool that you land in. You can do some bodysurfing in another pool called the Boogie Blast. It has waves for surfing. You can also ride in an inner tube on the Master Blaster. The ride's track is like a roller coaster of water that moves you up and down. You climb as high as a two-story building. Then you drop into the water.

Sample Answer:

One of the best places on a hot day is Wild Waters. The first ride to head for is the Turbo Slide. It's a huge water slide that twists and turns through a tunnel. You zoom down and fly through the air before hitting the water. The next ride is the Boogie Blast, where you can bodysurf in a pool that has real waves. Another favorite is the amazing Master Blaster. It's like a roller coaster of water. As you climb to the height of a two-story building, hold on, take a big gulp of air, and scream as you plunge headfirst into the deep water!

B. Use proofreading marks to fix the possessive noun in each sentence.

1. My two best friends' favorite ride at Wild Waters is the Turbo Slide.
2. Jeremy and Ahmed love swooshing through the slide's tunnel.
3. During the summer, the park's hours are from 10:00 a.m. to 8:00 p.m.

140 VOICE Daily 6-Trait Writing • EMC 6025 • © Evan-Moor Corp.

Name: ____________________ **Week 2 • Day 4**

Voice Be sure your voice matches your purpose.

Where would you like to go on a class trip? Complete the chart to plan a paragraph persuading your teacher to take you there. List three things that would be exciting to see or do there. Then write descriptive words and strong verbs about each of those things. Sample Answers:

Name of Place: Futureland

Things to Do or See	Descriptive Words	Strong Verbs
1 ride the Tower of Tomorrow	colossal, lightning-fast, breathtaking	fall, rush, scream, zoom
2 watch the Robot Olympics	metallic, whirring, suspenseful, clever	crush, zap, race, score
3 play in the Gravity Garden	funny, surprising, weird, informative	leap, dangle, bounce, float

© Evan-Moor Corp. • EMC 6025 • Daily 6-Trait Writing VOICE 141

DAY 3

Read the rule aloud. Then guide students through the activities.

- **Activity A:** Read aloud the paragraph. Ask: *Do we know how the writer feels about the water park?* (No, she describes it without showing her feelings.) Have students name some of the weak verbs used. (**is, like, has, do, can, ride, moves, drop**)

  Ask: *How could the writer have made her paragraph more exciting and entertaining?* (by adding exciting details about the rides, using more emotional words and strong verbs)

  Read the words in the box. Then have students brainstorm additional strong verbs and adjectives that might be used to rewrite the paragraph. List students' suggestions on the board. Then have students complete the activity in pairs or individually. Afterward, have volunteers read their revisions.

- **Activity B (Convention):** Review how to form singular and plural possessive nouns. Then have students complete the activity.

DAY 4

Review the rule. Guide students through the activity.

- Brainstorm with students different places they would like to go. (e.g., an amusement park, a museum, a zoo) Then say: *If you want to persuade me to take you there, you'll need to give me good reasons and use strong, descriptive language that shows your emotion. You'll need to convince me that it's worth the time it will take away from our regular classwork.*
- Use the sample answer on the reduced page to the left to model completing the chart with details that show emotion and enthusiasm.

DAY 5 *Writing Prompt*

- *Use your chart from Day 4 to write a paragraph persuading your teacher to take your class on a trip. Use an exciting voice to show your enthusiasm.*
- *Be sure to spell possessive nouns correctly.*

Name: ______________________________

Voice

The voice you use depends on your purpose. For example, you can use your voice to persuade.

A. Read the e-mail Dani wrote to persuade her cousin to visit. Then:

- Underline three activities that Dani listed to persuade Ellie.
- List six emotional words that Dani used to persuade Ellie.

Dear Ellie,

Are you looking forward to summer vacation? I am! I'm writing with some amazing news. Are you ready for this? Pete and the Pugs will be performing at this year's county fair—our absolute favorite band! Don't you just love the band's new song, "Chili Dog"? So I begged and begged my parents, and guess what! They said they'd get us tickets! So you must come and visit me in July. We'll have other awesome things to do while you're here, too. You can borrow my sister's tennis racket, and we can play every day at the high school. Also, our town's new water park, Wild Waters, just opened. We would have a blast there! So try to e-mail me back sometime, because I think the concert tickets probably go on sale kind of soon.

Hugs from your cousin,

Dani

________________ ________________ ________________

________________ ________________ ________________

B. The last sentence of the e-mail isn't very persuasive. Rewrite it in a stronger voice to persuade Ellie to write back to Dani right away.

____

____

C. Circle the possessive nouns in Dani's e-mail. Write them next to their meanings below.

(of this year) ________________ (of my sister) ________________

(of the band) ________________ (of our town) ________________

Name: ______________________________

Voice You can use your voice to be entertaining.

A. Ethan wanted to write a funny paragraph about eating hot dogs. His purpose was to entertain, but some of the language he used sounds more formal than funny. Use proofreading marks to replace the words in bold with more entertaining words and phrases from the box.

Entertaining Words and Phrases			
tickle the taste buds	splattered	head straight for	mouthwatering
a huge, sloppy mess	if you ask me	slaps on heaps	

Hot Dogs

For the most **flavorful** hot dogs in town, I **recommend** Charley's Burger Place. Most customers' favorite meal there is the Charley Burger. However, **in my opinion,** the best thing on the menu is Charley's chili dogs. They really **are quite delicious**. First, Charley **applies generous amounts** of mustard and ketchup. Next, he adds a special chili sauce. I always have to ask for extra napkins because the hot dogs can be **difficult to eat.** One time, I even **managed to drip** chili on my shoes! It was worth every bite, though.

B. Write the plural possessive form of each word in parentheses to complete the sentences.

1. The ________________ trays were loaded with plates of steaming food.
   (server)
2. The customers inhaled the ________________ spicy aroma.
   (hot dog)
3. After dinner, the ________________ bellies were full.
   (boy)
4. Their ________________ wallets were empty!
   (parent)

Voice Be sure your voice matches your purpose.

A. Kim's assignment was to write an exciting description. However, she didn't use a very exciting voice. Read what Kim wrote. Rewrite the paragraph in a more exciting voice. Use the words in the box to help you.

Exciting Words						
amazing	colossal	dare	dark	deep	hottest	longest
plunge	roaring	soar	splash	thrilling	wild	zoom

A Day at the Water Park

A trip to Wild Waters on a hot day is a lot of fun. You will like the park's Turbo Slide. The slide has twists and turns through a tunnel. At the tunnel's end is a pool that you land in. You can do some bodysurfing in another pool called the Boogie Blast. It has waves for surfing. You can also ride in an inner tube on the Master Blaster. The ride's track is like a roller coaster of water that moves you up and down. You climb as high as a two-story building. Then you drop into the water.

____

____

____

____

____

B. Use proofreading marks to fix the possessive noun in each sentence.

1. My two best friends favorite ride at Wild Waters is the Turbo Slide.
2. Jeremy and Ahmed love swooshing through the slides tunnel.
3. During the summer, the parks hours are from 10:00 a.m. to 8:00 p.m.

Name: ______________________________

Voice Be sure your voice matches your purpose.

Where would you like to go on a class trip? Complete the chart to plan a paragraph persuading your teacher to take you there. List three things that would be exciting to see or do there. Then write descriptive words and strong verbs about each of those things.

Name of Place: ______________________________

Things to Do or See	Descriptive Words	Strong Verbs
1		
2		
3		

VOICE
Using Voice in Poetry

DAY 1

Read the rule aloud. Then guide students through the activities.

- **Activity A:** Explain that Ebenezer Brewer was a famous writer who lived in the 1800s. Then read the poem aloud. Explain any unfamiliar words, such as **humble** and **eternity**. Then say: *Brewer wanted to write about the importance of little things, so he used images of drops of water and grains of sand, comparing them to minutes in time.*

  Have students answer questions 1 and 2. Then ask: *What do you think Brewer was trying to say?* (Eternity is made of little moments, just as the ocean and earth are made of drops of water and grains of sand.) For question 3, discuss how the images contribute to the voice of the poem. Elicit that Brewer's images of small but important things give the poem a simple, quiet voice.

  Convention: Use the poem to point out that each line of a poem usually begins with a capital letter, even if the line is not a complete sentence.

- **Activity B:** Say: *In the poem, "drops of water" is an image used to describe moments in time. When I think of time, I picture wrinkles on an old person's face. What do you picture?* Have students complete the chart and share what they wrote.

Name: ____________ **Week 3 • Day 1**

Voice Images are pictures that a writer creates with words to describe something. Images can add voice to a poem.

A. Read the poem. Then answer the questions.

Little Things by Ebenezer Brewer

Little drops of water,
Little grains of sand,
Make the mighty ocean,
And the pleasant land.

Thus the little minutes,
Humble though they be,
Make the mighty ages
Of eternity.

1. In the first stanza, what are two small things that Brewer writes about? What are the two big things that they make up?
   Small things: drops of water   grains of sand
   Big things: ocean   land
2. In the second stanza, what small thing does Brewer write about? What is the big thing?
   Small thing: minutes
   Big thing: eternity
3. How would you describe the voice of this poem? Circle the words.
   funny   (simple)   exciting   (serious)
   (thoughtful)   mysterious   (quiet)

B. "Little Things" uses images to describe something invisible—time. For each invisible thing below, write an image that could describe it.

Something Invisible	Image Sample Answers:
1. time	wrinkles on a face
2. friendship	two people hugging
3. summer	bright sun shining on a crowded beach

144 VOICE   Daily 6-Trait Writing • EMC 6025 • © Evan-Moor Corp.

DAY 2

Read the rule aloud. Review: *Syllables are how words are divided.* Guide students through the activities.

- **Activity A (Convention):** Read the poems aloud. Point out that some forms of poetry, like haiku, do not require capitalization. However, the use of capitalization should be consistent within a poem. Have students complete the activity. Then review the answers, explaining that a haiku always has a 5-7-5 syllable pattern, and a cinquain often has a 2-4-6-8-2 pattern.
- **Activity B:** Say: *The words you choose contribute to your voice.* Model by saying: *You might want to write **cloudy**, but you need more syllables. Instead, you could use **overcast**. That word would make your poem sound more spooky or serious.* Have students complete the activity.

Name: ____________ **Week 3 • Day 2**

Voice Certain kinds of poems have a specific number of syllables. This gives the poems a rhythmic voice.

A. Read each poem. Then:
- Use proofreading marks to make the use of capital letters the same at the beginning of each line.
- Write the syllables in each line of the poem.
- Circle the words that describe the voice of the poem.

Haiku

	Syllables
loud, icy pebbles	5
Marbles falling from the sky	7
hail plonks on the roof	5

Voice: (funny) (informal) serious quiet (lighthearted)

Cinquain

	Syllables
Garbage	2
smelly, stinky,	4
Throwing, crushing, piling,	6
Filled with things we no longer want	8
the dump	2

Voice: formal (sad) enthusiastic (informal) (funny)

B. Read each word. Think of a word that has a similar or more specific meaning but a different number of syllables. Write the word.
Sample Answers:
1. scary terrifying   3. red rosy
2. tree redwood   4. run gallop

© Evan-Moor Corp. • EMC 6025 • Daily 6-Trait Writing   VOICE 145

Name: ______________________ **Week 3 • Day 3**

Voice You can bring your own voice and ideas to a common poetry form, such as haiku.

Write a line to complete each haiku. Be sure that the line has the correct number of syllables (in parentheses) and matches the use of capitalization in other lines. Then draw a picture to illustrate your haiku.

Sample Answers:

1. **Subject:** the sun
   - (5) Yellow like pencils
   - (7) Always sketching a new day
   - (5) Drawing happiness
2. **Subject:** a cat
   - (5) the cat wakes and yawns
   - (7) it stretches from front to back
   - (5) tail up in the air
3. **Subject:** winter
   - (5) bundled up in coats
   - (7) children scurry into school
   - (5) the year's coldest time

146 VOICE Daily 6-Trait Writing • EMC 6025 • © Evan-Moor Corp.

DAY 3

Read the rule aloud. Then guide students through the activity.

- Review the haiku pattern: *A haiku has three lines: the first and third lines have five syllables, and the middle line has seven.* Model completing the first haiku. Ask: *What is this poem about?* (rising sun) Then brainstorm words and phrases that convey the same thought. List ideas on the board and have students help you form a five-syllable phrase to finish the poem.
- You may want students to work in pairs or small groups to complete the second and third poems. Encourage students to repeat your process of brainstorming words and phrases, and then forming them into a five- or seven-syllable line that makes sense in the haiku. Have students complete the activity.
- **Convention:** When students have completed their poems, ask: *Does each line in your poems match the capitalization of the other lines?*

Name: ______________________ **Week 3 • Day 4**

Voice Use your own images and voice to write a haiku.

Haikus are usually about nature. Think of two things in nature that you would like to write a haiku about, such as animals, flowers, weather events, or bodies of water. Then use the chart to plan your poems.

Sample Answers:

	Haiku 1	Haiku 2
Subject:	iris	waterfall
Words related to the subject:	purplish-blue, slender stem, delicate blossom	rushing, roaring, misty, tumbling, rocks, pool, dramatic
Images that come to mind:	reaching up to the sun, towering over other flowers	a curtain of water, an angry river frothing at the mouth

© Evan-Moor Corp. • EMC 6025 • Daily 6-Trait Writing VOICE 147

DAY 4

Read the rule aloud. Then guide students through the activity.

- Say: *A haiku is usually about one simple thing.* Model completing the activity. For example, say: *I like iris flowers. When I think of an iris, I picture a purplish-blue color, and the way it shoots up from the ground. It usually towers over the other flowers.*
- Have students complete the activity, using two topics of their choice. If time permits, have students share their answers in pairs or small groups, offering suggestions of additional images to include. Then have students discuss which voice would best suit their topics and ideas.

DAY 5 *Writing Prompt*

- *Choose one of the subjects you wrote about on Day 4 to write a haiku. Be sure that the first and third lines have five syllables, and the second line has seven. Remember to let your voice come out in your haiku.*
- *Be sure to use consistent capitalization at the beginning of each line in the poem.*

Name: ______________________________

Week 3 • Day 1

Voice

Images are pictures that a writer creates with words to describe something. Images can add voice to a poem.

A. Read the poem. Then answer the questions.

Little Things by Ebenezer Brewer

Little drops of water,
Little grains of sand,
Make the mighty ocean,
And the pleasant land.

Thus the little minutes,
Humble though they be,
Make the mighty ages
Of eternity.

1. In the first stanza, what are two small things that Brewer writes about? What are the two big things that they make up?

Small things: ____________________ ____________________

Big things: ____________________ ____________________

2. In the second stanza, what small thing does Brewer write about? What is the big thing?

Small thing: ____________________

Big thing: ____________________

3. How would you describe the voice of this poem? Circle the words.

funny　simple　exciting　serious

thoughtful　mysterious　quiet

B. "Little Things" uses images to describe something invisible—time. For each invisible thing below, write an image that could describe it.

Something Invisible	Image
1. time	
2. friendship	
3. summer	

Name: ______________________________

Week 3 • Day 2

Voice Certain kinds of poems have a specific number of syllables. This gives the poems a rhythmic voice.

A. Read each poem. Then:

- Use proofreading marks to make the use of capital letters the same at the beginning of each line.
- Write the syllables in each line of the poem.
- Circle the words that describe the voice of the poem.

Haiku

	Syllables
loud, icy pebbles	____
Marbles falling from the sky	____
hail plonks on the roof	____

Voice: funny informal serious quiet lighthearted

Cinquain

	Syllables
Garbage	____
smelly, stinky,	____
Throwing, crushing, piling,	____
Filled with things we no longer want	____
the dump	____

Voice: formal sad enthusiastic informal funny

B. Read each word. Think of a word that has a similar or more specific meaning but a different number of syllables. Write the word.

1. scary ______________________
2. tree ______________________
3. red ______________________
4. run ______________________

Name: ______________________________

Week 3 • Day 3

Voice

You can bring your own voice and ideas to a common poetry form, such as haiku.

Write a line to complete each haiku. Be sure that the line has the correct number of syllables (in parentheses) and matches the use of capitalization in other lines. Then draw a picture to illustrate your haiku.

1. **Subject:** the sun

    (5) Yellow like pencils

    (7) Always sketching a new day

    (5) ______________________

2. **Subject:** a cat

    (5) ______________________

    (7) it stretches from front to back

    (5) tail up in the air

3. **Subject:** winter

    (5) bundled up in coats

    (7) ______________________

    (5) the year's coldest time

Name: ______________________________

Week 3 • Day 4

Voice Use your own images and voice to write a haiku.

Haikus are usually about nature. Think of two things in nature that you would like to write a haiku about, such as animals, flowers, weather events, or bodies of water. Then use the chart to plan your poems.

	Haiku 1	**Haiku 2**
Subject:		
Words related to the subject:		
Images that come to mind:		

WEEK 4 VOICE

Writing from Different Points of View

DAY 1

Read the rule aloud. Say: *A **point of view** is the way a character see things and how he or she tells the story. For example, in "The Three Little Pigs," the wolf and the pigs would have very different versions of the same story!* Then guide students through the activities.

- **Activity A:** Say: *Each of these stories is told from a different character's point of view: a girl named Aubrey, her dad, and Bowser, their dog.* Read aloud the first version. Ask: *Does this sound like it's told by a kid, a parent, or a dog?* (a kid) Then ask: *How does Aubrey's voice sound? What emotions does she reveal?* (e.g., frustration) Say: *Your characters' emotions should come out in the voices you give them.* Repeat for the other versions.
- **Activity B (Convention):** On the board, write **should have, should've, should of,** and **shoulda.** Circle **should have** and **should've** and say: *Only these two are correct. One is a contraction of the other.* Then say: *In speech, we often shorten **should have, would have,** and **could have** to **shoulda, woulda,** and **coulda,** but in writing they're incorrect. It is also incorrect to write **should of, would of,** or **could of.** These are often confused with the contractions **should've, would've,** and **could've.*** Then have students complete the activity.

DAY 2

Read the rule aloud. Then guide students through the activities.

- **Activity A:** Have a volunteer read aloud what each character says. Ask: *What words or phrases show their points of view?* (e.g., Sofia: "so upset," "our team is the BEST"; Trent: "that's OK," "should've practiced more") Briefly brainstorm what else each character might say, based on his or her point of view. You may want students to complete the activity in pairs, using role-play to imagine what each character would say. Review responses as a class.
- **Activity B (Convention):** Review the common mistakes people make with **could have, would have,** and **should have.** Then have students complete the activity.

Name: ______________________ **Week 4 • Day 1**

Voice Everyone has a unique point of view and a unique voice.

A. Read each version of this story about a girl, her dad, and their dog. From whose point of view is each version told? Circle the name. Then write an adjective to describe the voice.

1. **Point of View:** (Aubrey) Dad Bowser **Voice:** upset

We were in the living room watching TV, waiting for our lasagna to cool. Well, we (should have) known better than to leave it on the table, because the next thing you know, my dog Bowser walked in with lasagna all over his snout! I (could have) cried. I had worked so hard to make that lasagna after school, and I was so hungry! Now everything was totally ruined.

2. **Point of View:** Aubrey (Dad) Bowser **Voice:** tired

After a very long day, I finally got to sit down for a few minutes and watch TV. The lasagna smelled delicious, and we were only minutes away from enjoying it. Suddenly, I heard the rattle of Bowser's collar in the kitchen. I (could have) gotten up and checked on him, but I was too comfortable to move. So that's how Bowser ended up having lasagna for dinner, and we ended up having takeout pizza!

3. **Point of View:** Aubrey Dad (Bowser) **Voice:** excited

Oh boy, it's dinnertime! Where's my bowl? I am STARVING! Ooooh, what's that yummy smell? Whatever it is, it's right on the edge of the table, so that must mean it's mine. YUMMMM! That's delicious! I (would have) behaved better today if I'd known I was going to get a reward like this! I'll go show the family how much I love them. They're the best!

B. Circle the phrases *should have, could have,* and *would have* in the story versions above. Write them as contractions.

should've could've would've

150 VOICE Daily 6-Trait Writing • EMC 6025 • © Evan-Moor Corp.

Name: ______________________ **Week 4 • Day 2**

Voice When you write a story, think about what kind of voice your character would have. Use that voice to write from his or her point of view.

A. Read what each character says about losing a softball game. Then write what else he or she might say. Use the same voice and point of view.

Sofia says:

"I am so upset! I can't believe that the other team won. What's so great about them, anyway? Our team is the BEST! Sample Answer: We pitch the best, we hit the best, and we run the best. I hate losing. Next time, we're going to play our best game ever, and we will WIN!"

Trent says:

"I think our team could've done better, but that's OK. Maybe our team should've practiced more. The other team had some good players, so I can see why they won. Even though we lost, I had fun at the game. I scored more runs than I ever did before. Woo hoo!"

B. Use proofreading marks to fix the incorrect forms of *could have, should have,* and *would have.*

1. "You ~~should of~~ should have seen the home run I hit yesterday," boasted Emily.
2. "I ~~woulda~~ would have made it to the game on time if my sister hadn't gotten sick," explained Rudy.
3. "We ~~could'uv~~ could have scored a lot more runs, but our best hitter had a sore arm," said Louis.

© Evan-Moor Corp. • EMC 6025 • Daily 6-Trait Writing VOICE 151

Name: ______________________ **Week 4 • Day 3**

Voice When you write a story, give each of your characters a unique voice. Imagine how each character would react in a given situation.

Read each character description. Then read the problem. Imagine what each character would say about it.

The Characters:

Berto, a nervous, shy boy who is afraid of the dark

Kiara, a confident girl who is captain of her softball team

Mr. Savio, a calm, experienced teacher

The Problem: The power suddenly goes out in the school. The lights are off, and the classroom has no windows. It's pitch-black! Sample Answers:

Berto would say: Ahhhhhh!!!! What happened? I wish I had a flashlight! What are we going to do?

Kiara would say: Hey, cool, the power must have gone out! If anyone wants to borrow my flashlight, I've got one in my backpack.

Mr. Savio would say: Everyone stay calm. The power has just gone out, but everything is fine. I'll open the door to let some light in. I'm sure the power will be back on momentarily.

152 VOICE Daily 6-Trait Writing • EMC 6025 • © Evan-Moor Corp.

Name: ______________________ **Week 4 • Day 4**

Voice When you develop different characters, think about their different points of view. Give each character a unique voice.

Read about Gio's problem. Then fill in the chart to create two characters who have two different opinions about what Gio should have done.

The Problem: Gio received money for his birthday. He could have saved it for a skateboard, but he bought a lot of candy instead. Then he ate all of the candy at once and got sick!

Sample Answers:	Character 1	Character 2
Character's Name:	Yesenia	Nolan
Two words to describe personality:	happy, candy-lover	responsible, smart
Reaction to Gio's problem:	thinks Gio shouldn't have eaten all of the candy at once	thinks Gio should have kept the money and put it in his piggy bank
What character would say to Gio:	"Gio, if you had only eaten a little candy each day, it would have lasted longer!"	"Gio, a skateboard would last longer than candy. If you had stuck to your plan and saved your money, you could have had one by now."
Two words to describe voice:	amused, sympathetic	mature, frustrated

© Evan-Moor Corp. • EMC 6025 • Daily 6-Trait Writing VOICE 153

DAY 3

Read the rule aloud. Then guide students through the activity.

- Read aloud the character descriptions and the problem. Then ask: *How might a frightened, nervous kid react if the lights suddenly went out?* (e.g., shriek, panic) *How about a confident team captain?* (stay calm, offer to help) *A teacher? (try to keep control of the class)* Have volunteers role-play the three characters and what they might say.
- Have students complete the activity. Remind them to think about each character's voice as they write. Ask: *Which person might use exclamations? Who might use commands? What kinds of words would he or she use?*

DAY 4

Review the rule. Guide students through the activity.

- Read the problem aloud and invite students to share their own opinions about what Gio did. Then say: *You know how you feel, but your job as a writer is to put yourself in your characters' shoes.* Model this by using the sample answers on the reduced page to complete the chart. For example, say: *Personally, I wouldn't have spent the money on candy. But I'll create a funny character who loves sweets and doesn't blame Gio for buying the candy. She just thinks he shouldn't have eaten it all at once! She'd probably tell him that in a lighthearted voice.*
- Have students work in pairs to brainstorm characters and complete the activity.
- **Convention:** Remind students to write phrases such as **should have** and **could have** correctly.

DAY 5 *Writing Prompt*

- *Use your ideas from the chart on Day 4 to write a dialogue between the characters you created. Have them discuss what Gio did with his birthday money, expressing their particular points of view.*
- *Be sure to use* ***should have, could have,*** *and* ***would have*** *correctly.*

Name: ___________________________

Voice Everyone has a unique point of view and a unique voice.

A. Read each version of this story about a girl, her dad, and their dog. From whose point of view is each version told? Circle the name. Then write an adjective to describe the voice.

1. **Point of View:** Aubrey Dad Bowser **Voice:** ______________

We were in the living room watching TV, waiting for our lasagna to cool. Well, we should have known better than to leave it on the table, because the next thing you know, my dog Bowser walked in with lasagna all over his snout! I could have cried. I had worked so hard to make that lasagna after school, and I was so hungry! Now everything was totally ruined.

2. **Point of View:** Aubrey Dad Bowser **Voice:** ______________

After a very long day, I finally got to sit down for a few minutes and watch TV. The lasagna smelled delicious, and we were only minutes away from enjoying it. Suddenly, I heard the rattle of Bowser's collar in the kitchen. I could have gotten up and checked on him, but I was too comfortable to move. So that's how Bowser ended up having lasagna for dinner, and we ended up having takeout pizza!

3. **Point of View:** Aubrey Dad Bowser **Voice:** ______________

Oh boy, it's dinnertime! Where's my bowl? I am STARVING! Ooooh, what's that yummy smell? Whatever it is, it's right on the edge of the table, so that must mean it's mine. YUMMMM! That's delicious! I would have behaved better today if I'd known I was going to get a reward like this! I'll go show the family how much I love them. They're the best!

B. Circle the phrases *should have, could have,* and *would have* in the story versions above. Write them as contractions.

______________ ______________ ______________

Voice

When you write a story, think about what kind of voice your character would have. Use that voice to write from his or her point of view.

A. Read what each character says about losing a softball game. Then write what else he or she might say. Use the same voice and point of view.

Sofia says:

"I am so upset! I can't believe that the other team won. What's so great about them, anyway? Our team is the BEST! ______________________________ ______________________________ ______________________________ ______________________________"

Trent says:

"I think our team could've done better, but that's OK. Maybe our team should've practiced more. ______________________________ ______________________________ ______________________________ ______________________________"

B. Use proofreading marks to fix the incorrect forms of *could have, should have,* and *would have.*

1. "You should of seen the home run I hit yesterday," boasted Emily.
2. "I woulda made it to the game on time if my sister hadn't gotten sick," explained Rudy.
3. "We could'uv scored a lot more runs, but our best hitter had a sore arm," said Louis.

Name: ______________________________

Week 4 • Day 3

Voice

When you write a story, give each of your characters a unique voice. Imagine how each character would react in a given situation.

Read each character description. Then read the problem. Imagine what each character would say about it.

The Characters:

Berto, a nervous, shy boy who is afraid of the dark

Kiara, a confident girl who is captain of her softball team

Mr. Savio, a calm, experienced teacher

The Problem: The power suddenly goes out in the school. The lights are off, and the classroom has no windows. It's pitch-black!

Berto would say: ______________________________

____

____

____

Kiara would say: ______________________________

____

____

____

Mr. Savio would say: ______________________________

____

____

____

Name: ______________________________

Voice

When you develop different characters, think about their different points of view. Give each character a unique voice.

Read about Gio's problem. Then fill in the chart to create two characters who have two different opinions about what Gio should have done.

The Problem: Gio received money for his birthday. He could have saved it for a skateboard, but he bought a lot of candy instead. Then he ate all of the candy at once and got sick!

	Character 1	Character 2
Character's Name:		
Two words to describe personality:		
Reaction to Gio's problem:		
What character would say to Gio:		
Two words to describe voice:		

WEEK 5 VOICE
Using Voice in Persuasive Writing

DAY 1

Read the rule aloud. Say: *One way to persuade people is to make them feel a certain way.* Then guide students through the activities.

- **Activity A:** Read aloud both editorials. Then ask: *Which one is more persuasive?* (Editorial 2) *Why?* (It uses an exciting voice. It makes the cleanup sound fun and easy, states what it wants readers to do, and gives them a choice to make.) Ask: *Which editorial makes its readers feel important?* (Editorial 2) *How?* (It makes it seem like those who join the cleanup will be making a difference.) Then point out that Editorial 2 has two questions that directly address the reader. Say: *Speaking directly to your readers is a good way to get their attention and make them think about your topic.*
- **Activity B (Convention):** Have students find the sentences in each editorial that contain items in a series. (sentence 3 in Editorial 1; sentences 4 and 7 in Editorial 2) Review the rules for commas in a series. Have students complete the activity.

Name: ______________________ **Week 5 • Day 1**

Voice When you write persuasively, think about the emotions you want your reader to feel.

A. Read each editorial. Then answer the questions.

Editorial 1

Earth Day is coming up on April 22. There is a lot of trash around. You can see soda cans, plastic bags, and other litter everywhere along Dodge River. It's good to pick up trash so that everything looks clean. Also, it helps birds and other animals, who often mistake litter for food. They can get sick from it, so come pick up trash on Earth Day.

Editorial 2

What will you be doing this April 22? If you're smart, you'll be having fun and helping out on Earth Day. Here's a simple way to participate: join the Dodge River Cleanup. We have gloves, bags, and hats for everyone. There will be a big party afterward, too, so bring your friends! April 22 doesn't have to be just another day. You could spend it hanging out with your friends, cleaning up your environment, and saving the wildlife. It's your choice. Which will you do?

1. Which editorial makes the event sound more fun? Editorial 2
   Underline three phrases that the writer used to do this.
2. Which editorial makes the cleanup job sound easier? Editorial 2
   Circle one word and one sentence that the writer used to do this.
3. Why do you think the writer of the second editorial used the phrase "If you're smart"?
   Sample Answer: The writer knows that most readers want to believe they are smart.

B. Use proofreading marks to fix the use of commas.

1. Celia, Marcus, Julio and, Cassandra planted a garden on Earth Day.
2. They pulled weeds dug up rocks and planted vegetables.

156 VOICE Daily 6-Trait Writing • EMC 6025 • © Evan-Moor Corp.

DAY 2

Read the rule aloud. Say: *When you write with a confident voice, your writing is more convincing to your readers.* Then guide students through the activities.

- **Activity A:** Review the definition of **opinion statement.** (a sentence that clearly states how you feel) Then ask: *Which statement is stronger? 1) I think our school should probably have uniforms. 2) Our school should require uniforms.* (statement 2; it takes a specific, confident stand) Read the example on the page aloud. Ask: *What makes this a strong opinion statement?* (e.g., the words **don't go**) Have students complete the activity.
- **Activity B:** Read aloud both reviews. Ask: *Which seems less confident and persuasive?* (the first) *What words or phrases make the voice sound weak?* (e.g., **pretty good, you might go**) Have students work in pairs to rewrite the review.
- **Activity C (Convention):** Use the opinion statement example in Activity A to review comma usage in complex sentences. Then have students complete the activity.

Name: ______________________ **Week 5 • Day 2**

Voice Use a strong, confident voice when you write persuasively.

A. Read each topic for a persuasive paragraph. What would your topic sentence be? Write it as a strong, confident opinion statement.

Example: **Topic:** avoiding the worst restaurant in town
Opinion statement: If you want to enjoy your food, don't go to Angie's Pizza.

1. **Topic:** joining a specific club or team Sample Answers:
   Opinion statement: Join the Save Our Oceans Club to be a part of something that truly makes a difference!
2. **Topic:** making the school day longer
   Opinion statement: Camden Elementary's school day should be longer to allow for homework time and tutoring from teachers.

B. Write an *X* next to the movie review that does not have a confident voice. Then rewrite it to make it sound more confident.

☒ The Flying Finkelsteins is a pretty good movie. Mr. and Mrs. Finkelstein are superheroes trying to teach their kids how to fly. I enjoyed the scene where they all jump off the roof of their house together. If you have time this weekend, you might go see The Flying Finkelsteins.

☐ Little Bo Beep is the funniest movie ever! It's about a robot who thinks he's a sheepdog. Bo Beep tries to protect his flock of sheep from mutant coyotes—with hilarious results! If you want to laugh your head off, go see Little Bo Beep today!

Sample Answer: The Flying Finkelsteins is an excellent movie. Mr. and Mrs. Finkelstein are superheroes who are trying desperately to teach their kids how to fly. The best scene in the movie is when they all jump off the roof of their house together. I won't give away what happens, but let's just say that you should definitely go see this movie right away!

C. Use proofreading marks to insert the missing commas.

1. If you have any books that you don't want please donate them to the library.
2. Although plastic bags are convenient they can also be harmful.

© Evan-Moor Corp. • EMC 6025 • Daily 6-Trait Writing VOICE 157

Name: ____________________ **Week 5 • Day 3**

Voice When writing persuasively, use a strong, confident voice to appeal to your reader's emotions.

A. Read this persuasive paragraph. Then rewrite the paragraph so it has a stronger persuasive voice. Be sure to:

- Appeal to your reader's emotions.
- Be confident in your writing.

Marshall Elementary School is collecting pennies, nickels, and dimes for The Children of the World Fund. This organization builds schools all over the world. It helps some children get an education. Pennies may not seem like they're worth very much, but they can add up to a lot of money. Most people have some spare change hiding around the house. If every family in town gave twenty-five or fifty cents, it might make a difference.

Sample Paragraph:

Can you spare a few cents? If you have loose change lying around, I have a way for you to donate it to a great cause. Marshall Elementary School is collecting pennies for The Children of the World Fund. This organization builds schools all over the world. While we have plenty of schools here in the U.S., there are some places in the world where kids are not as lucky. It's amazing what can happen if everyone donates even the smallest amount of money to a cause. On behalf of the children of the world, I urge you to contribute not just pennies but nickels, dimes, and quarters. You'll be glad that you did.

B. Use proofreading marks to insert the missing commas.

1. Please remember to bring in canned vegetables, meat, and soup for the food drive.
2. If you want to help distribute food, you should be at the Community Center at 5:00.
3. Not everyone can afford to give money, so they donate their time instead.

158 VOICE Daily 6-Trait Writing • EMC 6025 • © Evan-Moor Corp.

Name: ____________________ **Week 5 • Day 4**

Voice When you plan your persuasive writing, think about the reasons and voice you will use to convince your reader.

Use the opinion diagram below to plan a paragraph persuading people to contribute their time or money to an important cause at your school. Use one of the ideas below, or think of your own.

- Volunteer to be a homework tutor.
- Help start and run a new after-school club.
- Donate computers or art supplies to the school.
- Help raise money to pay for a class field trip.

Sample Answer:

Opinion Statement: Citizens of Springfield should donate art supplies to our school.

Reason 1: Our school budget has only enough money for paper and pencils.
Examples: We are almost out of construction paper, and half of our colored pencils are broken or missing. We also need paint, butcher paper, and modeling clay.

Reason 2: Our art can be displayed at school and in the community for everyone to see.
Examples: We can create sculptures and murals to decorate city buildings and enhance community pride.

Reason 3:
Examples:

Possible Objection: Some people may think other subjects are more important than art.
Response to Objection: Art helps us improve our creativity and critical-thinking skills, which we need for every subject.

© Evan-Moor Corp. • EMC 6025 • Daily 6-Trait Writing VOICE 159

DAY 3

Read the rule aloud. Then guide students through the activities.

- **Activity A:** Read the paragraph. Say: *The writer gives reasons for donating, but the voice could be a lot stronger. It does not appeal to the reader's emotions or tell the reader exactly what to do.* Go through the paragraph, discussing ways to improve it. For example, ask: *How do you want the reader to feel? Happy? Fearful? Important? What strong opinion statement could you add? What could you say in order to show that building schools is a serious issue?*
- Have students rewrite the paragraph on their own. Then invite students to read their revisions aloud. Discuss the changes that each student made to make the voice sound more confident.
- **Activity B (Convention):** Have students find and circle the commas in the paragraph in Activity A. Use them to review the use of commas in compound and complex sentences and in a series of items. Then have students complete the activity.

DAY 4

Read aloud the rule. Then guide students through the activity.

- Brainstorm various projects or activities that your school needs help with and ways that people in your school or community could contribute. (e.g., directing a play, chaperoning field trips, buying books for the library)
- Use the sample answer on the reduced page to model completing the diagram. Remind students that a good argument also includes possible **objections**, or reasons your audience might disagree with you, and then provides a response that addresses those concerns. Then have students complete the diagram independently.

DAY 5 *Writing Prompt*

- *Write a persuasive paragraph urging your readers to contribute their time or money to an important cause at your school. Use your ideas from Day 4 to help you.*
- *Be sure to use commas correctly.*

Voice When you write persuasively, think about the emotions you want your reader to feel.

A. Read each editorial. Then answer the questions.

Editorial 1

Earth Day is coming up on April 22. There is a lot of trash around. You can see soda cans, plastic bags, and other litter everywhere along Dodge River. It's good to pick up trash so that everything looks clean. Also, it helps birds and other animals, who often mistake litter for food. They can get sick from it, so come pick up trash on Earth Day.

Editorial 2

What will you be doing this April 22? If you're smart, you'll be having fun and helping out on Earth Day. Here's a simple way to participate: join the Dodge River Cleanup. We have gloves, bags, and hats for everyone. There will be a big party afterward, too, so bring your friends! April 22 doesn't have to be just another day. You could spend it hanging out with your friends, cleaning up your environment, and saving the wildlife. It's your choice. Which will you do?

1. Which editorial makes the event sound more fun? ______________

   Underline three phrases that the writer used to do this.

2. Which editorial makes the cleanup job sound easier? ______________

   Circle one word and one sentence that the writer used to do this.

3. Why do you think the writer of the second editorial used the phrase "If you're smart"?

   ____

   ____

B. Use proofreading marks to fix the use of commas.

1. Celia, Marcus, Julio and, Cassandra planted a garden on Earth Day.
2. They pulled weeds dug up rocks and planted vegetables.

Name: ____________________

Voice Use a strong, confident voice when you write persuasively.

A. Read each topic for a persuasive paragraph. What would your topic sentence be? Write it as a strong, confident opinion statement.

Example: **Topic:** avoiding the worst restaurant in town
Opinion statement: If you want to enjoy your food, don't go to Angie's Pizza.

1. **Topic:** joining a specific club or team
   Opinion statement: ____________________

2. **Topic:** making the school day longer
   Opinion statement: ____________________

B. Write an *X* next to the movie review that does not have a confident voice. Then rewrite it to make it sound more confident.

☐ The Flying Finkelsteins is a pretty good movie. Mr. and Mrs. Finkelstein are superheroes trying to teach their kids how to fly. I enjoyed the scene where they all jump off the roof of their house together. If you have time this weekend, you might go see The Flying Finkelsteins.

☐ Little Bo Beep is the funniest movie ever! It's about a robot who thinks he's a sheepdog. Bo Beep tries to protect his flock of sheep from mutant coyotes—with hilarious results! If you want to laugh your head off, go see Little Bo Beep today!

____

____

____

____

C. Use proofreading marks to insert the missing commas.

1. If you have any books that you don't want please donate them to the library.

2. Although plastic bags are convenient they can also be harmful.

Name: ______________________________

Voice

When writing persuasively, use a strong, confident voice to appeal to your reader's emotions.

A. Read this persuasive paragraph. Then rewrite the paragraph so it has a stronger persuasive voice. Be sure to:

- Appeal to your reader's emotions.
- Be confident in your writing.

Marshall Elementary School is collecting pennies, nickels, and dimes for The Children of the World Fund. This organization builds schools all over the world. It helps some children get an education. Pennies may not seem like they're worth very much, but they can add up to a lot of money. Most people have some spare change hiding around the house. If every family in town gave twenty-five or fifty cents, it might make a difference.

B. Use proofreading marks to insert the missing commas.

1. Please remember to bring in canned vegetables meat and soup for the food drive.
2. If you want to help distribute food you should be at the Community Center at 5:00.
3. Not everyone can afford to give money so they donate their time instead.

Name: ____________________

Voice

When you plan your persuasive writing, think about the reasons and voice you will use to convince your reader.

Use the opinion diagram below to plan a paragraph persuading people to contribute their time or money to an important cause at your school. Use one of the ideas below, or think of your own.

- Volunteer to be a homework tutor.
- Help start and run a new after-school club.
- Donate computers or art supplies to the school.
- Help raise money to pay for a class field trip.

Opinion Statement:

Reason 1:

Examples:

Reason 2:

Examples:

Reason 3:

Examples:

Possible Objection:

Response to Objection:

Proofreading Marks

Mark	Meaning	Example
♆	Take this out (delete).	I love ~~to~~ to read.
⊙	Add a period.	It was late⊙
≡	Make this a capital letter.	First prize went to maria. (≡ under m)
/	Make this a lowercase letter.	We saw a /Black /Cat.
——	Fix the spelling.	This is our ~~hause~~ house.
∧ with ,	Add a comma.	Goodnight∧, Mom.
∨ with '	Add an apostrophe.	That's Lil's bike.
! ∧ ? ∧	Add an exclamation point or a question mark.	Help!∧ Can you help me?∧
∧	Add a word or a letter.	The ∧red pen is mine.
# ∧	Add a space between words.	I like#∧pizza.
——	Underline the words.	We read <u>Old Yeller</u>.
“∨ ”∨	Add quotation marks.	“∨Come in,”∨he said.